Contents

FAITH AND THE HISTORIAN

Faith and the Historian

CATHOLIC PERSPECTIVES

EDITED BY

Nick Salvatore

UNIVERSITY OF ILLINOIS PRESS
URBANA AND CHICAGO

Manufactured in the United States of America
1 2 3 4 5 C P 5 4 3 2 1
∞ This book is printed on acid-free paper.

Library of Congress Cataloging-in-Publication Data
Faith and the historian : Catholic perspectives /
edited by Nick Salvatore.
p. cm.
Includes bibliographical references and index.
ISBN-13: 978-0-252-03143-4 (cloth : alk. paper)
ISBN-10: 0-252-03143-1 (cloth : alk. paper)
ISBN-13: 978-0-252-07382-3 (pbk. : alk. paper)
ISBN-10: 0-252-07382-7 (pbk. : alk. paper)
1. History—Religious aspects—Catholic Church.
2. Catholic Church.
I. Salvatore, Nick, 1943–
BR115.H5F28 2007
261.5—dc22 2006027174

Acknowledgments

The conference from which this volume grew could not have occurred if not for the encouragement and support of Professor James Turner of the University of Notre Dame, who was then also the director of the Erasmus Institute on that campus. His willingness to underwrite major parts of the conference's costs (the Institute's funding comes from an anonymous donor, the Pew Charitable Trusts, and the University of Notre Dame) was most generous. Kathleen L. Sobieralski of the Erasmus Institute gave her skill, attention, and energy to all the necessary details required to create the possibility of a meaningful conference. Further assistance came from the following programs at Cornell University: the American Studies Program; Cornell United Religious Work; and the School of Industrial and Labor Relations, which were led at that time by, respectively, R. Laurence Moore, Robert L. Johnson Jr., and Edward J. Lawler. Our collective appreciation to all.

FAITH AND THE HISTORIAN

Introduction

In March 2001, a small group of historians of American life gathered at Cornell University to share their thinking on how an experience with Catholicism had affected their approach to history.[1] Not all the participants were practicing Catholics, but all who gave papers, whatever their current beliefs, were born into Catholic families and thus had been "touched by Catholicism" in a serious manner. How, we collectively wondered, had that experience influenced our historical work?

The origins of this conference lay in the occasional discussions between the two co-organizers, Steve Rosswurm of Lake Forest College and me, that began in the late 1990s. While I worked on an article about Herbert Gutman's influence on writing the history of American working people (which included a discussion of religion), the biographer in me wondered about how familial values may have framed Gutman's historical thinking, and that of other historians too. This had interested me for some time and, in the process of work for that article, I came across a pointed comment by John McGreevy that whetted my curiosity again. In the introduction to his first book, *Parish Boundaries,* McGreevy wrote that the "underlying argument" in discussions of class in contemporary historical writing generally assumed "that consciousness formed as a laborer is more important than consciousness developed in the home." I remain quite sympathetic to McGreevy's historiographical point, but it was another inference that touched a more personal vein. How did that "consciousness developed in the home"—varied as it may be—affect those of us who wrote history? That our historical sensibilities did not begin with that first graduate seminar was obvious, but how an experience with faith might have influenced my professional work remained more elusive. Discussions with Steve revealed a common interest, and thus emerged the idea for a conference and, ultimately, this volume.[2]

The focus on Catholicism was partly personal and partly professional. We were quite aware of other collections that gave historians the opportunity to publicly discuss the origins of their work. Although many of these collections emphasized intellectual influences and historiographical trends, there had been some discussion of religious influences as well.[3] Yet Catholicism, we felt, remained less explored, an oddity given the increasing numbers of professional historians from Catholic backgrounds in recent decades. It seemed a theme worth exploring beyond our private interests.

From the beginning, our efforts revolved around two central ideas. First, we purposely used the broad phrase "touched by Catholicism" to describe one prerequisite. With this wording, we indicated an interest in a wide variety of experiences, including "cradle-to-grave" Catholics; those raised in that faith who later left (and in some cases even later returned); and converts to Catholicism (although none of the contributors were, in the final analysis, converts). The second guideline concerned the essays themselves. We were not looking for traditional historiographical pieces, important as their discussions can be; rather, we sought more personal essays and extended an invitation to historians to reflect on some of the deeper influences that framed their professional work. Thus, the prospectus, which was widely distributed over the Internet and by more traditional methods, said, in part, that we "wish to avoid the celebratory as well as the maudlin. We do not envision essays that are primarily expressions of faith (or the lack thereof); nor are we looking for essays that desire to 'settle scores,' be they old or new. Rather, we seek essays by historians for whom Catholicism proved to be a formative experience and who are willing to explore in a public fashion this aspect (and perhaps others) of their lives as it has influenced their professional work." This invitation to move from the professional to the personal, and back again, proved unattractive to some, as they felt their historical work should stand on its own. While this was certainly a reasonable approach, others responded to the invitation with enthusiasm.

One consequence of this emphasis on a broad personal dimension was that we made a decision early that we would include only published historians. We did this not to ignore younger scholars; rather, the very nature of the essays—a dialogue between the private and the public, the personal and the professional—required it. In addition, a reader curious about themes raised in a particular essay could then have easy access to the author's published work. Unfortunately, this meant that a number of smart and interesting proposals were not accepted. Of the draft papers presented at the conference in 2001, six are included here. In addition, two pertinent essays, revised and expanded versions of previously published work by Anne Butler and Mario García, have been included.[4]

The experience of twentieth-century Catholicism reflected in these essays is broad, although certainly not all-encompassing. The ages of the authors (birth dates range from 1927 to 1959) indicate that our experiences of adolescence, that critical time, included the Depression and war, the "prosperous" 1950s, and the "turbulent" 1960s and 1970s. Although these different American moments influenced us, equally important were the developments within Catholicism. Those born before 1950 grew to maturity within families deeply influenced by a church tradition that prized Catholic institutions, a strict moral theology, and, to varying degrees, looked askance at secular culture. These authors, whose cohort spans two generations, largely lived in a Catholic subculture, where priests were honored, religious sisters respected, and the authority of the Church itself questioned rarely. Although experienced differently (e.g., as a minority in a more rural and Protestant community; in the emerging suburbs after 1945; in the urban, ethnic parish), this was a church culture that profoundly reflected, still, the "ultramontane" revival of the mid-nineteenth century.[5] As a number of the essays suggest, Vatican II and the social and political turmoil of the 1960s burst upon this world with stunning force. Spurred by changes in the larger society as well as from Pope John XXIII's *aggiornamento* (opening to the world), Catholicism and modernity once again engaged in what was, at first, a mood of hopeful expectations. For these essayists, already in their twenties or older when the transformations of the 1960s began, the impact varied greatly even if the "touch" of a traditional Catholicism remained deeply embedded.[6]

It was different for a third generation represented in this collection, those born in 1950 or after. It was precisely these same changes, so dramatic in the experience of many in the older group, that was more often the norm that framed their religious experiences. Certainly by adolescence if not before, the power of that Catholic subculture, dominant into the 1950s, had sharply receded. As Catholics became more middle class and suburban after 1945, that historic Catholic quality that Charles Morris dubbed "its prickly apartness" ebbed as well. Even before Vatican II, many practicing Catholics no longer perceived modern (and decidedly secular) American culture as a major "occasion of sin" that bore for those who indulged the prospect of eternal damnation. By the mid-1960s, what had been a subterranean rivulet now seemed an all-too-public flood. Vatican II, with its emphasis on religious freedom, an understanding of the role of history and culture on the "immutable" teachings of the church, and the importance of the laity in the collective life of the church community, made obsolete overnight—or so it seemed—a century of American ultramontanism. The famous bastion of orthodoxy for the young, the *Baltimore Catechism,* with its theological nibblets doled out in singsong phrases suitable for memorization, suddenly encouraged individual thought. The reversal of what but a few years before had been deemed heretical in matters of faith, coupled with the use of English in the liturgy, symbolized even for the youngest that the Church could, and did, change. For believing American Catholics, the opening line of *God's Grandeur,* a poem by the nineteenth-century British Jesuit Gerard Manley Hopkins, took on new meanings: "The world is charged with the grandeur of God," Hopkins extolled. "It will flame out, like shining from shook foil." And all of this occurred during the 1960s as well.[7]

This expectation of continued fundamental change within the faith tradition framed the youthful experiences of this third cohort in ways significantly different from the other two. Nevertheless, all of the contributors to this volume were touched by these forces in their own ways. For some, the sacred and secular upheavals of that decade instigated a basic reevaluation of their religious tradition that would revitalize their faith commitment. Others discovered that the faith of their youth simply could not engage the new sense of the possible evident in the music, the politics, and the explosion of ideas sprung loose, in secular fashion, "like shining from shook foil." Still others at first welcomed the change symbolized by the merging of the two sources of upheaval as personified in the person of a nun, standing in the sanctuary, by the altar, often still in her traditional religious dress, strumming the guitar during Mass. But as the reaction set in, as Church authorities sought to check what they now considered the excesses of Vatican II, the Church's role in their lives diminished for some essayists, to say nothing of American Catholics in general. A turning point here, of course, was the 1968 publication of Paul VI's encyclical, *Humanae Vitae,* which declared that, as a matter of faith for all Catholics, the use of birth control to regulate family size was forbidden. Given that a papal commission had suggested the opposite course, the negative reaction was intense, particularly in America.[8]

Regardless of individual resolutions, the historians here, like American Catholics more broadly, had to confront certain fundamental tensions propelled by their experiences of the past and their understandings of these new possibilities. In one respect, the changes associated with Vatican II spoke directly to our professional historical sensibilities. If history and culture—historicism, in the language of our graduate seminars—now might modulate the absolutist and ahistorical insistence that church doctrine never changed, that might resolve certain tensions between one's professional thinking and one's faith. Or it might until the retrenchment under John Paul II reasserted more than once the all-encompassing assertion of doctrinal immutability and papal infallibility. But there was a more complex layer of tension as well. If, as Peter Steinfels has noted, Catholicism acknowledged "that its claim to be ahistorical and immutable was unfounded, or once it acknowledged that yesterday's heretics were in fact today's 'separated brethren,' could historical consciousness and ecumenism stop short of total relativism?" In the long continuum of responses to this question, from the historians in this collection as from a wide swath of American Catholics in thought and deed since the 1960s, reside clues to understanding the vitality of contemporary American Catholicism and to the changed tone of the faith for those who remained joined with that communion. In those responses as well one can find an understanding of those who have left.[9]

What follows are the essays by eight historians touched by Catholicism on the meaning of that experience and its effect on their professional work. The essays are presented in broad chronological order, organized more by generational cohort than by specific date of birth. The essays are reflections, in some cases even meditations, and were never intended to conform to the structure and methodology of the historical article for a professional journal. Still, we have tried to shed some light on the inner processes that create that very work.

Nick Salvatore

Notes

1. The participants included, as presenters, James Barrett, University of Illinois at Urbana-Champaign; David Emmons, University of Montana; Maureen Fitzgerald, College of William and Mary; Philip Gleason, University of Notre Dame; Joseph McCartin, Georgetown University; John McGreevy, University of Notre Dame; Steve Rosswurm, Lake Forest College; Nick Salvatore, Cornell University; and Christopher Shannon, University of Notre Dame. Those who commented on the papers were Mark Noll, Wheaton College; David O'Brien, College of the Holy Cross; Albert Raboteau, Princeton University; Robert Sullivan, University of Notre Dame; and Leslie Woodcock Tentler, Catholic University of America.

2. Nick Salvatore, "Herbert Gutman's Narrative of the American Working Class: A Reevaluation," *International Journal of Politics, Culture and Society* 12, no. 1

(1998): 43–80; John McGreevy, *Parish Boundaries: The Catholic Encounter with Race in the Twentieth-Century Urban North* (Chicago, 1996), 4.

3. See, for example, L. P. Curtis Jr., ed., *The Historian's Workshop: Original Essays by Sixteen Historians* (New York, 1970); Paul A. Cimbala and Robert F. Himmelberg, eds., *Historians and Race: Autobiography and the Writing of History* (Bloomington, IN, 1996); Bruce Kuklick and D. G. Hart, eds., *Religious Advocacy and American History* (Grand Rapids, MI, 1997).

4. My thanks to Dave Emmons for calling these essays to my attention in the months following the conference.

5. John McGreevy describes *ultramontanism* as "a cluster of shifts that included a Vatican-fostered move to Thomistic philosophy, a more intense experiential piety centered on miracles and Vatican-approved devotions such as that of the Sacred Heart, an international outlook suspicious of national variations within Catholicism, and a heightened respect for church authorities ranging from the pope to parish priests. All this was nurtured in the world of Catholic parishes, schools, and associations, whose members understood themselves as arrayed against the wider society." See McGreevy, *Catholicism and American Freedom: A History* (New York, 2003), 12–13.

6. On the American Catholic encounter with modernity, particularly in the 1790s, the 1890s, and the 1960s, see Jay Dolan, *In Search of an American Catholicism: A History of Religion and Culture in Tension* (New York, 2002). For an insightful analysis of these issues following Vatican II (1962–1965), see Peter Steinfels, *A People Adrift: The Crisis of the Roman Catholic Church in America* (New York, 2003).

7. Charles Morris, *American Catholic: The Saints and Sinners Who Built America's Most Powerful Church* (New York, 1997), 323–34 (the quote is on page vii); Dolan, *In Search of an American Catholicism,* 180–89; Steinfels, *A People Adrift,* 32; W. H. Gardner and N. H. Mackenzie, eds., *The Poems of Gerard Manley Hopkins,* 4th ed. (London, 1967), 66.

8. On this encyclical and the American reaction to it, see Steinfels, *A People Adrift,* 255–67.

9. Ibid., 37.

PHILIP GLEASON

1 *Becoming (and Being) a Catholic Historian*

I am (although I am not fond of the expression) a "cradle Catholic," and I hope to be a cradle-to-grave Catholic. For me, Catholicism is not a matter of looking back on the influence of a no-longer-operative "identity." Being a Catholic is, rather, so closely linked with my past and present sense of myself that autobiography seems the only way to approach the task of reflecting on the connections between my religious faith and my professional training and work as a historian. Since autobiography should start somewhere near the beginning, I begin with some notes on how religion interacted with family circumstance and early experience in shaping the temperament I later brought to the study of history.

I grew up in Wilmington, Ohio, a town in the southwestern part of the state with a population in my boyhood of just under six thousand. My father, a very progressive farmer who developed a prize-winning strain of hybrid seed corn, died in 1932, two weeks before my fifth birthday. My recollections of life on the farm are disconnected vignettes because, after struggling along with hired help for three years, my mother rented the farm and we moved into town in 1935. There couldn't have been a lot of money, but I never felt we were poor. No doubt the absence of a father's example and influence made a great, but unknowable, difference in the kind of person I became. Yet our family life was happy and I felt secure—except when my mother spoke, as she sometimes did, of returning to the farm when my two brothers and I were old enough to run it. Though it was just a fantasy on her part, it filled me with dread because I knew nothing of farming and was dismayed at the prospect of undertaking any such thing.

Wilmington was a Protestant farming community, overwhelmingly "old American" in ethnic makeup. It had three or four Jewish merchants, and about the same number of Greek and Syrian families; Italian and Slavic names were conspicuous by their absence. The town did, however, have a couple of "colored sections," in one of which there was a "colored" grade school. De facto segregation extended only through elementary school since there was but one high school, which African Americans attended, though they were few in number.[1] In these respects, Wilmington did not differ from neighboring communities, but the many Quakers living in the town and surrounding countryside made it distinctive in religious terms.

Yet aside from being conscientious objectors, the Quakers seemed to me no different from other Protestants. True, Catholics didn't make many distinctions among the separated brethren in those days, but in addition to that fact, the Quakers of Wilmington belonged to the tradition that had shifted away from strict silent worship and adopted the organizational forms of conventional Protestantism. Wilmington College was (and still is) a Quaker institution, besides which the local Friends had an imposing "Quaker church," a parsonage, and a minister (the Reverend A. Ward Applegate), just like the Methodists, Presbyterians, and Baptists. Growing up in this religious environment, I naturally assumed that Quakers were among the major Protestant denominations. It was quite a shock to learn, many years later, that their numbers are minuscule—no more than 200,000 nationwide—a discovery that should perhaps have made me more sensitive to the limitations of one's own experience than it actually did.

Since there was no Catholic school in Wilmington, I went through the public system. Virtually all of my grade school playmates and my closest friends in high school were Protestants. In fact, there were only three or four Catholics besides myself in my high school class of about eighty; none of the high school teachers was a Catholic, though my third-grade teacher was. Religion must have come up from time to time in conversations with my friends, but it wasn't really a matter of discussion, much less dispute. Although my elders occasionally spoke of Ku Klux days, there was no evidence of active religious hostility as I was growing up. Even so, I was quite conscious of the difference in religion and, in keeping with the then-prevailing spiritual arrogance of Catholics, felt that religion didn't mean nearly as much to my Protestant friends as it did to me.

Wilmington's Catholic church was dedicated to St. Columbkille, and people of Irish background constituted the largest single element in the congregation of a hundred or so families. But St. Columbkille's was nothing like the legendary ethnic parishes (Irish and otherwise) in places like Chicago. Father Theodore Stuber, the resident priest throughout all my time in the parish, was rather shy and withdrawn; he took no part in Wilmington's civic life and his pastoral activity was confined to strictly religious functions—offering Mass, hearing confessions, making sick calls, and so on. Except for an annual turkey supper (seventy-five cents a plate!) and sedate monthly meetings of the Married Ladies Sodality and the Catholic Ladies of Columbia, there was no community life in the parish not directly related to worship or religious education. The latter consisted of catechism classes taught mainly by Ursuline Sisters who came from a convent some thirty-five miles away. Gas rationing in World War II knocked out the Saturday afternoon classes, but catechism between the early and late Masses on Sunday morning continued to serve as the main occasion of social interaction among young people—and for the women who served rolls and hot chocolate—through the war years. A few years after the war, a Knights of Columbus chapter was organized in the parish, but by then I was away from Wilmington most of the time.

Yet despite its meager social dimension, St. Columbkille's was the focal point of our existence, more so than the school or any other institution outside the immediate family. This can only be accounted for in terms of its religious—indeed, its *sacred*—character, its being regarded as the House of God, the local embodiment of "Our Holy Mother, the Church." I had the impression that such was the case for the whole parish, and I know it was for my family. Our derivation was purely Irish, and we were proud of it, although we knew virtually nothing of family history beyond the fact that my two grandfathers were born in neighboring counties in Ireland and that we still had cousins living there. We had no formal connection of any sort with the strictly "ethnic" side of being Irish.[2] "Irish Catholic" is legitimately used as an ethnic label but, for me, *being a Catholic* was what mattered, and it had nothing to do with nationality ("ethnicity" not being a term available in those days). Being a Catholic was a strictly *religious* matter, which is to say it dealt with the questions that mattered most: the existence of God, the nature of reality, the meaning of human life, and the kind of person one should strive to be. The Church—which meant, of course, the Catholic Church—was the repository of *truth* on those questions, and it provided the channels of grace by which one could hope to gain eternal salvation.

I was an altar boy for years, and for a long time after that I struggled with (i.e., against) the feeling that I had a vocation to the priesthood—a possibility not definitively set aside until, after two years of graduate work, I spent an unhappy semester in a preseminary program at Notre Dame. The pious intensity of youth has long since faded, but my core beliefs were formed by the profoundly dualistic version of supernaturalism that characterized the Catholic Church before the Second Vatican Council. That religious sensibility, weathered by the doubts of a long lifetime and blurred by more recent theological emphases, remains embedded in my soul.

In speaking of the dualistic quality of pre–Vatican II supernaturalism, I do not mean to suggest a radically Manichaean duality of being, with two eternally warring forces of light and darkness, good and evil. Rather, what I have in mind are the multiple polarities that shaped the mental universe of preconciliar Catholicism—this world and the next, time and eternity, matter and spirit, nature and grace, body and soul. These dualities were an everyday part of the Catholic's religious vocabulary, while the college student who got even a smattering of the "Thomistic synthesis" was introduced to others (substance and accident, being and becoming, essence and existence, etc.) that were part of the philosophical system endorsed by the Church. This polarized religious mentality clearly embodied a ranking of importance. That is, Catholics who took their religion seriously could never forget that they were "citizens of two worlds," whose life in this world had to be oriented toward the world to come, because one's state of being in eternity was what *really* mattered.[3]

Looking back at this religious formation—so strongly "vertical," so supernaturally oriented, so focused on God—I can see that it colored my views in more ways than I had previously realized. Most obviously, perhaps, its emphasis on "piety," rather than "moralism," made me permanently skeptical of the effectiveness, or even the religious validity, of activist movements of the social-gospel type—an attitude, incidentally, quite in keeping with the Niebuhrian "realism" and insistence on God's "otherness" that dominated the American religious scene after World War II.[4] On a different level, I believe the temporal/eternal polarity makes more understandable the fact that I never felt the slightest tension between my "identity" as a Catholic and as an American. The absence of such inner conflict no doubt strikes younger Catholics (to say nothing of non-Catholics) as incredible. Given the rigidity, authoritarianism, and generally reactionary stance of the preconciliar Church, how could an American *not* experience a sharp tension between those two identities? For me, however, the issue never arose because the world was to be viewed *sub specie æternitatis,* with the "temporal order" being different from, and of lesser intrinsic importance than, the "spiritual order." Different principles applied to the two: democracy, freedom, and equality were excellent in themselves, but they were not absolute. To accept them as political postulates did not mean they applied in the same way to religious life. This view of the matter was, it seemed to me, quite in keeping with the nation's commitment to freedom of religion and the separation of church and state.

We didn't use the terminology of identity in those days, but the question was sometimes put as follows: "Are you a Catholic who happens to be an American, or an American who happens to be a Catholic?" My answer put me firmly in the former camp, because being a Catholic dealt with truths of transcendent importance, while being an American was, though deeply valued, a matter of passing "temporal" significance. Today, I would want to qualify the question and nuance my answer, but it would have to be essentially the same. For to reverse the order would make Americanism more of an absolute than it should be.

The priority assigned to matters spiritual should *not* be taken to mean that I was lukewarm about democracy or Americanism. As to the former, the family was ardently Democratic with a capital *D*, and Franklin D. Roosevelt had for us something of the aura of an epic hero. New Deal farm programs tided us over financially. My brothers and I played in and around the construction works of the Works Progress Administration (WPA), which gave Wilmington its sewage system, while the Public Works Administration (PWA) enlarged its high school. And I had a small boy's fascination with the camp life and outdoor work of the Civilian Conservation Corps (CCC), in which a couple of my uncles were for a time enrolled. It is clear in retrospect that all these experiences nourished a positive feeling about being American.

Then came World War II, with its mighty upsurge of patriotic feeling and sense of national unity in a noble cause—the defeat of totalitarian aggressors and vindication of "the values America stands for." I was in high school during the war years. For me, therefore, what Erik Erikson called the period of "ideological identity formation" coincided precisely with a tremendous nationwide revival of the ideology of democracy and Americanism.[5] My subsequent experience in the army—a year of uneventful occupation duty in Japan—expanded my horizons a bit, but did nothing to shake my belief that World War II was a "good war" and that the American system was the best on earth. By the same token, I was convinced that the United States was the indispensable bulwark of freedom against the threat posed by the Soviet Union and international Communism.

Such were my convictions at the time, but I did not realize then how deeply my consciousness as an American had been shaped by the New Deal and, especially, by the Second World War—which also, it should be noted, stimulated a "revival of religion" that lent new intellectual respectability to religious faith. Later, in graduate school, I came across "generational hypotheses"; that is, theories about how major social, political, or cultural events shape the lifelong outlook of young people who experience those events at a formative stage of their development. I found such theories intriguing, but they didn't really hit home until the 1960s. The crises of that decade—and especially their impact on young people, which was so different from what I experienced in the 1940s—made me a believer in the generational hypothesis, at least to the extent of convincing me that there was such as thing as the World War II generation, and that I most definitely belonged to it. Of this, more later.

Before my army service, I spent a year at Ohio State University, expecting to be drafted at any moment. When that didn't happen, I enlisted in the fall of 1946 so as to qualify for the benefits of the GI Bill, which I, and many other eighteen-year-olds who joined up at the same time, understood was soon to expire. When I got out of the army in 1948, I used the GI Bill to complete my college education at the University of Dayton, which I chose because it was Catholic and close to home. Even at the time, I sensed that the GI Bill was a tremendous social boon, and I came to realize more clearly over time that "upward mobility" was less a matter of individual effort than of broad social change. Being a direct beneficiary of that kind of change reinforced my conviction that America was, indeed, a good society.

Neither of my parents finished high school, and I was the first in my family to attend college. That background no doubt influenced my view of the purpose of higher education, which was that it should lead directly to gainful employment. In those days, good students at places like the University of Dayton didn't understand—or at least I didn't—that this could be done by continuing straight out of college into graduate school (on a fellowship, of course), and becoming a professor, a career that fulfils the goal of vocationalism while encouraging the illusion one has risen above so crass a consideration. My less ambitious solution to the problem of combining intellectual interests with preparation for employment was to major in education, with a teaching field in "social studies."

Most of my professionally oriented courses in such arcana as "life-adjustment education" and "nondirective guidance" were crushingly dull and left me feeling ill prepared to face a classroom of high school students. Hence I jumped at the chance to take an experimental civil service examination designed to identify bright prospects, who could then be picked up by various federal agencies and placed in special training programs for rapid upward advancement. That resulted in my spending the first year after college as a "Junior Management Assistant" in the Air Research and Development Command of the U.S. Air Force. The job was in Baltimore and was immensely important for me, not only because I learned that "management" was not my cup of tea, but also because I found at the Newman Club of the Johns Hopkins University a kind of intellectual companionship and stimulation that was altogether new to me. That experience—particularly my friendship with John Freccero, who later became a leading Dante scholar—was crucial to my decision to undertake graduate studies myself.

In the year I was waiting for my applications to graduate school to be reviewed, I did, in fact, teach school—in Xenia, Ohio, the town so affectionately described in Arthur M. Schlesinger Jr.'s recently published memoir.[6] My class consisted of forty-seven eighth graders, all but twelve of them boys, including one who was seventeen years old! Predictably, we had some tense moments, and the overall experience solidified my desire to move up the educational ladder. Yet there were also highly rewarding moments with the students, and years later I was delighted to learn that one of them, Laurence Glasco, had become a historian himself.

My own career as a historian began in the fall of 1953, when I started graduate work at Notre Dame. Although I was rooted in Catholicism, and to that extent conscious of being part of a larger world, I was hardly an example of what has been called "rooted cosmopolitanism."[7] On the contrary, I was so much the provincial in professional terms that Notre Dame and Fordham were the only graduate schools to which I had applied. Nor did I enter upon graduate work with the clear-cut goal of becoming a scholar. My ambition—unconsciously self-limited by temperament and life experience—was far more modest. All I had consciously in mind was to earn a degree that would enable me to "teach at the college level," ideally at my old alma mater, the University of Dayton. But by the end of the first semester, my teachers—especially Marshall Smelser, M. A. Fitzsimons, and Father Thomas T. McAvoy, C.S.C., the head of the history department—had revolutionized that impoverished conception of what I should aim at. Simply by taking for granted that graduate students in history would become *historians*—persons who researched and wrote history, as well as teaching it—they opened new horizons of possibility and planted in me the conviction that I, too, could become that kind of historian.

Looking back, it is clear that the "Catholic" elements in the outlook

I brought to the professional study of history were deeply intertwined with those deriving from my family background and the general frame of reference I had formed up to that point. I have already indicated the most fundamental features of my religious sensibility, insofar as I can identify them. Here I will simply reiterate that, for me, religious faith meant that human life is not complete in itself, but has its ultimate meaning in relation to a transcendent God and the divine purpose built into all created things. That obviously entails a "foundationalist" position on values and the conviction that there is such a thing as the nature of things. It also entails a lively awareness of the limitations on human possibility, and a like sensitivity to the human capacity for evil. Indeed, I have never understood how intelligent people could take seriously the kind of millennial future promised by Marxism, and it has always seemed to me that anyone not invincibly self-deceived could verify the doctrine of original sin by a few moments of introspection.

If such an outlook is anti-utopian, it might also be described as a tragic sensibility. Whatever one calls it, it accords with the temperamental conservatism I recognize in myself. The same premises are, however, equally congenial to a species of relativism about earthly matters, which I associate with the insight that moral choices are not ordinarily between good and evil as such, but between divergent goods. I claim no originality for this insight, but I distinctly recall its becoming real for me a few years after I started teaching. My own experience likewise convinces me that religion is a powerful structuring element in the mental world of ordinary people, and therefore constitutes a much more important factor in the history of humankind than most historians seem to realize—especially historians of the United States, for whom religion tends to disappear after the colonial period.[8]

This religiously grounded outlook, though it has no doubt deeply influenced my approach to historical work, did not constitute a self-conscious scheme of interpretation, nor did it inspire my program of studies. I went to Notre Dame because—despite my small-town, public school background—I was, in moral and intellectual terms, the product of a Catholic world, and a Catholic university seemed the natural place for me to go. That decision largely determined the course of my professional career. I have never regretted the decision, but what I want to stress here is that it stemmed from the whole of my socioreligious formation, rather than from a more self-consciously purposeful religious motivation. I didn't start out with the idea of specializing in the history of Catholicism, or of becoming a "Catholic historian" in any apologetical sense. In fact, I knew virtually nothing about Catholic history when I started at

Notre Dame, and I remember being very surprised when I learned that in the 1890s controversies in the Catholic Church made headlines in leading secular newspapers.

As already noted, my career goals were unformed when I entered upon graduate work in history, which in those days featured broad preparation rather than the early specialization that is the rule today. Since it was a newcomer to the field—and academically suspect because Catholic—the department at Notre Dame overcompensated by setting up very stringent requirements.[9] One (then unappreciated) virtue of the program was that the length of time it took to complete the sequence of courses, written and oral exams, and theses (M.A. and Ph.D.), allowed students like myself to find themselves professionally. By the time I got my degree in 1960, I had more or less settled on American intellectual history as my specialty. I had, in addition, put the idea of a religious vocation behind me; gotten married; become a father; and taught at Notre Dame for three years, two as a teaching assistant and one as an instructor.[10]

Although I had not yet had the opportunity to teach it, the still-new and rather diffuse field of American intellectual history attracted me because it accorded with my intellectual temperament and research interests. My first scholarly publication, an article in *Agricultural History,* was based on my M.A. thesis, and two other early articles grew out of papers I had done for courses.[11] I can now see in them three indications of the pattern my scholarly development was to follow. First, they dealt with the kind of intellectual-cultural themes that continued to attract me, an attraction that I regard as a matter of personal temperament having no special connection to my religious beliefs. Second, they were articles, and I have remained an "article person" rather than a "book person," which is in keeping with my being more a "splitter" than a "lumper," though no historian can be exclusively either one or the other. Finally, they were discrete pieces, not parts of an overall research plan aimed at establishing me as an authority in a specific historical field. That too remained consistent, for my scholarly career developed, if not accidentally, at least opportunistically, in the sense that topics for research presented themselves, or were presented to me, and were taken up because they accorded with my intellectual disposition and/or the demands of time and place.[12] But these things build on each other, so while there was no predetermined plan, a pattern did emerge. By the late 1960s, I could describe myself as an intellectual historian with special interests in immigration, ethnicity, and American Catholicism.

My doctoral dissertation played a decisive role in the emergence of this pattern. It was a study of the Central-Verein, an organization of

German American Catholics established in 1855, which at the turn of the century developed an interest in social reform. That was a surprising development in view of the conservative line taken by German Catholics in the socioreligious controversies of the late nineteenth century, and it presented me with an interpretive puzzle.[13] My being a Catholic made the topic more congenial than it might otherwise have been, but I didn't choose it for that reason. It was suggested to me by my director, Father McAvoy, and the availability of most of the sources at Notre Dame made it particularly attractive. The project turned out to be an excellent one. Not only did it get me into Catholic history and the history of immigration/ethnicity; it also gave me an understanding of how social, institutional, and intellectual factors interact; it sensitized me to the importance of historically contingent events (in this case, World War I); and it showed me how individuals can influence larger social developments, but only if the circumstances are favorable. In substantive terms, it left me persuaded that, to the extent that it is corporatist in inspiration, "Catholic social teaching" is ill-suited to the American scene.

Methodologically, I learned from the dissertation that a book-length project is quite a different matter from an article. But the fundamental illumination I gained from the exercise concerned the *constructedness* of written history. After struggling as I did to make sense of the evidence and to give a coherent account of the Central-Verein's development, I could never again regard history as something that one simply discovered. The historian has to impose order on the evidence. Of course, that order cannot be imposed arbitrarily; it must not only accord with the evidence, it must grow organically out of the evidence. I firmly believe that such was the case in my account of the Central-Verein and its interest in social reform. But finding out by direct experience that history does not happen in chapters had something like the force of a revelation. My newly acquired sense of what I thought of as the fragility of the finished product made me a lot bolder in evaluating history as written by others. It also confirmed my attraction to the aesthetic dimension of writing history—for example, the delight one experiences on perceiving intelligible connections in the evidence that make it possible to turn a difficult corner in composition. For, as the elder Arthur Schlesinger noted in commenting on an essay written by his son, who was then a student at Phillips Exeter: "There is always a little thrill one gets from saying things well."[14]

In professional terms, quite a bit happened between 1960, when I finished the dissertation, and 1968, when the revised version was published as a book. By the latter date, I had already gotten tenure on the basis of a half-dozen or so articles (which would be quite a long shot at today's Notre Dame). That was the most significant immediate result of my breaking into print, but publishing also gives one visibility, which builds on itself through contacts with other scholars and invitations to undertake new projects. Two requests from colleagues at Notre Dame illustrate the point, and one of them introduced me to a field of research—the history of Catholic higher education—that taught me most of what I know about American Catholicism and resulted, thirty years later, in my most ambitious book.[15] The articles also put me in contact with historians elsewhere, whose interest in my work came across to me as validating my full membership in the guild. From the viewpoint of career development, two of these new contacts were particularly important: John Higham, who invited me to edit a volume in the Interpretations of American History series, of which he was an editor; and Timothy L. Smith, who encouraged me immensely by his enthusiasm for my work and greatly enriched my understanding of immigration history and religious history.[16]

These landmarks of professional development, important as they were to me, shrink to pathetic banality when set against the backdrop of national crisis. For, whatever later revisionists may say, the sixties was a decade wracked by crisis—the deepest, in my opinion, since the Civil War. Both Richard Hofstadter and Eugene Genovese went even further in a 1970 *Newsweek* symposium. Hofstadter called it "a multilateral crisis" unique in American history; Genovese saw it as unprecedented because "today, for the first time, the country faces a massive breakdown, manifested in every section, class and stratum, in faith in its ideals, institutions and prospects."[17] The coincidence of the civil rights/black revolution occurring at the same time as the Vietnam War was the key element in the national upheaval, but many other factors were involved—the coming of age of the baby boom generation, the discovery of poverty, the rise of the New Left, the outbreak of urban riots and campus upheavals, the emergence of the drug culture/counterculture, the sexual revolution, and women's liberation. And, for Catholics, there was also the Second Vatican Council, which set off a spiritual earthquake that transformed the religious landscape and added a new and shockingly unexpected element to the atmosphere of revolutionary instability that pervaded the national culture.

The combined effect of this seismic upheaval was a sweeping rejection of the past, an emphatic delegitimating of traditional authority, not only in religion and politics, but also in morality, education, and culture generally.[18] "Dissent," "change," and "relevance" were catchwords of the times. Young people—touted as the best-educated and most sensitive, idealistic, and committed generation America had ever produced—demanded immediate results. Reform as a goal gave way to revolution. Since the past had nothing of value to offer, history, the study of the past, suffered a precipitous decline. Thus, Mario Savio addressed the rebellious student body at Berkeley on "An End to History," and a participant in a mid-sixties symposium on the changing Church declared that "the past is irrelevant and the future will be essentially different."[19]

The turmoil reached its climax between 1965 and 1970, just as I was beginning to carve out a place for myself as a historian. It affected me deeply because it called into question in the most imperious manner what it meant to be a Catholic and an American, matters I had long regarded as already settled and firmly in place. Vatican II made significant revisions in the faith I had internalized, and not a few interpreters of the Council's meaning treated preconciliar Catholicism with near contempt—all of which had a severely destabilizing effect on my religious faith. The same was true in the political sphere. It was obvious the American system wasn't working as it should, and the ideals and institutions I had always cherished were being passionately rejected as the basest kind of hypocrisy. I don't mean to overdramatize my state of mind—life did go on without serious disruption—but the sense of crisis was real; I felt it personally, and it inevitably carried over into my historical work. Although it influenced what I was doing in the field of American Catholic history most directly, there was also some carryover in the area of immigration/ethnicity. But before looking into those matters, a few words about how the crisis affected my historical understanding more broadly considered.

First of all, the sixties gave me a much livelier awareness of the degree to which we are social beings. One factor here was the stark contrast between the social shaping of the World War II generation (to which I belonged) and that of the Vietnam War generation (to whose formation I was a dismayed witness). But the realization of our social nature came through even more vividly from the unnerving discovery that our "personal" convictions depend so heavily on their also being held by those around us. For when people we think of as sharing our deepest views repudiate them, it affects us—especially if we feel a particular respect for, or identification with, the people in question. And when the phenomenon reaches the scope and intensity of a societywide crisis of confidence—a massive breakdown of faith in ideals and institutions, as Genovese put it—few individuals can escape its impact. This did happen in the 1960s, and it made me realize that *we are all involved in each other's crises of faith.*[20]

Another, and not unrelated, result of living through the sixties was a new appreciation of *change in history.* To adapt Cardinal Newman's terms, that experience transformed what had been a merely "notional" idea of historical change into a "real" grasp of the raw actuality of change. I later drew on this deepened sensitivity in discussing the bitter divisions that arose among Catholic churchmen in the "Americanist controversy" of the 1890s. The following passage represents my most sustained effort to formulate the insight gained from having experienced latter-day controversies:

> Those who remember the 1960s can testify that the ground shifts rapidly in a time of ideological conflict. The dynamic of history takes over—which is only a grandiose way of saying that the understanding people have of public issues, and the stands they take, are transformed by the very process of change that is going on. Action taken demands counteraction; that in turn must be met by still further action in continuing ding-dong fashion. Opinion stated prompts immediate rebuttal, and that requires counter-rebuttal in the same manner. Attitudes, beliefs, and institutions that seemed firmly fixed are questioned, discredited, toppled over. Ideas that would have been called extreme a short time before, now attract wide support and become platforms for action. As ideological factions crystallize, a person feels obligated to take a stand, to choose up sides. . . . And once one adopts a position . . . it is difficult not to impute the worst motives to the opposition, not to portray their thinking in terms of its direst possible consequences.[21]

Besides enriching my understanding of change in a period of crisis, what happened in the sixties provoked my thinking on other historical issues. The generally antihistorical temper of the times, along with revisionist demands among professional historians for a "usable past," piqued an already existing interest in what I loosely thought of as "the philosophy of history." There was also a good deal of talk among literate Catholics about our newly acquired "historical consciousness." Curiously, however, historical consciousness was frequently taken to mean that history, as ordinarily understood, could be entirely dispensed with because each age had its own unique character; hence, the experience of past ages had nothing to do with ours, which was to be understood strictly on its own terms.[22] All this provoked an interest in how past and present are related, and in the issue of present-mindedness in historical writing. These themes, which reflect the impact of the sixties most directly, recurred in many of the essays on Catholic history that I wrote in that decade and later.

In reflecting on these matters, it occurred to me that Robert E. Park's concept of "marginality" was applicable to the situation of American Catholics like myself. I hesitate to use the expression because what Park meant by it, and what I mean by it, is *not* the same as "marginal" or "marginalization" as those terms are used today—that is, in reference to a person's, or group's, being left out, shunted aside, or otherwise disregarded by mainstream society. For Park, "marginality" referred primarily to the psychological situation of second-generation immigrants, persons of mixed racial background, or others who found themselves uneasily straddling the frontier where two cultures meet and overlap. Belonging to two cultural worlds, yet distanced from each by attachment to the other, the marginal person may experience a good deal of inner stress, but he or she is uniquely qualified to observe both cultures with a combination of the insider's sympathy and the outsider's detachment.[23]

By analogy, a sudden and profound *historical* shift can render a person formed in earlier times, but called upon to accommodate to the new shape of things, "marginal" to his or her own history. Vatican II certainly qualified as a sudden and profound shift in the world of American Catholicism, and it placed me, at least, in a state of Parkian marginality. That is, acquaintance with the new, as well as the old, version of Catholicism constituted a displacement of perspective that threw both past and present into a new light. The wholesale rejection of preconciliar Catholicism certainly made the past problematic in ways it had not been before. But the same was true of the present, for what warrant existed for believing that the Church's new teachings were any better grounded than the old? The inner tension this entailed for me obviously bore directly on religious faith itself, which had the effect of deepening the sense of crisis I felt.

The events of the sixties did not immediately suggest the idea of marginality. That came to me as a retrospective insight when I was putting together the collection of essays entitled *Keeping the Faith,* which was published in 1987. In the introduction, I make the claim that the interaction of past and present is the unifying principle tying the collection together. Trying to explain to the reader (and to myself) just what that meant brought home another retrospective insight, one that now seems perfectly obvious; namely, that the relation of past and present is multifaceted and can be approached from any number of directions. I had, in fact, done that without being conscious of doing so when I wrote most of the essays included in that volume. A classified listing of those approaches covers much of what I have written in the field of American Catholic history.[24]

1. *Theoretical Approach.* The only time I tackled the relation of past and present in a direct theoretical way was in the introduction to *Keeping the Faith* and in chapter 10 of that book, "History, Historical Consciousness, and Present-Mindedness." In the introduction, I developed the above-mentioned notion of marginality and its relation to the post–Vatican II situation of American Catholicism. Chapter 10, written specifically for the book, critiqued what I considered undue present-mindedness on the part of three other Catholic historians and outlined my own position, which I called a "methodological confession of faith." The faith in question, I should emphasize, is strictly *methodological*—that is, it's about doing history, not how religious faith bears on doing history. The latter no doubt influences the former; however, in relation to the past-and-present issue, the overriding need is the keep the historian's present-day commitments, religious or otherwise, from steering his or her work toward an outcome in line with those commitments. Present-day concerns inevitably, and quite legitimately, suggest historical topics for study. But the cornerstone of my methodological faith is the conviction that the historian's primary responsibility is to *the past, not the present.* And I am further convinced that whatever value historical work may actually have for the present will depend on how faithfully the historian meets that primary responsibility.

2. *Commemorative Approach.* Essays marking commemorative occasions obviously involve past and present. They are also particularly challenging, since those who commission or request them are likely to expect more in the way of "relevance" than the historian is capable of delivering. I wrote two, one for the 1976 bicentennial and the other for the centenary of the Third Plenary Council of Baltimore (1884), the last of the national gatherings of American bishops held in the nineteenth century. The latter was the easier one to deal with in terms of relevance, because I focused on education, and Baltimore III was a major landmark in the development of the parochial schools; for that reason, it was often referred to (usually negatively) in the controversy over Catholic schools in the 1960s. In the case of the 1976 bicentennial, I used as a prism the writings of Catholic observers on three earlier commemorative occasions: the golden jubilee of independence in 1826; the centennial of 1876, and the sesquicentennial of 1926. This triangulation limited the evidence to be considered, but at the same time threw important changes in Catholic thinking into sharp relief.

3. *Reversals of View.* A striking shift in contemporary opinion can also awaken curiosity about the past. Thus, when American Catholics in the 1960s turned against the Middle Ages, which they had formerly revered as the high point of western civilization, it prompted me to investigate the genesis, development, and function of medievalism in American Catholic thought. Exploration of these themes made clear that collective images of the past are both shaped by, and contribute to the shaping of, a people's understanding of their contemporary situation. My research also reinforced a previously existing interest in romanticism, which played so large a role in the great medieval revival of the nineteenth century. That fact made American Catholics' rejection of the Middle Ages even more intriguing because (except for their antimedievalism) Catholics seemed to share fully in the romanticism that permeated American culture in the 1960s. Without attempting to solve that puzzle, I wrote a popular article on "Our New Age of Romanticism" in 1967, and again drew attention to romantic parallels in a later article on the Catholic upheaval of the sixties.[25]

4. *Historical Background Approach.* This angle of approach to the past-and-present problem resembles the one just described, but differs in being primarily intended to illuminate a contemporary issue by showing how it is related to, or grew out of, the past. My work on the history of Catholic higher education illustrates this approach—indeed, it began in response to an invitation to do a "historical background" chapter for a book of essays on Catholic colleges in the 1960s. But the first such instance was an article examining the role of immigration in American Catholic intellectual life, the weaknesses of which were widely deplored in the late 1950s.[26] That essay combined my interest in intellectual history and what I had learned from my dissertation on the Central-Verein.

5. *Analogy Approach.* The dissertation itself had no contemporary stimulus other than the all-important fact that completing it was essential to my academic survival. But in revising it for publication in 1968, it dawned on me that similarities existed between the "identity crisis" that struck German American Catholics as an ethnic group early in the twentieth century and the situation of American Catholics as a religious group in the 1960s. The perception of that analogy, sketched in the last chapter of the book, was worked out in greater detail in my essay "The Crisis of Americanization," originally published in 1969, which argued that the forces of social assimilation were affecting Catholics and the Church itself in much they same way they had earlier affected European immigrant groups.

The mention of *Americanization* opens a different perspective on my approach to American Catholic history. For, to quote a passage written more than thirty-five years ago, I regard Americanization—meaning adjustment to the social, cultural, and political norms of American society—as "the great theme in the history of the Catholic Church in the United States."[27] Its salience has, however, varied over time. In the 1880s and 1890s, differences of opinion about what Americanization required in concrete terms (in education, for example) led to deep divisions among churchmen that culminated in a furious controversy over what was explicitly labeled "Americanism." Two generations later, a great outpouring of research on those battles marked the coming of age of Catholic historical scholarship in the United States, and at the same time reflected a heightened self-consciousness about the relation of religion and culture on the part of a new generation of American Catholic intellectuals.[28]

In keeping with the World War II generation's positive attitude toward the nation, that body of scholarship generally sided with the Americanizing "liberals" of the late nineteenth century. The historiographic consensus, broadly speaking, was that the accommodation to American ways urged by the liberals was justifiable in prudential terms, and did not endanger the religious faith of Catholics. Thus "Americanism" was not a "heresy," as the conservatives charged, because it did not touch upon the central doctrines of faith but was confined to social and cultural issues that were in themselves religiously "indifferent." This interpretation, as it now seems to me, depended on (or at least accorded with) the pervasive dualism of preconciliar Catholic thought, which made so sharp a distinction between matters temporal and eternal.

Since Vatican II, scholarship on Americanism has shifted in ways that lend support to that opinion. The old polarities—along with supernaturalism itself—are now definitely out of favor among Catholic intellectuals. They have been largely displaced by immanentist and historicist tendencies that invest "this world" with an intrinsic religious significance it lacked when seen *sub specie æternitatis,* as a kind of antechamber to "the next life." As this new way of looking at things "secular" took hold, historians of American Catholicism began to discover genuinely *theological* issues in Americanism. Thus, whereas the older generation dismissed the charge of heresy as a "phantom," more recent investigators are able to detect the real thing. But they do not necessarily regard that finding in negative terms, since what was considered heresy in the preconciliar Church can now be interpreted as a theologically acceptable correction of Catholic teaching. Consider the example of Dennis P. McCann, who is admittedly not a historian but a specialist in religious studies. He insists that American Catholics must "own up to the Americanist heresy," but then goes on to hail it as a good thing. In fact, he proposes that "Americanism," as recovered and generalized from systematic reflection on the historical past, should be appropriated and applied in the here and now as a normative principle governing religious thought and action.[29]

By making liberal democracy the touchstone of authentic Catholicity, McCann carries his Americanism too far for me. For although I too regard Americanism as a good thing, I also believe it is possible to have too much of a good thing. No doubt my ambivalence is traceable in large part to my formation in the old dualistic outlook. But "Americanism" and "Americanization" are not transparent terms. On the contrary, they are extremely abstract and capacious, not to say vague or even vacuous. What they mean in any given context depends on how they are defined—which, since the terms are used so loosely, must usually be inferred or guessed at. To insist on the need for distinctions should not be conflated with ambivalence. However, a keenness for making distinctions also bears the mark of my formation in the preconciliar Church—although I never studied enough of St. Thomas to claim that as the source!

Americanization/assimilation also, of course, figures prominently in studies of immigration and ethnicity. As noted earlier, my perception in the late sixties of an analogy between the Central-Verein's assimilation-induced identity crisis and the situation of American Catholics led me to work out the parallels in the essay on the Church's "Crisis of Americanization." But most of what I have written in this area reflects my interest in matters of definition. I am referring to the essays analyzing the language used in the discussion of ethnic interaction and tracing changes over time in the meaning of terms/concepts like *melting pot, assimilation, cultural pluralism, minority group,* and *identity.*[30]

Thanks to my dissertation, I got into this area of research a full decade before the "ethnic revival" began in the late 1960s. That phenomenon, along with the tremendous upsurge in immigration since 1970 and other sociocultural changes, gave the study of immigration/ethnicity far greater "relevance" than it had earlier. But while the subject took on new interest, it did not have, for me, the same degree of intense personal relevance that changes in the religious sphere had. This was so despite the fact that Catholics—most notably, Andrew Greeley, Michael Novak, and Geno Baroni—played leading roles as advocates and popularizers of the "new ethnicity." Their work (which I have discussed elsewhere)[31] shared the interpretive outlook of the new research on immigration/ethnicity being done by academic historians. The latter, which poured forth in great abundance, was radically revisionist; in fact, it turned the prevailing interpretive framework upside down.

To oversimplify for the sake of clarity, the older viewpoint—of which Oscar Handlin was the outstanding representative—rested on two fundamental assumptions: first, that assimilation or Americanization was a reality, a social process that had actually taken place in the history of immigration to the United States; second, that despite the social, cultural, and psychological costs entailed, assimilation was a good thing because "Americanization" meant that immigrants became full participants in the freest, most democratic nation on the face of the earth. By the early 1970s, the new conventional wisdom among historians of immigration—and even more so among spokespersons for ethnic minorities—held just the opposite. According to this view, immigrants had most emphatically *not* assimilated—the melting pot, as the cliché had it, "never happened"! Which was all to the good, because America was an oppressively racist and imperialist society that no decent and halfway intelligent person would want to be "assimilated" to.[32]

My immersion in the history of the Central-Verein left me with no doubt whatsoever that assimilation of immigrants had, indeed, taken place. But I was equally convinced that it was such a highly complex process, which touches on so many facets of individual and group experience, and upon which so many variables impinge, that generalizations about it are subject to almost infinite qualification.[33] Thus, while assimilation is a reality, the concept is not a very useful analytical tool unless applied with a high degree of theoretical self-consciousness and precision of specification. In other words, matters of definition are crucial in this area. And as I see it, the revisionist claim that assimilation simply didn't "happen" is valid only if the process is defined as one that removes every vestige, every lingering memory, of the immigrant's ancestral heritage. That, I willingly grant, did not happen in the past, and does not happen now. But it is wildly exaggerated to conclude from this fact that nothing legitimately called assimilation "happens" to immigrants over the course of time and generational change.[34]

The ideological aspect of the revisionists' position was unacceptable to me for reasons that require little elaboration. I was willing to grant the existence of genuine social evils, the folly of stubborn adherence to mistaken policies, and the overall failure of the nation to live up to its ideals. But given the ideological convictions whose formation I have already described, I could not accept the view that the "American Creed" itself was a fraud, a hypocritical smokescreen, and that assimilation was in reality an effort to domesticate immigrants to a social system of race-, class-, and gender-based oppression. Moreover, the expectations of social harmony and spiritual renewal entertained by some champions of cultural pluralism seemed to me unrealistic, not to say utopian.[35]

Another critical reaction to the newer literature on immigration/ethnicity is more closely related to my being a Catholic. I am referring to the widespread tendency (noted earlier as common among historians in general) to overlook, or deprecate, the importance of religion as an independent variable, a causative factor to be taken seriously on its own terms in interpreting people's actions or analyzing historical events. Perhaps the most frequently encountered form this tendency takes in immigration history is the implicit assumption that "ethnicity" is not simply a more inclusive category than religion, but also a more basic reality. According to this view, "religion" doesn't count for much in terms of historical explanation, because considerations of ethnicity, race, class, gender, or power provide deeper insights into what was really going on, even though the historical actors in question may have formulated the issue in terms of religion.[36] To repeat, my own experience convinces me of the power of religious belief in shaping a person's view of life and giving direction to his or her actions. Historians who neglect or disvalue the causal significance of religious faith run the risk of seriously distorting past reality—especially perhaps in immigration/ethnic history, where religion is so often central to a people's sense of group identity, and where religious institutions so often dominate their organizational life.

To speak of "distorting past reality" of course raises a question about this essay itself. How close does it come to past reality, to the ways in which religious faith affected, and was affected by, my professional involvement in history for five decades? All I can say is that I have done my best to avoid distortion. Self-deception is, to be sure, an ever-present danger, especially in an undertaking of this sort. As to memory itself, even St. Augustine acknowledged in his profound meditation on that subject in book ten of his *Confessions:* "I cannot totally grasp all that I am."[37] It may be comical to suggest comparison with that great exemplar, but the point applies in this case too. And however unimpressive the results, this effort to trace out the interaction of faith and professional activity confirms for me another of Augustine's observations: "I have learned many things I never knew before . . . just by writing."[38] I hope others will be encouraged to do the same.

Notes

1. According to the 1940 federal census, 5,450 (91 percent) of Wilmington's 5,971 residents were native-born whites; 64 (1 percent) were foreign-born whites, and 457 (8 percent) were African Americans. Slightly more than one in five of its residents twenty-five years of age and older had completed high school. The town has since more than doubled in size and moved modestly upscale. An abandoned Air Force base where glider pilots trained in World War II has served since 1980 as the national hub for Airborne Express; a few years ago, *Time* magazine (December 8, 1997) featured Wilmington as a "hot small town" whose (rapidly disappearing) bucolic charm made it a magnet for jaded yuppies.

2. There was, however, one quite essential connection with Irish organizational life. In the early 1920s, when the "troubles" in Ireland aroused intense feeling and activity among Irish Americans, my parents-to-be met at an Irish rally in Columbus, Ohio, where my mother lived and where my farmer father was visiting a relative.

3. In November 1950, the American bishops issued a pastoral letter on education entitled "The Child: Citizen of Two Worlds," which contains the following language: "[The child] must be seen as a citizen of two worlds. He belongs to this world, surely, but his first and highest allegiance is to the kingdom of God . . . [and] his chief significance comes from the fact that he is created by God and is destined for life with God in eternity." Hugh J. Nolan, ed., *Pastoral Letters of the American Hierarchy, 1792–1970* (Huntington, Ind., 1971), 421.

4. On piety and moralism, see Joseph Haroutunian, *Piety versus Moralism: The Passing of New England Theology* (1932; repr., Hamden, Conn., 1964); for Reinhold Niebuhr's influence on several leading historians, see Michael Kammen, *In the Past Lane: Historical Perspectives on American Culture* (New York, 1997), 28.

5. For the ideological revival, see Philip Gleason, *Speaking of Diversity: Language and Ethnicity in Twentieth-Century America* (Baltimore, 1992), chap. 7; for ideological identity formation, see Erik Erikson, *Identity: Youth and Crisis* (New York, 1968).

6. Arthur M. Schlesinger Sr. grew up in Xenia and described it in *The Rise of the City* (1933; repr., Columbus, Ohio, 1999), 62–63, and in his memoir, *In Retrospect: The History of a Historian* (New York, 1963), 3–6. The younger Schlesinger never lived in Xenia, but knew it from visits to his grandparents. See Arthur M. Schlesinger Jr., *A Life in the Twentieth Century: Innocent Beginnings* (New York, 2000), chap. 1. Xenia is about twenty miles from Wilmington; I bought my first car for the commute to my teaching job at what was then called Xenia Township School.

7. For rooted cosmopolitanism, see David Hollinger, *Postethnic America: Beyond Multiculturalism* (New York, 1995), 5, and the authorities cited there.

8. For an interesting (and rare) example of a major historian's analysis of the neglect of religion, see William H. McNeill, "Carl Becker, Historian," *The History Teacher* 19 (November 1985): 98–100. However, the critique of Becker's "resolute secularism" is much softened in the chapter about him in McNeill's *Mythistory and Other Essays* (Chicago, 1986), 160–61. For U.S. historians' general neglect of religion, see David M. Kennedy, "A Vexed and Troubled People," *The History*

Teacher 28 (May 1995): 420–21; Kammen, *Past Lane,* 13–15; and Jon Butler, "Jack-in-the-Box Faith: The Religion Problem in Modern American History," *Journal of American History* 90 (March 2004): 1357–78.

9. Doctoral work in history did not really begin at Notre Dame until after World War II. For evidence that Catholicism was regarded by mainstream historians as incompatible with true scholarship, see Peter Novick, *That Noble Dream: The "Objectivity Question" and the American Historical Profession* (Cambridge, U.K., 1988), 174n., 203n., 366n. As late as the 1980s, a prominent American historian still deemed it needful to emphasize in a letter of recommendation that the Catholic academic background of the person being recommended should not, in that case, be considered a negative factor.

10. I will not attempt to cover teaching in this discussion; for brief notes on the subject, see Philip Gleason, "Reflections on Teaching," *American Catholic Studies Newsletter* 26 (Spring 1999): 11–13.

11. These articles are "The Attitude of the Business Community toward Agriculture in the McNary-Haugen Period," *Agricultural History* 32 (April 1958): 127–38; "A Scurrilous Colonial Election and Franklin's Reputation," *William and Mary Quarterly,* 3rd ser., 18 (January 1961): 68–84; and "*Moby-Dick:* Meditation for Democracy," *The Personalist* 49 (October 1963): 499–517. My first publication unrelated to any graduate school requirement was "From Free-Love to Catholicism: Dr. and Mrs. Thomas L. Nichols at Yellow Springs," *Ohio Historical Quarterly* 70 (October 1961): 283–307.

12. Conscious of the fortuitous quality of my own career pattern, I found it reassuring that A. J. P. Taylor accentuated the same thing in an amusing memoir of his development as a historian entitled "Accident Prone, or What Happened Next," *Encounter* 49 (October 1977): 52–61.

13. For the revised, published version, see Philip Gleason, *The Conservative Reformers: German-American Catholics and the Social Order* (Notre Dame, Ind., 1968); for an abbreviated version of my solution to the interpretive puzzle, see Philip Gleason, "An Immigrant Group's Interest in Social Reform: The Case of the German-American Catholics," *American Historical Review* 73 (December 1967): 367–79.

14. Arthur M. Schlesinger Jr., who quotes this line (*Life in the Twentieth Century,* 89) goes on to say: "This . . . sentence for some reason has lingered in my mind ever since [the early 1930s]. It remains true."

15. The results of these requests were: Philip Gleason, "American Catholic Higher Education: A Historical Perspective," in *The Shape of Catholic Higher Education,* ed. Robert Hassenger (Chicago, 1967), 15–53; and Philip Gleason, ed., *Contemporary Catholicism in the United States* (Notre Dame, Ind., 1969). The book published thirty years later is Philip Gleason, *Contending with Modernity: Catholic Higher Education in the Twentieth Century* (New York, 1995).

16. The result of Higham's invitation is Philip Gleason, ed., *Catholicism in America* (New York, 1970). Thanks to Tim Smith, I was able to participate in a rewarding series of conferences on immigration and religious history that he organized in the 1970s.

17. Richard Hofstadter, "The Age of Rubbish," *Newsweek,* July 6, 1970, 20–23; Eugene D. Genovese, "A Massive Breakdown," *Newsweek,* July 6, 1970, 25–27; quotations on 21, 25.

18. I agree here with Robert Bellah's assessment of the 1960s: "Far more serious than any of the startling events of the decade was the massive erosion of legitimacy of American institutions—business, government, education, the churches, the family—that set in particularly among young people." Bellah, "The New Religious Consciousness and the Crisis of Modernity," in *The New Religious Consciousness*, ed. Charles Y. Glock and Robert N. Bellah (Berkeley, Calif., 1976), 333–34.

19. Mario Savio, "An End to History," in *The Berkeley Student Revolt: Facts and Interpretations*, ed. Seymour Martin Lipset and Sheldon S. Wolin (Garden City, N.Y., 1965), 216–19. The quotation in the text is from James E. Beichler, ed., *Law for Liberty: The Role of Law in the Church Today* (Baltimore, 1967), 78.

20. For the crisis of faith as it came through to me, and my efforts to analyze it, see Philip Gleason, *Keeping the Faith: American Catholicism Past and Present* (Notre Dame, Ind., 1987), chaps. 7–8, esp. 136–39, 172–77.

21. The passage is from an essay entitled "The School Question: A Centennial Retrospect" originally published in 1984; it is quoted here from Gleason, *Keeping the Faith*, 134. For Newman's distinction between notional and real assent, see his *Grammar of Assent* (1870; repr., New York, 1964), esp. chap. 4.

22. From lecture notes of mine dated September 23, 1966, it seems probable that I first heard this view expounded a few months earlier at a meeting in Chicago of the Catholic Commission on Intellectual and Cultural Affairs.

23. This paragraph and the next are adapted from Gleason, *Keeping the Faith*, 5–7. See also Robert E. Park, "Human Migration and the Marginal Man," *American Journal of Sociology* 33 (May 1928): 881–93; Everett V. Stonequist, *The Marginal Man* (New York, 1937); and Milton M. Gordon, *Assimilation in American Life* (New York, 1964), 56–57.

24. Unless otherwise indicated, all the essays referred to in next five paragraphs may be found in Gleason, *Keeping the Faith*.

25. Philip Gleason, "Our New Age of Romanticism," *America* 117 (October 7, 1967): 372–75; for the second discussion of romantic parallels to the sixties, see Gleason, *Keeping the Faith*, 92–96. For another review of the Catholic scene touching on many romantic elements, see Andrew M. Greeley, *Come Blow Your Mind with Me* (Garden City, N.Y., 1971).

26. Philip Gleason, "Immigration and American Catholic Intellectual Life," *Review of Politics* 26 (April 1964): 147–73; for the background chapter on Catholic colleges, see above, note 15.

27. The quotation is from the headnote to the first selection in Gleason, *Catholicism in America*, 10.

28. For discussion of the points made in this and the next two paragraphs, see Gleason, *Speaking of Diversity*, chap. 11.

29. See Dennis P. McCann, *New Experiment in Democracy: The Challenge for American Catholicism* (Kansas City, Mo., 1987), chap. 1 and 163, 165.

30. Aside from my article "American Identity and Americanization," in *Harvard Encyclopedia of American Ethnic Groups*, ed. Stephan Thernstrom, Ann Orlov, and Oscar Handlin (Cambridge, Mass., 1980), 31–58, these essays in semantic history are collected in Gleason, *Speaking of Diversity*.

31. See Gleason, *Keeping the Faith*, chap. 2, "Immigrant Past, Ethnic Present."

32. For a fuller discussion, see Philip Gleason, "Crèvecoeur's Question: Historical Writing on Immigration, Ethnicity, and National Identity," in *Imagined Histories: American Historians Interpret the Past,* ed. Anthony Molho and Gordon S. Wood (Princeton, N.J., 1998), 120–43. See also Russell A. Kazal, "Revisiting Assimilation: The Rise, Fall, and Reappraisal of a Concept in American Ethnic History," *American Historical Review* 100 (April 1995): 437–71.

33. The complexity is well illustrated in Elliott R. Barkan, "Race, Religion, and Nationality in American Society: A Model of Ethnicity—From Contact to Assimilation [and comments thereon]," *Journal of American Ethnic History* 14 (Winter 1995): 38–101.

34. In his *Assimilation in American Life,* Milton Gordon makes many useful distinctions and concedes that "behavioral or cultural assimilation" has taken place on a large scale. But his seven-stage "model" of assimilation sets so stringent a standard for completion of the social process that his book was widely assumed to have completely discredited the "myth" of assimilation. For discussion, see Gleason, *Speaking of Diversity,* 72–75.

35. For examples, see Gleason, *Speaking of Diversity,* 40–41, 52, and 78.

36. For example, in discussing group conflict in colonial Pennsylvania, Alan W. Tully states that "religious groups became the focal point of ethnic interaction in politics." Putting it this way, instead of simply saying religion was a more important factor than differences in language and nationality, which were also involved, suggests that "religion" was merely a vehicle through which the more basic something-or-other called "ethnicity" expressed itself. See Tully, "Ethnicity, Religion, and Politics in Early America," *Pennsylvania Magazine of History and Biography* 107 (October 1983): 503–4. For an extended critique of the tendency to treat "ethnicity" in this fashion, see Wilbur Zelinsky, *The Enigma of Ethnicity: Another American Dilemma* (Iowa City, Iowa, 2001).

37. I use Frank Sheed's translation (*The Confessions of St. Augustine, Books I–X* [New York, 1942], 180) because that is where I first encountered the passage, but Garry Wills, *Saint Augustine's Memory* (New York, 2002), is a more accessible translation of book ten and it includes Wills's splendid commentary and notes.

38. Quoted in Peter Brown, *Augustine of Hippo: A Biography* (Berkeley, Calif., 1967), 273.

ANNE M. BUTLER

2 *Personal Landscapes of Catholicism: From East to West*

On the always-turbulent landing approach to the Salt Lake City airport, one feels the West rise up in greeting. The intermountain West, embraced by the northern Rockies in one direction and the Sierra Nevada in the other, awaits. Snow-topped peaks soar stunningly into the air, the out-of-place Great Salt Lake lies still upon the valley floor, the brown and parceled land reflects its unforgiving aridity—sharp reminders that one is about to enter a magnificent, unparalleled arena of contested spaces and conflicted peoples.

Other national regions may claim landscapes of beauty and legacies of contention. The West, however, with its stereotypical cast of characters, its odd history braided into its extravagant geography and excessive climate, its chronicle muddied by fact and fancy, its heritage shaped by love and hate, takes a singular place in the American odyssey.

What other section of the country managed to emerge as an enduring symbol of national identity and unity, as it harbored, even fostered, dissent, disagreement, and discrimination? Where are there such diverse vistas with mixes of people and cultures, so that the resulting package of natural environment and human experience is used to explain the very essence of American democracy? What other segment of this country promoted itself and has been promoted as the source of American "character" and the guardian of national "values"? The scene below the descending airplane seems to answer, "Here, it all happened here; this is the West."

For many years, I thought I knew the West. Although I lived in the East, my research about nineteenth-century frontier women had taken me more than once across the spaces west of the Mississippi River—Montana, Wyoming, Texas, Colorado. I had crisscrossed these states time and again, visiting their cities and towns, conversing with their residents, thinking about their histories.

When in 1989 a professional opportunity offered the chance to become both associate editor of a scholarly western history journal and modern-day pioneer, pulling up stakes, leaving kin, and setting forth on a life adventure, I accepted. I learned quickly that I did not know the West and even less so my new state of residence, Utah, the heartland of the Church of Jesus Christ of Latter-day Saints. This, the fortress of the Mormons, was now to be my home.

In this place of much beauty and few people, a newcomer comes to understand that anyone—Native American, Christian, Jew, Buddhist, Muslim, faithful, atheist, or agnostic—outside the lodge of Mormonism is classified as a "gentile." While this homogenous, all-purpose labeling may seem ironic, arrogant, or amusing, it prods one to think about heritage and belief. In Utah, as a scholar of the American West and a researcher in the field of Catholic history, I found myself pushed to examine my personal intellectual and spiritual moorings. Ultimately, I had to determine what sort of "gentile" I would be in the Beehive State? If in 1847 Brigham Young actually had gazed across the Great Salt Lake Valley and announced, "This is the place," where, in his Zion, would I stand?[1] Would Utah bring me closer to my own religious core, or draw me into a community known for its aggressive proselytizing? How, if at all, would my current research about the experiences of Catholic nuns in the nineteenth-century American West help me to sort out these questions?

In the first instance, it had not been easy to move to the West, where Catholicism, like everything else, is separated by great distances. Not a great deal has changed since 1899, when a missionary of the Sisters of St. Dominic recorded, "The Catholics were few and far between. . . ."[2] While Catholic clusters pepper the urban map, as in Santa Fe or San Francisco, the faithful, always thinly distributed across the vast rural terrains, remain so.

One drives for many miles with no sign of the familiar church and rectory, school and convent complex. Parish schools and mission stations, once operated by small bands of religious sisters, closed years ago. In out-of-the-way towns and on isolated Indian reservations, humble Catholic churches stand in lonely, silent salute to the Church of Rome.

Today, many western Catholics live through cold winters and hot summers, much like their forebears, holding to a hardscrabble life far from the centers of their faith. For them, an itinerant priest, like the circuit riders of yore, pressed by the call of many, visits and moves on. His presence infuses the spirit and he leaves giving assurances he will return in four, six, or ten weeks. Before him stretches hundreds of miles of empty road, treacherous weather, and other Catholics, who watch and wait for his arrival.

In the meantime, perhaps a single nun, willing to exchange her motherhouse community for a tiny apartment, takes on a complex array of support services and educational activities for the remote Catholics. She prepares families for baptisms and confirmations, she comforts the sick, leads prayer, sustains her neighbors. Town folk, even Catholics, know little of the origins of these western parishes and have long forgotten whether Ursulines or Benedictines or Franciscans struggled to establish schools and hospitals for their pioneering ancestors. Indeed, they may be unclear about the congregation from which their one sister journeyed to staff their hamlet parish. Is she a Sister of the Holy Family from San Francisco, a Holy Names Sister from Portland, or perhaps a Daughter of Charity from St. Louis? The local religious knowledge of the people seems uneven, as is understanding of the historical connections to the larger American Catholic community. Despite demography and technology of the modern world, much of western Catholicism retains its mission aura of yesteryear.

In contrast, in Baltimore, Maryland, cradle of American Catholicity, Catholicism surrounds the city, caresses its people. The Catholic community traces its spiritual and cultural roots to the era of Archbishop John Carroll, consecrated in 1790. In downtown Baltimore stands the architectural masterpiece of Benjamin Latrobe, the Basilica of the Assumption, the first Catholic cathedral in the United States. The old St. Vincent de Paul church, as it has for decades, beckons to those who work and play at Baltimore's harbor. Close to the Maryland penitentiary in the heart of the city, St. Frances Academy, operated by the Oblate Sisters of Providence, still educates African American students, a daring initiative started during slavery by this first religious congregation for black women in the United States.

Unlike the West, drive in any direction and witness the fruits of Baltimore's early religious heritage. Catholic schools, hospitals, colleges, seminaries, convents, community centers, cemeteries, hospices, retirement homes, monasteries, retreat centers, novitiates, and soup kitchens fill the horizon. These institutions of religious identity operate inside small row houses and on large campuses; they fill the spaces of the inner city and the outer suburbs. They are found in grand Victorian structures and modest modern dwellings. Among them are buildings owned by Jesuits, Sulpicians, Carmelites, Redemptorists. List the workers in this urban vineyard and a partial litany includes Sisters of the Good Shepherd, Mission Helpers of the Sacred Heart, Josephite Fathers, Daughters of Charity, Xaverian Brothers, Mercy Sisters, Christian Brothers, and Franciscans.

It was to this Catholic world that I came as a teenager. From northern farm to southern city, from foster parents to biological mother, from Christian Science Sunday school to Roman Catholic Mass—dramatic changes awaited me in the Baltimore of 1952. Before all this transition rained down on me, I was not uninformed; I had heard about Catholics; in fact, I even knew that I was one, baptized in St. Joseph's Church in Somerville, Massachusetts, when I was six weeks old.

For close to thirteen years, however, I, along with four other youngsters, had lived as a foster child in a small rural community outside of Boston. On a bitterly cold January 1, 1940, my mother, buffeted by a slew of misfortune, brought me, a year-old toddler, by train to this country town, where I was to stay for six months. The months evolved into years, forming what came to be my childhood.

It was a life of ordinary routines, marked by both a touch of sternness and a portion of indulgence. Our guardians were well into their fifties, their two children grown to adulthood and off to their own lives. We "rescued" children played and grew in a sort of no-nonsense atmosphere, expected to be well-behaved, do our chores, go to school, and make limited commotion. Like friends with "real" parents, we had Christmas stockings dangling from the mantel and gifts hiding under the tree, fees for school field trips, outfits on Easter, uniforms for Girl Scouts, and birthday parties with cake and ice cream.

Our lives were not lavish, but neither were they spare. Not one of us questioned our place at this hearth. We never fretted to each other that perhaps these guardians would pack our bags and send us away, if we, like all children, failed to be perfect. No Dickensian world with pathetic waifs here. Safe, secure, and loved, we gave little thought to whether this was "normal." We were a family together.

We counted among us two boys and three girls—a pair of brothers, an older teenager, a Panamanian of African heritage (I was thirty-five before old photographs brought that fact to my attention), and me, the youngest. The older ones teased the younger, but also took us fishing off the rocky Atlantic Coast, taught us to play the piano, and protected us beyond our farm.

For the five of us, this was "home." It included yearlong, seven-days-a-week care, with July lazed away at a cottage on Nantasket Beach as the guests of our foster parents; the room and board—and everything else in the world of a child—was four dollars a month, totaling, since the July charge was canceled, but forty-four dollars per year—with no comment or change in treatment when absent parents fell behind in visits, letters, or payments.

Our foster mother had one rigid stipulation for this motley assortment of children: all must attend the same church—hers. There would be no Sunday tour about the town, coordinating services and programs, dropping off and picking up at the various houses of worship. There would be no mix of theologies among us, no conversations about who believed what and why, just as there would never be a whisper about one child's nappy head, another's alcoholic father, or everyone's divorced parents.

So, Sunday mornings saw me, with my staunchly Republican foster parents and ersatz siblings, off to the Christian Science church. There I learned about Mary Baker Eddy and her teaching that none of us should smoke tobacco, drink alcohol, or seek medical care from a physician.[3] We did our Sunday School readings, recited the Lord's Prayer, sang hymns, and absorbed the Eddy prescriptions for "well-being," most of which seemed grounded in a conviction that a cheerful attitude conquered all. Talk of violence, mendacity, ill fortune, or death was not permitted; indeed, we were taught that people did not die, they were just "away."

Illness, consequently, was not exactly permitted in our home. When some childhood complaint laid us low, we could miss school for a day or two. A toothache warranted a hot flannel compress. Measles, mumps, and chicken pox were looked on as "normal" maladies of the young, but upset stomachs and sore throats were expected to be gone by five o'clock, when we should be dressed and ready for supper. We tried to comply, for we did not want our guardian to resort to calling the Christian Science practitioner to "read" for us. She was a kindly woman who would spend time with Eddy's writings on our behalf, but she also advised that we drink large cups of steaming hot water laced with lemon and some other foul brew, a concoction none of us could tolerate.

Despite this rather hodgepodge approach to medical science, we all survived. Fortunately, we were a healthy lot with few fevers or life-threatening mishaps among us. We had no regular doctor, but every two months I dutifully walked from my classroom to the office of the school dentist, who charged fifty cents per visit; he must have been better than adequate—I have never lost a tooth. When one of us incurred a bloody injury or a possible broken limb, our guardian called a neighbor on the next farm—a prominent Boston pediatric surgeon of extraordinary goodness—who decided, in a courtly and kindly manner, if Mary Baker Eddy should be set aside in favor of medical intervention.

On weekends and holidays, my guardian often made arrangements for me to visit with my own kin. It was a complicated trip, but by the age of six, I was permitted to travel alone, with various relatives or friends waiting at the transfer points to make sure I hopped on the correct connection. I took three buses, or "the cars," as they were known, to the city where, among my biological father's people, an entirely different religious and social world enveloped me.

There, a huge collection of relatives waited with a good strong dose of Boston Irish Catholicism, complete with drinking, smoking, swearing, and bickering. They also threw in a fierce loyalty to Democratic politics, an unflagging devotion to the Joseph P. Kennedy family, and a regular reliance on doctors, medicines, and hospitals.

Nobody had much use for Protestants and certainly not the English. The scars were too fresh for those who had emigrated to escape Ireland's troubles, only to find themselves in service to Boston's elite, so scornful of the Irish. My great-uncles spoke in bitter language about New England's discrimination, and my great-aunts said nothing better about their domestic service in the homes and dinner clubs of wealthy Protestants. As for the reality of sickness and death—the Irish knew plenty about that, as I saw in more than one family wake.

My father's aunt, legally blind and with a tongue like a razor, was my caregiver and it was with her that I stayed. On the Friday nights in Somerville, I knew fish—usually haddock or cod—would be on the supper menu, because that was "Catholic," as much so as the baked beans and brown bread of Saturday night was "Boston." While my aunt, in her one-room, shared-bath quarters, prepared the meal over a gas burner, she recited the rosary along with Richard Cardinal Cushing. His singular strong accents resonated from the radio and through the little tenement room. I knew better than to speak during the cardinal's prayers, but I did not mind for his was a mesmerizing voice. My early Catholicism may have skipped the usual timetable for catechism instruction, but I did know how to recite a Hail Mary.

Every Saturday shopping trip included a visit to a Catholic church, so that I could light a candle. I loved to do this and always prayed for my mother, whose features and voice I found hard to recall. Often, I sat lost in a cavernous old pew, while my aunt fumbled about in her blindness to find the way into the confessional. With her shadowy vision, she feared missing the kneeler and crashing to the floor, for such scenes had wounded her pride more than once. Despite her caustic ways, I learned from her that something special happened in that darkened space, where Catholics entered into a special dialogue that brought the comforting balm of forgiveness. Even she, woman of biting words, however, could not dragoon my father into the performance of that religious duty. I wondered if she was right, that he would stay out of bars, "straighten up," and "keep his nose clean," should he too slip behind the heavy velvet curtains, as well as "take the pledge."

After the detour to church, we stopped to see my great-grandmother, Ma Ryan, a somber, sad woman. I thought her intimidating and a bit mysterious. As a young wife, she with my great-grandfather had "come on the boat from the Old Country," bringing with them the first of their thirteen children, my grandmother, destined to die from tuberculosis before the age of thirty-three. Ma had lost husband, children, and kinfolk, enough so that she only wore widow's black; she was always dressed for the next funeral. Her gloomy house was filled with photographs of the dead relatives, holy pictures, rosaries, palm, and crucifixes; she gave me cake and milk in her cavernous kitchen because my great-uncle sat alone and forbidding in the shuttered dining room, making his way through yet another bottle of Four Roses whiskey. These were poor people and theirs were not cheerful homes, but their Catholicity could not be missed.

Sunday mornings my aunt and I set out for a fast-paced walk along treacherous brick sidewalks for the square in Somerville. It was my charge to be her eyes, watching for broken and warped bricks so she did not fall, as we raced along for eleven o'clock Mass at St. Joseph's church. At her command, even my father, the former altar boy, consented to attend, when he was around.

Mass began on the hour in the upstairs church and on the half hour downstairs. The number of people overwhelmed me. A crush of worshipers hurried up and down the front steps, moving in and out for one liturgy or the other. Outside the nave, ushers sat at little tables, stacks of coins before them, as they made change for the "seat collection." One could see how this practice, with its lightning-fast exchange of quarters, nickels, and dimes, gave rise to the Protestant rumor that Catholics "had to pay to get into church."

Once inside, I loved the richness of the main church interior, the sun's rays bringing light to the stained-glass windows, the beauty of the vestments, the saintly statues, the aroma of incense, the ringing of bells, the sounds of murmuring Catholics, standing, kneeling, and sitting in a confusing array of motion. What were all these people doing? Whatever it was struck me as infinitely more compelling and dramatic than the sanitized proceedings at the First Church of Christ Scientist.

Each of my domestic camps looked on the other as slightly suspicious. My great-aunt found the school lessons from Mrs. Eddy's *Science and Health with Key to the Scriptures* tucked in my coat pocket to be amusing, but she greatly admired my Christian Science foster mother. They, joined in their care of me, enjoyed a warm friendship for many years. Nonetheless, my great-aunt thought the Christian Science religion "odd," and she often remarked that Mary Baker Eddy was "crazy" and "quite a dame," whose "own son tried to have her committed to an insane asylum." Occasionally, her inner gall boiled over, and she "warned" me that someone in that Protestant foster family would encourage my guardian to "get rid" of this little Catholic. My father encouraged me to do as told by my guardians, including go to church in a willing way, and promised to visit me, a vow he had trouble keeping over the years. My foster family occasionally implied there was something unsavory about Catholics, who certainly had too many children. These little jabs aside, there was a pleasant enough truce between the two lodges. I was the most fortunate of youngsters, for I loved and was loved in both of these wildly divergent and contradictory environments.

Yet, this bifurcated religious training did leave an odd tattoo on my identity. I never felt a comfortable fit under either roof. As my teen years approached, I could not hold seriously to the teachings of Mary Baker Eddy. The shockingly sudden and very real death of my foster father swept away any vestiges of attachment I felt for Eddy's ideas. This good man died as much from medical ignorance and misuse of medications as he did from the heart attack that felled him. Even at my young age, I understood the mistake he had made.

I, the only child left of the five, stayed on one more year with my foster mother. We had a special, warm time together; she never again required that I attend the Christian Science church.

Still, my own clan beckoned to me, but my immersion in Catholicism had been too erratic to give me a foundation. Over the years, I had learned quite a lot, but not in a systematic way that made a religious framework. In 1952, I left New England to live with my mother and her new husband. With her own life stabilized, my "out-of-the-church" mother moved quickly to address my religious status, sending me for instruction at the parish, seeing that I received the sacraments, getting me to Mass each Sunday, turning me over to the nuns for my high school education.

Catholic presence and lore permeated the life of Baltimore, my new home. Over time, renowned prelates, such as James Cardinal Gibbons and Lawrence Cardinal Shehan, personified that presence for the entire community. Shehan, born and raised in Baltimore, educated in the old parish of St. Ann's, and cut from the fabric of the city, stood out as a local son who rose among the clergy, returned to his hometown, and remained connected to its people. A man who cared deeply about justice and peace, Shehan used the pulpit to articulate his spiritual and intellectual defense of racial equality and moral citizenship.[4] He embodied the best in a Catholic life, and Baltimoreans of every persuasion appeared to appreciate that about him.

It was with the School Sisters of Notre Dame, however, that I figured out how to be a Catholic. A congregation of dedicated teachers, the School Sisters mapped out a pedagogy predicated on academic achievement and spiritual growth. They guided by example; they inspired by demeanor. They illuminated for their students the meaning of Catholic womanhood, in which they expected their charges to reach for secular and religious excellence in the pursuit of a faith-based life. From them, I, a refugee from a rocky religious background as fractured as my parents' marriage, began to learn the meaning of the rituals of faith that had off and on been part of my Boston life. Unlike most of my classmates who had sat through plenty of Catholic lessons, I devoured the religious curriculum, especially the third year devoted to Church history. The lives of the saints, the impact of the popes, the doctrinal controversies—I could not learn enough about these matters. I always scored perfectly on Sister Augusta's tests in religion class.

Outside of school, for the first time, my friends were all Catholics, and they knew their way around the language of scapulars, rosaries, and genuflecting. Their homes had sick-call sets and palm from the previous Easter. Their mothers went to daily Mass, their fathers placed a St. Christopher statue on the car dashboard, their families began the evening meal with grace. They reframed my Boston childhood, placing me at the heart of those earlier years and eliminating my lingering feelings of being an outsider in my own Catholic past.

Clearly, a major component of Baltimore Catholicism was drawn from its network of schools. Elementary schools attached to every parish contributed to the cultural conversation of young adults. We knew each other by parishes, not by neighborhoods. I went to Catholic schools and, as an adult, I taught for a total of ten years in several Catholic schools. My son attended the alma mater of his father, my daughter that of her mother—no better place for my children than with Jesuit priests and Notre Dame sisters.

Did someone have a joke about mother superior or the elderly monsignor? Do not tell it to me. I had no patience with sarcasm or humor directed at those who had thrown me a Catholic lifeline. In Baltimore, my Catholic awareness had been able to take shape, giving me a spiritual base from which to consider my life and fermenting a cultural loyalty that embedded itself in my thinking.

I credit that Popish world with leading me toward my university studies. Although I had married at an early age and dropped out of college, the intellectual exhortations of my nun teachers continued to echo in my head. Eventually, I pushed myself to finish my undergraduate degree and moved on to graduate work at the University of Maryland, anxious to explore at last my lifelong interest in the American West.

Such a solidly eastern institution might seem an unlikely place to pursue nineteenth-century history that occurred beyond the Mississippi River, but such an assumption would be inaccurate. A prominent western historian, Walter Rundell, led the history department as chair, and the proximity of the National Archives with its rich regional records sealed my scholarly future. Rundell proved to be something of a Methodist male version of the School Sisters of Notre Dame. He had high standards and expected his students to meet them, on time and without complaining. My Catholic school training transferred well to the secular campus and to his oversight.

In my first semester at Maryland, in search of a subject for a graduate research paper, I settled on the subject of prostitutes in the American West. I cannot claim that some weighty intellectual concept fueled my choice, nor did it connect to my Catholic sentiments. I simply wondered whether the lives of prostitutes had been as glittering and glamorous as every Western movie portrayed. Thus began, somewhat by chance, a project that emerged as a major research commitment for me, one that brought me many publishing opportunities and considerable attention in the media.[5]

Predictably, I suffered through every bad joke and sly remark about my dissertation topic, which some did not hesitate to dismiss as questionable scholarship. Over the years, colleagues, even high-ranking university administrators, seemed to have no hesitation about asking me salacious personal questions or requesting "good" phone numbers. Thanks to my mentor, I learned how to counter such comments, using just a hint of the icy tone learned from my imperious great-aunt as a way to stifle the jocular remarks.

At the same time, the emerging field of women's history further legitimated prostitution as an appropriate arena for scholarly consideration. With a growing call for "history from America's underbelly," more scholars recognized that the size of a group, its "respectability," or its fame should not be the only standards for historical research. Better to look for the social, economic, and political impact of women, especially those overlooked in our writing of the past. Historians of many stripes moved women from ethnic and minority communities out of the shadows and to the center of their research. No subfield benefited from this shift more than western history, where the rich diversity of its many peoples begged for scholarly attention.

Eventually, prostitutes, with their lives woven through western vice districts and the annals of regional crime, led me to women incarcerated in penitentiaries. Although prostitution usually remained the concern of town or county officials, a prostitute charged with a major felony often found herself in the hands of state and territorial authorities for punishment. In these circumstances, women rather frequently entered male penitentiaries in the nineteenth-century West. Many archivists and librarians had warned me that western prison records would not yield information about women inmates, but I learned otherwise. Convinced that, like prostitutes, incarcerated women had something to reveal about western institutions, I undertook a second project that I hoped would add to our knowledge of race, class, and gender in the American West.[6]

I did not anticipate that these two groups of women—prostitutes and female prisoners—would return me to my earlier high school interest in Catholic history. Yet I began to notice that newspaper accounts of criminal women often contained a reference to local nuns, a point that quickly caught my attention. Commonly, a reporter noted that a poverty-stricken prostitute had died at the hospital of the Catholic sisters or that nuns were making Sunday visits to a nearby prison. I began to see that Catholic sisters in many western places and from many different congregations had reached out to the poor and the suffering in the American West, when there were few civic institutions to provide services to local constituencies.

Once my search revealed that by 1890 between six and nine thousand sisters lived west of the Mississippi River, I knew they represented a significant population of single women carving a space in a region largely regarded as male-centered and family-dominated. Given the stereotypical notions of nuns as quiet, sheltered women, locked away from the world, their presence in such wide-open towns as a Virginia City, Nevada, or a Butte, Montana, raised a broad range of questions: how and when had these women arrived in the West; under what conditions had they traveled; why had they come to the chaotic frontier; what were their relationships with the bishops and priests of the West; how did they support themselves; what were their worldly and spiritual expectations; how had secular persons viewed them; what relationships did they share with the people around them; and how could the outcomes of their western lives be assessed in religious and secular terms? Clearly, nuns had undertaken their ventures deliberately, earning a living, delivering social services, strengthening their congregations, and advancing their church in the American West. I came to see the sisters in a larger context, one that underscored their importance as culture brokers, Catholic workers, and community builders in the West. For me, located in the East, the linkages between criminal women and nuns suggested the fabric of gender, as well as that of Catholic history in the West, was far more interwoven and intricate than we had suspected.

This was my scholarly grounding when, in 1989, I moved to the history department of Utah State University, where I was to teach and act as an editor of the *Western Historical Quarterly.* My Catholic experience, forged in the breeding grounds of American Catholicity, deeply influenced my personal thinking and the research agenda that I brought to the West. As I turned toward the mountains and valleys of the West, I did so acutely aware that eastern Catholicism largely held an honored social, economic, and political place, thanks to generations of immigrants who brought their religion and ritual from a number of Old World homelands. Together, they muted their national differences in the commonality of their religious allegiance. They created a world where people either were Catholics or generally recognized the role of the Church in the building of local community. As a consequence, one, unless a late-bloomer Catholic like me, did not need to think about religious identity; it was widely known and instantly accessible. Although I had been tardy in finding this atmosphere, the church of my baptism and the schooling of my adulthood directed me toward my life in the West.

Within the religious component of my life, this sense of community culture, this feeling of spiritual closeness, this citywide visual affirmation of Catholicism evaporated when I relocated to Utah. Overnight, I moved to a frontier Catholicism—a world where my religion receded from a position of importance, prestige, and social acceptance to that of a missionary church. Utahans were not acquainted with nor particularly interested in the warp and woof of eastern Catholic life. I entered a community that, in the main, looked on Catholics—regardless of character or conduct—as "mysterious" and "peculiar," perhaps even "seditious."

It took me a while to understand that Catholicism may have added to some of these perceptions with its own historic controversies. They stemmed from conflicts between Catholics and Native Americans, Catholics and Protestants, and Catholics and Catholics. While it might seem that these relationships left only a legacy of wounded minds and hearts, such did not prove to be the case. The clashes and controversies also imparted positives and gave spiritual vigor to the establishment of Catholicism in the West, necessarily forcing participants to examine themselves and their most cherished beliefs, sometimes making adjustments to both.

Among themselves, Catholics frequently allowed bickering and ill will to prevail. Squabbles among Catholics often centered on the rancor that surfaced among immigrants of differing national origins. These quarrels intensified because of an American church that waffled about whether to retain its European character or adopt a New World flavor.[7] Teaching sisters and priests, whose cultural backgrounds and native languages rankled local Catholics, absorbed the brunt of these arguments. German settlers opposed the arrival of French-speaking sisters, French Catholics grumbled about an Irish pastor, and Irish immigrants rejected German-speaking nuns.

As I learned more about this unrest, I thought that none of this should be surprising because the American West took shape as a contentious space marked by social, economic, and political conflict. That was the early story of Catholicism, one that often resonated with disagreement, hardship, laxness, and indifference. In a contested West, Catholics waded through disagreements with native populations, rivalry with Protestant opponents, and their own arguments. Although not always attractive, these abrasive encounters infused the western Catholic experience with life and helped to shape its distinct and hardy character.

With its shaky beginnings so often mired in friction played out in a fractious environment, western Catholicism managed to grow into a faith with a strong regional identity. As I perused the records of missionaries from several decades, gone were the priestly accounts of hiking through hip-deep snow to carry the sacraments to a dying miner or of building a wilderness chapel with Indian people. Gone were the most poverty-driven days of pioneer convents; sisters no longer wrote of living in abandoned chicken coops and gathering berries to survive. The challenging environment remained, but modern people acquired skills and technology to help them combat the most trying aspects of western isolation.

Eventually the faith steadied, moving into the twentieth century with its practitioners more comfortable in western life than had been the pioneer faithful. While the West remained the same, a land of grand mountains, crashing rivers, dry plains, and deep valleys, its Catholic folk accepted their remoteness from the centers of American religion. They relied, as western people were known to do, on each other for solace and support. Theirs was not to be a Catholicism grounded in the oldest arenas of the U.S. church, as I had known in Baltimore. Yet it proved to be a faith woven together by the power of individual spirit and community bonding, always attached to the Vicar of Christ.

Accordingly, like all frontier institutions, the Catholic Church in the West drew on the skills of adaptation and accommodation for survival. If there were but few houses of Catholic worship to catch my eye as I drove from Salt Lake City, through Ogden, Brigham City, and Nibley on the way to Cache Valley, one could not miss the vital role of the laity, as well as the cooperation between pastor and parish that marked western churches. Small groups of Catholics, bound by the essential beliefs of their church, created a Christian family atmosphere within their spiritual space. The physical manifestations of Catholicism appeared simple, but the spirit of Christian involvement in the maintenance of Catholic life came to be writ large.

Still, within this Utah community, where the religious and political power of Mormonism circumscribed life, Catholic scholarship lacked a significant local grounding. Not only was it peculiar to be a Catholic, but even more so to study Catholics, especially nuns. More than once I sensed a puzzled cool response, a slightly strained courtesy when I spoke about my Catholic research. After all, had not only a scant handful of Catholic sisters lived in the nineteenth-century West? What could be compelling about these silent, black-robed women? In a dramatic and fast-paced "Wild West," what possible historical import had these anonymous women shut away in locked cloisters?

Through my research, by now including more than fifty religious congregations with western mission houses, I knew how wrong-minded such notions were and had learned of the nuns' importance—as women, as Catholics, as religious, and as westerners. The community chronicles, superiors' correspondence, profession registers, and pioneer memoirs with which I had worked for several years gave witness to the sisters' impact on the emergence of western communities and the transformation of American religious life. Out of little-used papers in convent archives had arisen, among others, Mother Emily Power of the Sinsinawa Dominicans, Mother Xavier Ross of the Sisters of Charity of Leavenworth, Mother Pancratia Bonfils of the Sisters of Loretto, Mother Joseph of the Sacred Heart Pariseau of the Sisters of Providence, Mother St. John Pradinaud of the Sisters of Charity of the Incarnate Word—all forceful women who led other forceful women in the building of the West.[8]

While their stories filled me with zeal, these women and I worked alone, as I grieved for the tortured Catholic history of the Intermountain West. So I, with my documents from pioneer convents, trudged along in the West—certainly not cut off from my church, but not convinced that this Catholic research of mine measured up as legitimate in LDS Utah or even among my academic colleagues, both Mormon and non-Mormon.

A graduate student's pursuit of a thesis topic in history changed my perceptions. Initially, the student planned to edit an extensive collection of letters written from the 1930s to the 1950s by five biological sisters to their mother. Among these sisters, raised in the Methodist religion, one, at the age of twenty-nine, had converted to the Catholic faith and entered a California convent. Eventually, my student chose to omit four of the sisters and limit the thesis to an examination of those letters from nun to mother.

In her analysis, the student sought to demonstrate how the sister developed new familial bonds with members of her religious congregation. At the same time, over several years, the sister renegotiated parent and sibling ties, strained by her conversion and vocation. The result was a paper that explored the diverse ways, in a pre–Vatican II world, the meaning of family, within a secular and religious context, shifted and expanded, despite competing loyalties.

My student, Utah born and Mormon bred, began this complex study with no knowledge of Catholicism other than perhaps some vague inaccuracies—Catholics pray to statues, the pope wants to "take over" the United States, nuns enter convents because of failed romances. She did not know any Catholics, few attended school with her, none lived around her, she had never seen a nun, and had never spoken to a Catholic on the subject of religion. Many of her Mormon friends thought her choice of such an alien research topic perplexing, startling, or worrisome.

Undaunted by these responses and problems, she launched her study. This student, unwilling to accept the letters at face value, wanted to understand the woman who wrote them and her way of life. The student came to me with long lists of questions about Catholic belief and culture—some easy to answer, others grounded in complex theology or complicated ritual: what is a novena, what was a habit and why were there so many different ones, what is a postulant, what is a holy day of obligation, why were nuns prohibited from eating in public, what is the difference between a sister and a nun, when and what is the Feast of the Sacred Heart, what are liturgical colors, why do they exist, what is meant by the Mystical Body of Christ, what happens at Mass, what do Catholics believe?

Some of the questions surprised me; did not everyone know these things? Others sent me searching my Catholic reference books. Each question spawned a dozen more. Schooled in different religious tenets, we learned to be comfortable with each other as we entered into a remarkable conversation that explored the meaning of Catholic life and its impact on a religious sister. Our discussions ran for hours and increased in sophistication and exuberance as the subjects pushed the boundaries of our respective worlds.

Over time, my student perceived the way the sister's spiritual life, the mission of her congregation, and her personal accomplishment supported one another. She began to grasp the dramatic tension that existed between the families—one chosen, one given—and the strategies used by the sister to reconcile the two disparate worlds. She saw how this individual sister assumed a new identity within a religious community, even while preserving and nurturing biological family linkages.

At the outset, the religious congregation involved denied my student permission to work in the community archives, research that would have enhanced an appreciation for the congregation's mission. Because sisters, generally, are enthusiastic promoters of religious women's history and extend a hearty welcome to researchers, internal congregational matters almost certainly influenced that decision; my student was crushed, certain, my assurances aside, that her Mormonism explained her exclusion. Despite the setback, she proceeded, tracking other research leads, contacting sisters in another province of the congregation, and intensifying her use of Catholic literature.

The finished thesis, a graceful and intelligent paper, fell into the hands of a retired sister in the California community. Then in her early nineties and with a wealth of pedagogical expertise, she instantly appreciated the paper's careful scholarship, balanced tone, and winning argument. At this nun's invitation, student and professor traveled nearly eight hundred miles for a unique convent visit.

My Mormon student finally had the opportunity to meet and mingle with a remarkable group of Catholic sisters. She joined them at meals, walked through their gardens, sat in their community room, visited their chapel, and slept in their convent. Hour after hour, the sisters' long tradition as educators infused the lively conversations and affirmed the academic boldness of a student who, harnessing her intellectual and personal courage, entered an unknown religious and cultural arena. One evening, she sat in the sister's library and peppered her friends with an amazing array of questions—several of which made me smile with joy at the open exchange, the straightforward answers, the honesty, and the lack of guile by all. Finally, the student had the pleasure of coming face to face with the subject of her thesis—the now ninety-five-year-old nun whose spiritual life, professional endeavors, and letters to her family had so captured the novice scholar. When we left California, we took with us new friendships, a renewed excitement about the history of religious women, a deepened commitment to promoting their experiences through scholarship, and a greater awareness of the cross-cultural rewards of exploring religious frontiers.

This research episode brought Catholic history into a non-Catholic world and, through one student carpenter, built bridges, joining two cultures. It energized my life as a teacher and a scholar, reminding me that the pursuit of history need not be limited by individual faith or geographic location. It merely requires respect for ideas, freely given and fully engaged. Catholics and their buildings may be few inside the boundaries of Utah, but no artificial borders close off the life of the mind. Through intellectual rigor, thoughtful inquiry, personal dignity, and unflagging good humor, my Mormon student demonstrated the highest level of academic ecumenism to me and to a congregation of California sisters. Perhaps above all, my student and I had rollicking good fun doing religious history together. From her example, I found a way for my Catholic scholarly place to be more relaxed in the Great Basin Kingdom of Brigham Young. Inside myself pulsated an even stronger sense of my Catholicism and an empowered conviction of the inherent value in pursuing the Catholic history of the American West.

The cauldron of the nineteenth-century West produced many of the pieces that influenced the rich democratic heritage of the nation. Among them were divergent forces that gave western Catholics a religious foundation grounded in the West but bonded to the universal church. From these experiences and impulses, western Catholics built a legacy with which to face the challenges of America's modern Catholicism and to do so as champions of the enduring sacred elements of their faith and the unique events of the pioneer days of the American West. I am not certain that my Mormon student and I fully understood these elements at the time we shared our adventure in Catholic history. But I do know we both came away from our experience together with greater respect for each other and for ourselves, as well as a closeness to our own personal beliefs.

My immersion in the Mormon world of Utah proved interesting and informative. Ultimately, it toughened the roots of my eastern Catholic life, with its off-center origins and strange family structures. The Beehive State, home to the Latter-day Saints, did not suffocate my inner faith or my scholarly research. Bonded to the offbeat eastern Catholicism of my odd childhood and spiritual past, as well as the western Catholicism of my adulthood and intellectual present, I find myself comfortable with and grateful for both.

Notes

An earlier version of this article appeared as "Western Spaces, Catholic Places," in the *U. S. Catholic Historian* 18, no. 4 (Fall 2000): 25–39, and was the winner of the Arrington-Prucha Prize, offered by the Western History Association.

1. Among a broad range of Mormon history accounts, the work of Leonard J. Arrington is widely recognized. For example, see Arrington, *The Mormon Experience: A History of the Latter-day Saints* (New York: Knopf, 1979), or Arrington, *Brigham Young: American Moses* (New York: Knopf, 1985).

2. *Sisters of St. Dominic of the Congregation of the Holy Cross, Annals, 1890–1923*, 59, Dominicans of Edmonds, Archives, Rosary Heights, Edmonds, Washington.

3. There is an extensive literature concerning Mary Baker Eddy and the Church of Christ Scientist, which is headquartered in Boston, Massachusetts. For examples, see Stephen Gottschalk, *The Emergence of Christian Science in American Religious Life* (Berkeley: University of California Press, 1973); Julius Silberger Jr., *Mary Baker Eddy* (New York: Little, Brown, 1980); Gillian Gill, *Mary Baker Eddy* (Reading, Mass.: Perseus Books, 1998).

4. See Joseph Gallagher, *The Pain and the Privilege: Diary of a City Priest* (Garden City, N.Y.: Image Books/Doubleday, 1983), esp. 375–78.

5. Anne M. Butler, *Daughter of Joy, Sisters of Misery: Prostitutes in the American West, 1865–90* (Urbana: University of Illinois Press, 1985).

6. Anne M. Butler, *Gendered Justice in the American West: Women Prisoners in Men's Penitentiaries* (Urbana: University of Illinois Press, 1997).

7. Marvin R. O'Connell, *John Ireland and the American Catholic Church* (St. Paul: Minnesota Historical Society Press, 1988); Charles R. Morris, *American Catholic: The Saints and Sinners Who Built America's Most Powerful Church* (New York: Vintage Books/Random House, 1998), 82–85.

8. For congregational histories that introduce these subjects, see Mary Synon, *Mother Emily of Sinsinawa: American Pioneer* (Milwaukee, Wis.: Bruce Publishing, 1955); Sister Julia Gilmore, SCL, *We Came North: Centennial Story of the Sisters of Charity of Leavenworth* (St. Meinrad, Ind: Abbey Press, 1961); Sister M. Celestine Casey, SL, and Sister M. Edmond Fern, SL, *Loretto in the Rockies* (Denver: n.p., 1943); Sister Mary of the Blessed Sacrament McCrosson, *The Bell and the River* (Palo Alto, Calif.: Pacific Books, 1956; softcover ed. Seattle: Heath Printers, 1986); Sister Mary Loyola Hegarty, CCVI, *Serving with Gladness: The Origin and History of the Congregation of the Sisters of Charity of the Incarnate Word, Houston, Texas* (Milwaukee, Wis.: Bruce Publishing, 1967).

DAVID EMMONS

3 Homecoming: Finding a Catholic Hermeneutic

Early in the fall of 1990, I got a call from Albert Borgmann, a University of Montana professor of philosophy and one of the university's most distinguished scholars. The call was to invite me to the faculty's Philosophy Forum, a healthy mix of the solemn and the hilarious and one of the university's more durable and useful traditions. The topic for that October forum would be my recently published book *The Butte Irish: Class and Ethnicity in an American Mining Town, 1875–1925*, an account of the rambunctious and conspicuously Catholic Irish who dominated the world's greatest mining town. A number of faculty from various departments who had read the book were there, along with many other interested faculty and students. They all wanted a word with me about the book's deeper meanings, including, I came to learn, some meanings unknown to me.[1]

After a lively and generally favorable discussion, Albert handed down his philosophical verdict. The book, he said, was a result of a "hermeneutic of affection." I remember nodding my head knowingly; the Philosophy Forum is not a good place to display even partial ignorance. When the forum ended, I hurried back to my office to look up "hermeneutic." I wasn't entirely certain what it meant and I knew I had not consciously employed one. Borgmann meant the word in the usual way as the art or craft of interpreting the world through its various texts. But all historians do that. The more important word was "affection." I came to understand it better when I was introduced to its opposite, the hermeneutic of suspicion, and the uses to which those two words, *affection* and *suspicion*, have been put. The affectionate construct and retrieve past lives; the suspicious deconstruct and recast them.

Borgmann believed that I was predisposed to the former; that I couldn't be suspicious of the Butte Irish without being suspicious of myself. Self-analysis, including a healthy suspicion of one's own motives, may not be an inherently bad thing. But the deconstructor self-deconstructed is circular to the point of dizziness and in this instance, as in most, is the kind of thing historians are better off leaving to others. Albert hadn't said I had a Catholic "analogical imagination." I came later to wish he had. It would have meant that, analogically, I was in communion with these Irish and with God, that I shared some kind of traditional lore, almost in the sense of tribal culture, with the Irish and that both they and I saw God as "present in the world, disclosing Himself in and through creation." That kinship would have given me special access to the Irish's interior worlds. It would also have left me unwilling—perhaps totally unable—to engage in any reductionist theorizing when I gained that access, which strikes me as a very good thing indeed. In all events, I had become in ways I had not entirely understood a very active participant in my historical retelling.[2]

Hermeneutic is far too grand a word for all this. It also is one that implies a consciousness of purpose that simply was not there while I was reading and trying to interpret my various texts. There was no art or craft in what I was doing; there was only what I'd rather call a triggering mechanism, an actuating cause without material form or substance. For those not squeamish about these sorts of things, I would call it my animating spirit. I was only vaguely conscious of it at the time, which is the way with the immaterial parts of a person. My affection was not, then, a hermeneutic—unless such can be unconscious. It was merely my way of choosing my historical "friends"; that is, those for whom I felt an affection, and whose lives I wished to intrude upon and retrieve. After the forum, I recall wondering if perhaps I hadn't been too active a participant—and too affectionate and unsuspicious a one. Were there conscious interpretive strategies I should have used? Should "affectionate" have been among them? Certainly there was nothing about that particular approach that guaranteed success. I was relieved when Borgmann concluded that, on balance, my personal involvement had served me well.

But it was not so much whether my way of going about it had yielded good history or bad that interested me; it was the simple acknowledgment by one whose own work I greatly respected that I had brought to my history more than an objective impartiality and less than a withered and lifeless exercise in deconstructionism. Historians are supposed to tell the truth, or as near to it as they can get. Neutrality can easily become disengagement, and whatever truth emerges from that is likely to be too incomplete and sterile to be of much historical value. Critical theory can easily become reductionist, and what emerges from that is discursive and intellectually imperialistic. Still, there remained some confusion as to the full meaning of "affectionate." I understood that it meant more than just that I "liked" Butte's Irish and that from this chumminess came understanding. I hoped that affection meant only that I recognized the world they had made, that it was familiar to me. Familiarity does not necessarily mean affinity or fondness; it can mean the opposite. In this instance, it did not. I did enjoy the company of most of them, and I was always prepared to let them speak for themselves. But the simple idea that I liked these people and hence understood them left open the distinct and equally simple possibility that I liked them but did not understand. All of this aside, I was taken and encouraged by Borgmann's remark. I, too, believed that somehow I had come to know Butte's Irish, and in ways that were both deeper than tracking and interpreting documents and fairer than looking for subtexts through some critical theoretical prism.

But what really gave interest to this effort to understand what Borgmann had meant was that his comment was based on a misconception. He knew that I was Catholic; he may even have known that my background was distinctly working class. His comment, however, arose from his assumption that I was of Irish descent and that my interpretive strategy was an ethnic inheritance, the result of the intersection of ethnicity and scholarship. So common is this perception that I long ago quit trying to correct it. Let me correct it here: I am not Irish. My Catholicism is from the cradle, but the cradle was brought from southern Italy with my mother's parents. My father's family was from Oklahoma, ethnically mixed and, with the exception of my disinterested father, almost aggressively Protestant. The Italian Catholic side easily won whatever sectarian and cultural battles were waged over my youthful soul and its initial claims were seldom contested—and never by me. The Italians laughed more, for one thing, and served better food. I'm sure that more was involved than brio, but if I thought of myself as anything at all, it was Italian American and Catholic. My baptism and first communion were in Denver's St. Catherine of Siena parish; not at St. Patrick's, and certainly not at Bethel Baptist. Being Italian and Catholic was a part of the rhythm of my early life. Being Irish was not.

I can now say that I learned important lessons from my youthful Catholicism. I discovered that this was a faith deeply felt but lightly worn.

I learned that it was literally festive, proudly "irrational," and filled with mysteries. To use an old but useful word, it was earthy and nothing like the dour and repressive institution (especially on matters of sex) that its critics charged—evidence enough, perhaps, that St. Catherine's was not an "Irish" parish. I became convinced that the priests must have prayed daily for a tiny fraction of the temporal authority that many non-Catholics assumed—and feared—they had. It might also have begun to occur to me that St. Catherine's pews were filled with people of what might charitably be called modest means and equally modest dreams. Most were not strivers, and ambivalent at best about those who were. I came to understand that the Church contained and sustained a powerful sense of community. My grandmother was the cook at the rectory and always aware of who in the parish might have needed something and how the need might best be met. Hers was a small commonwealth, but a cooperative one. I learned later that parishes like St. Catherine's were the headquarters for what historians now call enclave cultures. Those who moved up in social class also had to move out of the enclave, and that was never easy. As the only member of my family to attend college, not to mention graduate from one, I learned that lesson from personal experience.

I may also have been made remotely aware of a political fact of life: Not all Democrats were Catholic, but all Catholics were Democrats. I assumed that was so because all the Catholics I knew were working class and, if not poor, at least fearful of becoming such. As with other early lessons, it required some seasoning—meeting rich Catholics, for example—before I fully understood that the "Catholic vote" was only partly the result of economic insecurity. Republicans, it seemed, had not quite outgrown the anti-Catholicism of their origins. Southern Democrats were scarcely more tolerant of papists, but in my world, Oklahoma was a foreign country and the real South was on another plane of existence altogether. Most of these lessons from a Catholic childhood were more cultural than theological or liturgical, but, for a historian at least, more useful for that reason. Historians who would understand past American workers must know something of the Catholicism of so many of them. Similarly, historians who would decipher past American politics must deal with the "Catholic vote" and the anti-Catholicism that accounted for it. Both sets of historians, in other words, must "speak Catholic" or at least be prepared to listen carefully when it is spoken.[3]

I would like to think that I obeyed that rule and paid attention to what Butte's Catholic Irish and reflexively Democratic workers had to say to me. That, however, is a method, not an interpretive strategy. Historians are supposed to listen. If I offered anything useful about Butte's Irish miners, if I made even partial sense of their lives, it had to have been because my whole and inherited approach—not just my method—was the right one. I had to have been not just an attentive listener but an empathetic and affectionate one as well. But because that approach—that animating spirit—owed nothing to tales of the Suffering Gael, the Great Hunger, perfidious Albion, or the little people, I had to look elsewhere for the source of my affection.

Always assuming that I did, in fact, come to understand these Irish, did that understanding perhaps arise from shared social class affiliation? I doubt it. I do not believe—nor did most of the Butte Irish—that a people's dominant affiliation is with their social class. And even if it is, the Butte Irish miners did work that I, and all my working-class relatives, could understand only in theory. They had an occupational rather than a social-class consciousness. I have a better feeling for the uncertainties of livelihood, for the fear, shared by all members of working-class families, of the wage earner being "out of work" (a most revealing phrase), but it would be fatuous for me to pretend to know what that underground world of the Butte mines was like. Technically, I suppose I was of the proletariat, but I had not been proletarianized.

If there was no shared ethnic affiliation and if shared class affiliation operated only sporadically, religion is about all that is left. But how did the religious connection play itself out? Perhaps my putative kinship with the Butte Irish resulted from the fact that the American Catholic Church was so overwhelmingly Irish that merely going to Mass was enough to leave me thinking and acting Irish. I do not dispute the Irish dominance of the American Church. There is no question, for example, that the mid-nineteenth century devotional revolution in Irish Catholicism was brought to America and made a part of American Catholicism. But by the time I entered it, the Church had shed the Jansenist influences of nineteenth-century Irish devotionalism and I would dispute any contention that that influence had ever had much effect on the parish of St. Catherine of Siena. I had not been Hibernicized either.[4]

I needed other explanations. One was to reverse the rejected notion cited just above and ask what being Catholic had to do with being Irish. There is powerful historical testimony that it had everything to do with it. The point is not, then, that the American Catholic Church was so Irish, but that the American Irish were so Catholic. Any Catholic, particularly if working class, could be expected to develop some understanding of Irish Americans. Such an understanding would not necessarily be sympathetic, or even empathetic, and would necessarily be incomplete, but it would always be there. It was with me. It was part of my birthright, involving beliefs and feelings, values and dispositions that made me think and act in certain ways.

This explanation still commends itself, partly because I believe all historians have these inheritances and the triggering mechanisms that are a part of them, and it makes perfect sense that this would be an aspect of mine. These are complex mental orientations and they are not learned in graduate school. They consist of a mix of formal training; the presence or absence of a religious faith; and a wild assortment of political, social, racial, and cultural background noises that are barely heard but always significant. They assert our essential values. In other words, I'm back to my animating spirit again. There is bound to be a fair amount of reading back—Wordsworth called it "after meditation"—as we try to trace and re-sound those noises and, in our writing, try to convert them into something like music, but that reading back is not in itself enough to doom the enterprise. Taking inventory is always useful, even if it involves a certain degree of unavoidable self-invention and self-delusion.[5]

That being so, it would be tidy at this point to be able to say that the background music that helped form my beliefs and values had its sources in the preconciliar Catholicism that I shared with thousands of American Irish, and that my uninterrupted faith life defined me and predisposed me to imagine and think in certain ways. I could then say that my understanding of the Butte Irish was instinctive, totally unlearned, that it arose because in God's Eternal Now and guided by the Holy Spirit, they and I prayed and received sacramental grace together, shared a commitment to the real presence, and believed that the Church was the mystical body of Christ. Some parts of that formulation may now be so; I hope they are. But for all of it to be true, I would have to have had a nonstop faith life, would have to have been from beginning to now an observant, even devout, Catholic. Unfortunately, I cannot say how many of Butte's Irish were all that, and I cannot even pretend that I was.

So I have to ask, what kind of Catholicism was it that formed my alleged hermeneutic? I confess (the appropriate word) that it was not until asked directly how the intersecting lines of faith and history affected my work that I began to think and read seriously about questions of religion and scholarship and to discover that others far more alert and sensitive than I had done likewise. Of those others, the most useful for me has been the ethnohistorian Greg Dening. I did not come to like Dening because he told me what to think but because he told me much of what it was that I had been thinking. He gave words and validation to my search for the sources of my mysterious affection for my subjects. That he is

Catholic—or was Catholic; I'm not certain of his present relationship with the church—should also be noted.[6]

I do not recall why or even when I stopped going to Mass. I know it was in the late 1950s and I was about eighteen. I could say I had a crisis of faith, but that would be inaccurate. Crisis suggests something principled and profound. My withdrawal was mindless and hopelessly superficial. I do not recall thinking that the Church had become sinister, and I had never been troubled by the fact that it seemed irrational. In fact, I liked that about it. The truth is that I had become spiritually lazy and intellectually arrogant and the Church had become an irritant and an irrelevancy. It was authoritarian and tried to tell me what to do and what to think—go to Mass on Sunday, David, and love your enemies. It is also the case that I was disappointed in my parish's response—or lack of response—to the black struggle for civil rights, but the Church's official position on this issue seemed to me enlightened if not always as bravely implemented as I would have wanted. Besides, my growing commitment to civil rights pitted me far more directly against the overt racism of my father and his Oklahoma relatives than it did against my mother and her confused and ambivalent Italian Catholic ones.[7]

Then came 1963. I had cast my first presidential ballot for John Kennedy. Even nonobservant Catholics understood that a vote for JFK was almost a sacred calling, certainly as close to a vocation as I would ever come. I am now convinced that Kennedy won because he promised a panel of Baptist preachers in Houston that although nominally Catholic, he was not a very good one and that he had no intention of becoming such. He kept his promise. I did not, however, suspect that in 1960 nor was I of that mind in 1963 when he was killed. As was the case with many millions of others, his assassination was a searing and defining moment. I make no claim to having felt a special grief, though I do recall thinking how grandly Catholics buried their dead. Other than that, my personal sorrow owed little enough to Kennedy's having been even marginally Catholic. And who was I to judge? I wasn't even on the margins, but I remembered enough to know that I had no business saying where he should be placed.

What followed after 1963 was so commonplace that I will spend little time discussing it. I opposed the war in Vietnam, attended teach-ins, and carried a few banners. But I could never bring myself to believe that that tragic war was the inevitable result of a corrupt and corrupting system. I persuaded myself that the war was an aberration and, although it reflected badly on those who waged it, did not arise from a systemic flaw, as my more radical friends argued. Besides, I was twenty-seven in 1966, married with a young daughter, an unfinished dissertation, and about to take a job in the History Department at Eastern Illinois University. More to the point, I did not even have to draw a draft number. Mine was and would remain a quiet rebellion. I was too old, temperamentally ill-equipped, and personally unthreatened to be a radical.

But my protest, however fainthearted, had meaning. My nation, always in my name, was committing terrible acts of violence in Vietnam, Cambodia, and Kent, Ohio. The America I had grown up in was dead. By 1970, it no longer mattered whether those acts and the cultural death they brought on were a consequence of bad policy or a reflection of a dirty and degenerate system. The violence had to stop and there was nothing I could do to make it stop. I could only distance myself from it, from the nation that engaged in it, and from the history of that nation. Since I was responsible for the second half of a U.S. survey course, the last of these was tough to do and took some time. The other two were easy. By 1970, I was as outside American politics and culture, as beyond the pale, as any despised nineteenth-century Paddy, though not aware of the analogy at the time. Fortunately, by then I had finished my degree and was teaching at the University of Montana; although the war protests were as desperate there as anywhere else in the country, Missoula, Montana, was about as distant from the ugliness and madness as one could get and still be on this planet.

I just recently discovered this small poem by Wendell Berry. I can only hope that I felt the deadliness of those years as strongly as he did, but his story, including the implied self-reproach it contains, is mine as well.

> *February 2, 1968*
> In the darkness of the moon, in flying snow, in the dead of winter,
> war spreading, families dying, the world in danger,
> I walk the rocky hillside, sowing clover.

If asked what I did during the war and the repression, assassinations, and scandals that accompanied and followed it, I could answer honestly that I skied, fished, rafted rivers, and wandered and scrambled through the woods and mountains. Dead nations and irrelevant faiths left me belonging only to myself, which was not, I thought then, such a bad thing at all. Living well, we had been told and pretended, was the best revenge. And living solely for self—doing it if it felt good—was the best and maybe the only way to live well.[8]

It was not, however, a shortcut to professional advancement and fulfillment. I had never taken being a "research historian" very seriously. I was not even certain I knew what one was. My undergraduate degree at the University of Colorado was in classics and philosophy, with strong "minors" in varsity baseball and socializing. My Greek language professor said I was the Greek ideal. I knew better. I was merely confused. At the urging of this same professor, I applied and was admitted to the University of Wisconsin for graduate study in classics. At the last moment, I declined Wisconsin and in 1961 presented myself to the University of Colorado's history department as a potential graduate student in American history. I had taken only the U.S. survey courses as an undergraduate—and earned low Cs both semesters. The department admitted me and then, with the exception of some quite welcome assistantships and fellowships, left me alone. To say that my graduate training was essentially self-directed is to understate. It had no direction at all, and I left Colorado in 1966 with scarcely more understanding of what being a historian meant than when I started.

By the mid-1970s, however, I knew enough to understand that the more distance I put between myself and my nation, the more distant I felt from national histories. I was tired of teaching the history of America, its leaders and institutions, and more interested in the history of Americans, their social structures and cultural systems. I would leave America's national history to the diplomatic and political historians with their untested assumptions that national leaders—always privileged, white, Protestant males, not a single one of whom would have been comfortable at my family's dinner table or I at his—made America's history. I wanted to do social history, what Charles Tilly described as the history of "how the ordinary people live the big changes," which often was by not changing very much at all.[9]

Specifically, I wanted to study the people for whom I felt a genuine, if largely unexamined, affinity; namely, those whom the nation had ignored or maligned or exploited. The peoples' histories were like transparent overlays to the national historical base map. The people were in full view and full voice only on those transparencies. There were many of these overlays—ethnic, racial, gender, regional, and social class among them. I went to those that my instincts and background directed me: immigrant and ethnic working people, particularly in the West, where, according to western myths of origin and development, they were not supposed to be. I was only minimally concerned that I had had no training in social history; I figured I would read a lot and dance to the background music.[10]

It did not take me long to figure out that most of those ethnic working-class Westerners were also Catholic. That was of some interest to me historically, but it had no other effect. There wasn't any place for the Catholic Church in what I was doing. It never seemed as wicked as the Department of Defense, the Committee to Reelect the President, or Dow Chemical; indeed Pope John XXIII seemed an altogether kinder and wiser man than Lyndon Johnson, Richard Nixon, or William Westmoreland. But the Church was large and hierarchical; it had opposed radical remedies to corporate power and arrogance in the past and seemed inclined to do the same in the bleak and distorted present. I did not see it as a force for moral uplift. As for the Second Vatican Council, from what very little I knew, it had stripped the liturgy of its stateliness, surrendered to the Protestant "establishment," and, in the process, tried to reorchestrate much of that background music.

What was more important, in my mind, was that the Church belonged on the base map with all those other discredited national institutions. The fact that the nation had often evinced a deep distrust of the Church as essentially undemocratic was irrelevant. It *was* undemocratic; it *was* impossible to reconcile the Syllabus of Errors with the Gettysburg Address. The essential point, however, was that those bursts of American anti-Catholicism were all but over. Church and state were now cozied up, two bellicose Cold Warriors, each as lunatic as the other, both worshiping idols. From conversations overheard at St. Catherine's, it would be easy to believe that Catholic hostility to Communism and the Soviets had more to do with religion and closing down the churches than it did with private property and violations of its sanctity. J. Edgar Hoover, however, cannot have cared about the distinction—at least if his alleged preference for Fordham graduates is any indication. As far as I was concerned, the American retreat from the promises of Gettysburg had taken it as far from Lincoln's vision as the Catholic Church, at its most autocratic, had ever been. Neither nation nor Church was truly democratic or egalitarian or committed to social justice.[11]

This time my withdrawal was not just from a Church that had become irrelevant. This was a rejection from conscience; it had a gloss of seriousness about it. It was equal parts crisis of faith and deep disaffection. No rational person could believe the superstitions the Church offered up as truths; they were the solace for those who refused to think. The times required rational, more heroic sorts. I was aware of the Catholicism of Mario Savio, the Berrigans, Thomas Merton, and Dorothy Day, or, and more to the political point, that of Eugene McCarthy and Robert Kennedy. I even knew that Michael Harrington had once knelt at Catholic altars. But that was the point: He didn't kneel there anymore. His example and that of many of the others pushed me into the camp of the "lapsed Catholics." That had just the right dark and tragic feel to it.[12]

It also had a certain social cachet. I remember well one discussion at a colleague's house. It was the early 1970s and all present were profoundly "alienated." One among us—not I—expressed his envy for African Americans. They were participants in a vibrant and segregant culture, a detached brotherhood, and we envied them their solidarity. But this culture was also intensely counter to the dominant culture we had rejected. Blacks were visibly Other and, God, how we wanted to be Other. In the middle of this discussion, I mentioned that my mother's birth name was Celentano (or Celantino, she's not certain to this day)—wishing that that had been my father's—and that her parents had been born in Italy. I did not mention that my grandmother had been married at fifteen to a thirty-eight-year-old man she had never met, or that my mother and her sisters had spent five years in the Queen of Heaven Orphanage being both loved and roughly disciplined by Irish nuns, or that my stepgrandfather was from Palermo, Sicily, and knew people who had some unconventional ideas about the rule of law. No one present would have been prepared to deal with that full an accounting. I did, however, think they could handle being told that I had once spent my Sundays at Mass, mumbling in Latin and celebrating something called the Eucharist. I added that though still unavoidably and proudly half-Italian, I didn't do any of those other things anymore. I had become something different. Fortunately, no one asked what exactly it was that I had become. I had credentials. That was enough.[13]

Historians might now say that I was engaging in an act of "ethnogenesis," reinventing myself and claiming status as an American ethnic, an "in-between" person. At the time, I meant only to say that I was not the descendent of white, Anglo-Saxon Protestants. As such, I was outside the lines—not as far outside as Americans of color but far enough that I could duck some of the guilt for the sins of the American "establishment." The use of that word now causes acute embarrassment, but at the time it expressed something we thought profound. I also began to think more carefully about the hostility to Catholicism displayed by important parts of this establishment in previous incarnations. Papists were literally "enemies of the state," not because they were openly seditious but because their values were dissonant with those of the "righteous empire" of American Protestantism. That described me perfectly. I, too, was a quiet enemy of the state. It was wonderful, if also absurd, to think of myself as somehow associated with the targets of these ancient hatreds, even though I no longer believed what the Church taught. The larger point was that I didn't believe what the state taught, either.[14]

I later learned that had even my apostate Catholicism been known, I would not have been hired at Montana. The department chair was convinced that Catholics were born—or perhaps only baptized—incapable of original thought, so used to taking their cues from the clergy were they. By his reckoning, there were no ex-Catholics. Certainly there would be none, ex- or otherwise, in his history department. At that, I can now say that the years I was away from the Church were the ones I needed it most, both personally and professionally. I published my dissertation, wrote a few articles on topics for which I felt no passion or even connectedness—institutional history done as a means of getting tenured. My unhappiness with American policy and policy makers had formed in me what might, I suppose, be called a hermeneutic of disaffection. The heady experience of being slightly outside the lines was seductive, even though I knew that being truly Other required action, not just making inheritance claims. Being an ex-Catholic did not count for much. My other problem was that although some sort of affective spirit was beginning to make itself felt, it had no target. I had not found any immigrant Western workers to apply it to, and doubtless would not have known what to do with them had I found them. My emerging hermeneutic, even had I known I had one, was sterile. It yielded nothing.

I have already admitted that a lot of "after meditation" accompanies these inventories, particularly those that attempt to assess something as murky and intangible as the intersection between faith and history, but I was coming to understand that having a point of view, a place to stand on, was not in itself enough to make me a historian. I had always known that past human lives had meaning and an inherent relevance. I thought I had a problem finding topics but I now believe that finding topics is a function of knowing who you are and what you want to do. That usable topics might be those that I could treat "affectionately" rather than simply critically never occurred to me. Entering into the interior worlds of past generations is never direct or unmediated. In my case, it required that I be connected to something and have a world of my own from which I could seek entry. Mostly, however, I believe that I had become weary of radical self-containment, of being so totally unconnected. I was not living well and I no longer sought revenge.[15]

A variety of options was open to me. I could have done the perfectly respectable and common thing and connected with other historians, with intellectuals as social types or members of a distinct social class. But that connection never worked for me; my background music was not harmonious with that of some putative community of scholars. The connection could have been with a political ideology but that scarcely worked better. Ideologies lead inevitably to "systems analyses," which seem rigid and confining and place too great an emphasis on national histories. I had nothing in common with either the history or most of the historians who told it. The connection could, I suppose, have been with the cultural left, but it was and is insufferably smug, intolerant, and condescending. Its background music is not just inharmonious with mine; I find it jangling and discordant. I needed a real home; in mountaineering language, a belay to keep from falling.[16]

It was this search for a community, not an active and ongoing participation in one, that led to the Butte Irish—that and a great deal of luck. I was teaching in London in the spring of 1977 and decided to go to Easter Mass at the Brompton Oratory. I did not become aware until later that Brompton was as nearly preconciliar in its liturgy as any church in England. I just liked the looks of it and I knew how to get there. I thought of my attendance as going to a concert in a fine auditorium, nothing more. I looked forward to the performance—the celebration—and it did not disappoint. It was a wonderful Mass; the homily was thoughtful and perfectly delivered, the liturgy was as dignified, as "stately," as I suspected and hoped it would be; the music was spectacular. After Mass, I commented on all this to one of the parishioners. "Yes," he said with a slight grin, "we recusants do put on a good show."

But the feelings and the delights went well beyond the aesthetic. I was surprised by this, but even the simplest acts—genuflecting and making the sign of the cross for example—were like ritualistic handshakes. They signified membership in something special and mysterious. They conveyed to those around me that I was more than just a tourist; I knew the drill. Obviously, I did not take Communion, but I felt an enormous tug as I watched the others quietly make their way forward to receive, as I could clearly hear the Eucharistic ministers say, "the body of Christ," "the blood of Christ." Their murmured "amens" admitted them into a community "with all the angels and saints." It was unimportant whether I believed any of this. I envied them. I wished I could believe as they did, maybe even what they did.

My Easter experience, plus the fact that the nicest people I met in England were Irish, decided my post-London travel plans: I would go to Ireland, land of saints and scholars—and cheaper by far than the continent. I had eighteen wonderful days in what was then a distinctly foreign place. I did not attend Mass—the sources of my envy had always been essentially secular and I had not gone to Ireland as a pilgrim. At that, it could be safely argued that nothing in Ireland in 1977 was entirely secular. Like the Easter Mass, Ireland did not disappoint. I drank a quantity of Guinness in the company of some of the funniest and most affable people I had ever been around. I persuaded myself that their sociability arose from the fact that they truly knew one another and had for generations. I admit to seeing through a romantic haze and dimly, but everything they did seemed part of something larger than and outside themselves.[17]

One of the ways the Irish say "the people" is *an muintir.* I know that it is routine to warn that "there is no English equivalent," but in this instance, that is true. I also know that most of the Irish no longer speak in Irish. But they still think in it. *An muintir* can be used to describe a religious order; families, both nuclear and extended; the people of a village or household; a tribe or clan; members of an organization; the tenants on the same estate; or the "folk" of a townland or parish. I say "can be used" because this is a heavily laden word, to be saved for when the speaker wants to suggest a closeness, a degree of solidarity and connectedness, that passes understanding in English. *An muintir* is an organic thing, unself-conscious and uncontrived. Only infrequently, and then as a political artifice, is it used to describe the nation of Ireland. A cultural anthropologist might say that it delimits those who are eligible to come into the community's cave and warm themselves by its fire. And it extends back in time, taking in not just this generation of villagers or tenants but all who had trod the same ground or been connected to the same family, clan, parish, or tribe.[18]

Americans belong to families, and they say they belong to other organizations from bridge clubs to political parties and athletic teams. De Tocqueville rather famously described us as a band of joiners. But Americans do not belong as the Irish do when they use *an muintir.* There is, I suppose, some pretty standard social and cultural theory in all this—gemeinschafts and gessellschafts and their equivalents—but for me it became an entirely Irish phenomenon with long historical and religious bloodlines. It did not occur to me until later that defining those who get to come into the cave implies that there are many more—I among them—who would be left out in the cold. In 1977, this natural tendency of clans and *na muintirí* to exclude escaped me. It was enough just to be in Ireland and to imagine a social and cultural connectedness that was not a part of my experience and that I sorely missed and needed. I was as ready for Ireland as I have ever been ready for anything in my life. I realize that this was the Ireland of my imagination. So might the magical

Mass at the Brompton Oratory have been magical only for me and only at that time. I used to worry about those things. I don't anymore.

I returned to Montana with a proposal for my colleagues. I wanted to teach the history of Ireland. It was an odd request, but I assured the department that I would read everything I could, build a library as quickly as possible, and treat the course with the care its subject deserved. I did as I had promised. The course drew well; I even managed to persuade a graduate of University College–Dublin to take her M.A. at Montana. And I began to learn about the Irish and about the powerful and complex role the Church has played in their remarkable history. Being Catholic was a central part of being Irish or—and more accurately—being not-English. Their faith was no less real for being so initially politicized; what tied them to the Church was not always piety but contrariness. What kept them there, however, was belief.[19]

More important and more to the point, I began to go to Mass again, hoping to recapture some of what I had taken back from Easter and from Ireland. *Something* had worked at the Oratory; *something* had to be responsible for *an muintir,* or at least come close to replicating it. I had begun to realize that although disaffection separated me from some of the more repellent values of American culture, it separated me from everything else as well. I wanted to change that. Missoula has six Catholic parishes; I exercised my postconciliar right to choose and selected St. Francis Xavier, the oldest of the six by far, founded in 1873 and located on Missoula's north side near the railroad tracks. In the days when parish lines were drawn geographically, it was a solidly working-class congregation, with distinct ethnic (Italian, French Canadian, and Irish) components. Its building—ornately (some would say gaudily) decorated by murals and stations done by Br. Joseph Carignano, S.J.—was completed in 1893. It *looked* preconciliar. It still does. Obviously, it was a Jesuit parish, tended by priests who took seriously their clerical descent from the Black Robes of the northern Rockies. I sat in the back of the church, often wondering what I was doing there but somehow always made better by the experience. I felt at home—not in some grand sense of epiphany, but in the simpler and more commonplace sense of knowing where I was.[20]

I grant that I had considerable psychic capital invested in St. Francis Xavier and that that can blur one's vision. I even confess that the community I sought would be in large part one that I would have to construct, not some preexisting organic union to which I was born and that would once again embrace me. *Na muintirí,* however, cannot be constructed; they can only be. In that sense, my effort to find an existing *muintir* and sink into it was discredited at its origins. Discredited but not doomed.

Disconnectedness did not work for me anymore. In fact, it had never worked for me. It was time to try something else. I was a little like Zacchaeus; I had climbed the sycamore tree to observe, to "see Jesus." Belief would come later when, again like Zacchaeus, the incarnate God came "to stay at [my] house." It was not enough simply to sit in the sycamore tree. Coming all the way home required belief.[21]

For reasons that still escape me but for which I am grateful, belief came easily and naturally, almost as if I had never been away. I recall with relief Butte-born Fr. Tom Healy's laugh when I began my confession in 1980 with "bless me Father for I have sinned; it has been something like twenty-one years, give or take, since my last confession." This, he figured, was going to be a *long* confession. I will never forget my second first communion. I was visibly shaking when I took the chalice. Eighteen years later, Fr. Healy served as my director as I went through St. Ignatius's Spiritual Exercises, an extraordinary experience that attached me to a long and enduring tradition of Western spirituality, tightening and strengthening the belay rope that bound me to the Church.[22]

In almost every way that counted, I was a convert, drawn by the same powerful mix of the cultural and the spiritual that attracted Thomas Merton, Dorothy Day, Walker Percy, and thousands more. My mother's diligent attention to my early religious formation saved me a lot of time, but little else. Catholics, however, are not "born again" and they do not "witness," at least not without considerable squirming. It is for me, as noted, a faith deeply felt but lightly worn, so I will conclude this exercise in self-revelation by saying only that what I had done felt right and that I was quite unconcerned that my reasons for starting back had nothing to do with blinding flashes of revelation. With that I return to my triggering mechanism and the origins of my "affection": I did not understand the Irish because I was a Catholic. It was the other way around. I became a Catholic because I thought I understood the Irish and knew I envied them. The fact that both the understanding and the envy were of an Ireland hopelessly idealized are matters that troubled me once. Now they are just other mysteries, and Catholics are good at handling mysteries.[23]

My always-quiet radicalism began to take on a distinctively "Catholic" quality. I read what I could find on Catholic social teaching, and began generally to shed what remained in me of the secular left and to replace it with a more spiritually informed politics. I subscribed—predictably—to *Commonweal* and *America* and joined Pax Christi and what was then known as the Seamless Garment Network. Obviously, I was a natural for the parish Peace and Justice Committee formed by a young priest from Berkeley whose radicalism was genuine and fully informed by Catholic social teaching. Members of the committee arranged for the *Catholic Worker* to be available in the vestibule and for white crosses commemorating the Jesuit martyrs of El Salvador to be placed outside the church. We cooked at the Missoula homeless shelter and talked about peace and nonviolence. We spoke out also on life issues, sanctuary for Central American refugees (not a likely cause in Montana), debt relief for the Third World (which we never called that), immigration and race, the inequities and asymmetries of power built into a global market capitalism, and the American bishops' call for a preferential option for the poor.[24]

These were certainly not new issues for me, but the language—the discourse—though quieter than it had been before, was somehow more highly charged. That happens when meetings are opened and closed with prayers. I was not quite ready to join the "radical orthodoxy" movement, but I was and am still convinced of the inherent radicalism of Catholic social teaching. I mean "radical," of course, in the context of contemporary American values, and concede that Catholic values may only be oppositional. The distinction is not important. What counts is that I do not know if I would have returned to the Church had it not been for its commitment to social justice and its insistence that Catholics act on those commitments.[25]

That last point, or at least the way it worked itself out at St. Francis Xavier, is particularly significant. I was surprised that the Peace and Justice Committee encountered so little opposition—clerical or lay—to any of its initiatives. There are, after all, Catholics—and St. Francis Xavier has its share of them—who identify themselves on the basis of the maximum distance they can put between themselves and what they identify as American liberalism. Whatever unhappiness some parishioners may have felt when they found copies of the *Catholic Worker* stacked up next to the schedules of retreats and novenas was expressed quietly and respectfully. There are also, however, self-professed American liberals who reverse the formula and whose identities arise from the maximum distance they can put between themselves and what they perceive as Catholic autocracy. I make this point in the most general way and without complaint or self-pity. I was once one of these liberals. I now know better, although I admit that I have about the same chance of mediating these disputes as I had of stopping the Vietnam War.[26]

I was happy to be back, partly because being Catholic did not involve altering my political commitments at all, except to weave them of a stouter cloth. My own contrariness—similar in many respects to that of the Irish—was part of this. Being Catholic was a quiet act of defiance. I would be an anomaly to all but myself: a self-styled Catholic leftist, undeterred by those who believed that this was an oxymoron—if not simply moronic. Being misunderstood by the secular left was an important, if slightly perverse, part of my coming home and settling in. I would continue to seek grace, do "good works," and be on the "correct" side on most of the issues. The one obvious exception to the latter was my position on the abortion question, which the secular left sees as obdurate, reactionary, and disqualifying. I see it as the opposite and have been known to respond with impatience and some heat when my pro-life position is identified as "right wing." It is not. In my mind, the extreme pro-choice position is. As just noted, however, this is not a dispute easily mediated. As for my faith, it was not what I hoped it would be, but I had learned that "the desire to desire" was very Ignatian and hence eminently respectable, and I was patient.

And so I was a Catholic again, and nothing was quite the same. The changes were not dramatic or even visible. I still wandered the mountains, "sowing clover," but the mountains somehow looked different, more like sacred space than testing ground. If anything, closing with the Church widened the distance between me and the various political institutions that commanded my obedience. I retreated even further from American culture—including the secular counterculture. My allegiance and affection were and are with my Church. I was no longer an "enemy of the state," nor did I want to be, but neither was I its unquestioning ally. I do not find much to applaud in either its domestic or foreign policies, including George W. Bush's preferential options for the rich and the senseless invasion of Iraq. Many of those policies violate what my Church teaches and what I believe. This detachment is almost entirely nonpartisan; in fact, political parties play no role in it. Neither do liberals and conservatives, conventionally defined. I cannot accommodate myself to American politics and political values. They simply do not make sense to me. I remain as intensely political as ever, but only as a dazed and discouraged observer.

This ongoing sense of estrangement from national values heightens my sense of being Catholic and being Other and that still pleases me. It allows me to be in but not of American society; to be ambivalent (or schizophrenic) without being contentious—which is not a bad thing for a historian. I am clearly more willing than I once was to render unto Caesar, but I am also increasingly of the mind that in one sense the nativists are right, that the nativists were always right: Catholics are not a perfect fit for American society. Catholic values have often been in conflict with American policies and the dominant values of American life. They still are. There is, then, a certain continuity and legitimacy to my Catholic-based skepticism toward contemporary policies and values. Whether the Catholic Church in America is literally countercultural, or even subcultural, can be debated endlessly—which is to say, unproductively. At its best and truest, it offers a few of what I gently suggest are "alternative visions." In any event, that is what the Church is for me, an oppositional identity, "a people set apart."[27]

Other questions remained. Being Catholic had to influence my scholarship as well as my politics. It did, and in important ways. I am struck by the storytelling aspects of the Catholic liturgy, by the sheer historicism of the Mass. Past and present are conflated in ways that even the most vivid historical accounts cannot match. I appreciate the Church's regard for and reliance on tradition and the tested "virtues." The wonderful Jesuit historian John W. O'Malley has written that there is a "Catholic penchant for emphasizing continuities among historical happenings and minimizing discontinuities," and that this tendency arises from the Catholic doctrine that the seven sacraments were passed down, changeless, from Christ and the apostles. I'm happy to take O'Malley's word for it. Let the national historians deal with events and big changes; the historian of "ordinary" people learns quickly enough that they often live the changes by not changing very much.[28]

I like being in communion with the dead, even praying for them. All social historians—new, old, "soft," and "hard," including the most secular of them—should have some connection beyond the merely intellectual with the ordinary people whose lives they presume to retrieve. At every Mass, the greatest significance is invested in the most ordinary things of this world—bread, water, and wine. One result was that working with the transparent overlays of history, telling the stories of "common" people living everyday lives, took on new importance. Seeing God in all things—the Catholic "analogical imagination"—meant seeing God in past things, and the same God at that. Catholics bring back and connect to events and historical actors millennia old, and not by way of symbolic gesture. As Flannery O'Connor put it in an oft-quoted line about the Eucharist, "if it were only a symbol, I'd say to hell with it." Coming home left me more connected to the past than I had been before—and that is not a bad thing for a historian either.[29]

None of that, however, fully answers the practical question, What exactly does it mean to be a Catholic historian rather than a historian who happens to be Catholic? What principles guide me as I stumble toward answers to that question? This is the essential issue and, notwithstanding the stumbling, my answers need to be carefully considered and clearly stated. First, it means that I would never treat religious beliefs as if they were epiphenomena. *Religion mattered.* Historians who do not recognize that miss half the fun and much of the significance of studying the people who lived before them. Second, Catholics should not attempt to provide "Catholic" answers to historical questions. It is one thing to believe that God created all things, visible and invisible, and that God was thus an agent in human history, and quite another thing to write such into a historical narrative or to offer it up as a historical explanation. Those are outrageous ideas, and I reject them without a single pang of conscience. Reason and religion are certainly compatible, but they are not synonymous. However, *asking Catholic questions struck me as substantively different from offering Catholic answers.* This was not outrageous at all and this I was determined to do. I would draw my questions from the deep well of Church social teachings and ideas of justice and from my fixed position on the oppositional Catholic left, aware in a vague way that, as Greg Dening once wrote, historians should know "that the ultimate source of the questions they ask of the past is their reflective self." But even from this position, I was determined not to prescribe.[30]

To put it another way, if God is sovereign over history, then everything that has occurred has meaning. We need not—and cannot—know what this meaning is to believe that human lives possessed it. Being Catholic gives me what Keats called "negative capability"; I am "capable of being in uncertainties, mysteries, doubts, without any irritable reaching after fact and reason." My personal identity does not require that I have to have made up my mind about everything. That being so, I offer my third principle: *I believe that reason—pure or otherwise—is not the only means of finding historical "truths." The spirit can find them too.* As a Catholic, I believe that every human being has a soul and every human life dignity and value. That is not a "fact"; it is not even a rational statement because I cannot prove it. I like it more because of that.[31]

Which leads to a fourth precept: I believe that *identities are relational.* To argue that human lives have dignity is not to atomize those lives and then split the atoms. It is not a paean to individualism—the official American ideology—but a celebration of companionship. Catholics have no monopoly on this companionate ideal. I still recall that long-ago conversation about African American solidarity and would now add the importance of their Protestant churches in crafting and maintaining it. The Catholic Church, however, has a rich intellectual and cultural tradition of seeing relationships—indeed, seeing all society—as sacramental.

This gives added political meaning to the Church's insistence that good works done in "imitation of Christ" must accompany faith. We must seek justice; our relationships must be based on it. It is both the means and the ends of right relationships, both the source and the result of sacramental grace. Or so we are taught.

As a Catholic historian, my identity, as well as justice, means having the right relationships with the people of the past whose lives I intrude upon and mean to study, which leads to point five: *I reserve the right to choose my friends—my historical "subjects"—from those I know and for whom I feel an "affection."* I am involved in a relationship with those people. They are my companions, even though they live in that foreign country we call the past. To put it simply: Catholics in the past believed in mysteries that non-Catholics often found silly and absurd—or sinister and subversive. Catholics now, myself included, believe in those same mysteries, and non-Catholics still find them, if not silly and subversive, at least a bit strange. The past may be foreign but the people of the past, though they may do things differently there, are not. Historians should not be telling those people how they should have behaved or what their behavior really represented. That's what I meant earlier about academic imperialism. It arises from the hermeneutic of suspicion and is not just anachronistic but, based as it is on the historians' greater power, inherently unjust. It is no way to treat friends. It is not a right relationship. That tradition of grace, faith, good works, justice, and right relationships *may* give Catholics a significant advantage in trying to find that companionate ideal, may even make them more assiduous in the search. The best I can do is ask which relationships were most often determinative, how did the dignity and value of the lives I study manifest themselves, and did they do so in historically meaningful ways. And from this I take my sixth principle. It is the hyperlink between my being Catholic and being a historian. *I like talking to and asking questions of "friends."* Those friends need not be Catholic, but my interest in them must be more than merely academic. The connections have to be "affectionate."[32]

These six ideas were barely in the formative stage when I began my research on the Butte Irish. In fact, it wasn't until I was invited to participate in the discussions that led to this present collection of essays that I began to take those ideas beyond that formative stage and to investigate seriously their origins. As for the Butte book, it was equal parts cause and effect of my undeveloped sense of what being a Catholic historian should mean. Being interested in the history of ordinary people, as I had been for years, is one thing; believing that those people "without a history" also shared in God's divinity, as I was coming to, is quite another. Researching and writing *The Butte Irish* provided compelling evidence of that.[33]

In the first place, the stakes were suddenly higher. Work that had once been only interesting became riveting. I had found the richest collection of primary materials on any Irish town in America and I charged into it, my background music blaring. But it was more than just those records of Butte's Irish associations that I found engrossing. I began to read U.S. census enumerations for 1900 and 1910 and to count and chart every Irish man, woman, and child, immigrant and first generation, whose name appeared on them. Every handwritten line on the enumeration lists was a story, made more fascinating—and frustrating—because of such uncertain ending. I would stay up until 2:00 or 3:00 A.M., to the amazement and concern to my wife and children; no sane person could be mesmerized by a census list. I took considerable comfort from knowing that I was not alone in this. In his *Voyagers to the West,* Bernard Bailyn described his work with a "virtual emigration register" he found in London: "The work," Bailyn writes, "became engrossing. . . . My interest in these people grew greater. I wanted to trace every one of them, find out everything about them, probe their origins, the great transition in their lives, and their ultimate destinies." I know the feeling.[34]

For my part, this became an occasion for "discernment." All of those Jesuits at St. Francis Xavier had taught me that there are occasions when we absolutely know—we discern—that we are doing what we are supposed to be doing, what God wants us to be doing. Tracing until early morning the records of people ignored by history, carefully and painstakingly inscribing their names and relationships and what I could know of their lives onto oversized ledger sheets, and loving every minute of it, was such an occasion for me. Poring over the records of Butte's Irish associations with the same eagerness was another. Reading diplomatic pouches would not have kept me up until 3:00 A.M.—with all due respect to those historians who read diplomatic pouches.

I never thought that the Irish were special merely by reason of their Catholicism or that I had some kind of transcendent insight into their lives by reason of mine. It was all much simpler than that. I believed that past human lives had intrinsic, not just derivative, value and that the nonmaterial aspects of those lives were as important—as "real"—as the material. I took what little these obscure men and women told me as they answered the census enumerators' questions, and mine, and treated it seriously—which is to say as if their lives counted for something. I acknowledge that meaning and significance are not the same thing and that much of what I was doing at 2:00 A.M. was of no immediate historical value. But the longer view is the better one, and I now know that that time was not wasted, that it acquainted me with these people in a way nothing else could have. I knew their names, where they lived and worked, when they got to the United States, whether they could read or write, where their children were born, and how many of those children had died. The fact that my charts never made it into the book is unimportant; the lessons learned in the compiling of them did.

Among other useful services, those lessons helped me to deal with one of the most important and puzzling aspects of the early Irish Catholic experience in Butte. Like all historians, I went into my research with certain preconceptions. I was dealing with Irish miners in the late nineteenth and early twentieth centuries, working in the American West in industrial mines for a powerful corporation, the aptly named Anaconda Copper Mining Company (ACM). I knew the theories. If ever there was a formula for militant labor radicalism, it was to be found in that mix of elements, and so I prepared myself for the important task of exposing the details of the radicalism I knew I would find. The problem was I did not find any. I found instead that from 1878 until 1914, the Butte Miners' Union, the largest and most powerful local union in the world and dominated by combative and class-conscious Irishmen, engaged in not a single job action of any significance, bought preferred stock in the Anaconda Company, and signed long-term contracts that violated every standard of labor militancy. Why had the vast majority of Butte's Irish miners not behaved as they were supposed to? Why had they not at least impersonated the aggrieved and rebellious worker? Certainly they had known grief in abundance.[35]

My answers to those obvious questions are of no relevance here; how I arrived at them is. I felt then and feel even more strongly now that no fair answer would come by investigating only the material reality of their lives—how their lives were lived. The issue was what their lives had meant. That was a question of an altogether different sort and it was not one I could answer for them. They had to speak for themselves. When I began to "interrogate" these Irishmen, I understood that I could have limited the discussion to the purely secular and material; some of my questions were entirely that. But here was where background music and empirical research intersected harmoniously. If ever there was a time for Catholic questions, this was such a time. G. K. Chesterton's comment that "in America even the Catholics are Protestant" is undeniably funny, but as undeniably wrong. Butte's Irish were a part of a separate Catholic culture; so am I. We share in a timeless "community of memory." Mine were questions drawn from that community.[36]

In Butte, the Irish did more than just support the Church; they were the Church; they justified its existence. Catholics are taught that, and Butte's Irish had no trouble believing it. But I had a follow-up question. Was it not also possible that the Church justified and guided their existence? That was a historical as well as a Catholic question. Asking them if the Church justified their lives was a very personal part of my historical analysis, and for that reason a very important part, particularly in light of their refusal to behave the way they were supposed to. The only problem with asking the question was that I could not expect unambiguous answers. Some of these Butte Irish may have lived less for this world than for the next, may have sought sainthood more eagerly than a pay raise, may have rejected class warfare because it required violence or the threat of it, may have opposed socialism because private property was ordained by God, may even have loved their enemies. I cannot claim to *know* any of these things about these apparently conciliatory and certainly pragmatic Irish workers. This is a matter of scant significance; historians seldom really know anything. What counts is that I learned a lot about myself and about them merely by asking the questions.

More important than knowing the particulars, I came to believe that *their* faith, as surely as mine, affirmed the significance and dignity of their existence. Religion brought clarity to their living and hope to their dying. And so I speculate—a not uncommon indulgence of historians— that the Butte Irish refused to behave with the militancy some expected of them because Butte, *as it was,* provided them with what they wanted and needed most: steady work at wages sufficient to send money back to Ireland as well as earn for themselves and their families what an Irish immigrant had once called a "fair living." They were given job preference in Irish-run mines; they were surrounded by people of like mind and heart who loved them; and they belonged to a larger Irish and Catholic world, which was far different from being a member of the Elks or the Rotarians.[37]

In other words, they had transplanted and had the support of *an muintir.* A percentage of the wages earned the hard way in Butte made it back to Ireland to finance the only war that counted. Class wars were for those who did not have more important things to do. They did not live long; the actuarial realities of the work they did determined that, but when they died their lives were remembered and honored, and, if they could keep their sons out of the mines—and they tried—their children could dream. I am not describing the embourgeoisement of the Butte

Irish; theirs were quite legitimate working-class goals and they were seen and pursued as such. It is too easy to say now that these goals were not good enough and should not have been good enough then—and there was a time when I might have thought that, too. But unless I was willing to accuse them of lacking grit—an unthinkable charge—I had to try to understand them as they understood themselves. And they understood themselves as Irish Catholics.

They had their radical critics, some of them Irish. One of those, Joe Shannon, argued that religion generally and Catholicism in particular banked the fires of worker militancy or, in language so common as to be banal, was an "opiate." I assume he spoke for more than just himself and that his reference was partly to the much publicized Catholic belief in the sinfulness of socialism and other forms of political radicalism. Shannon was not alone, then or later, in making that charge. There were, however, and still are, a couple of serious problems with this argument. First, Shannon did not know what was being said in the pulpit. Neither do I with any certainty but I felt more compelled to ask than Shannon did. Second, Shannon cannot assume that the homiletic message—whatever its political content—was being listened to or heeded. He seemed to believe that lay Catholics bleated and behaved as told. He should have known better; he probably did know better. Even the priests knew better. As for me, I remembered St. Catherine's and how much it resembled the parishes in James Carroll's wonderful essay in *Commonweal* on "not skipping the sermon." Working people, particularly the men, had made a quite unofficial deal with their priests. The clergy could instruct them on everything from their sex lives to their drinking habits, but it could not tell them how to think on political matters, and it must never involve itself in matters relating to their relationships with employers. Every historian of labor in America should read Carroll's article.[38]

There was, however, another and I think more important aspect to the radical's hostility to religion. Dealing with it required that I accept the truth of the charge that Catholicism dampened enthusiasm for revolutionary solutions—but not for the usual reasons, and particularly not because the priests told the workers what to do and think and the workers meekly genuflected and obeyed. All I had to do was take seriously the possibility that their faith provided Catholic working people with a powerful and literally soul-satisfying alternative to both militant socialism and unmanly submission (and how often the radicals made references to a worker's manliness). To put it in the language of the social teaching of the Church, there was a Third Way, an essentially nonmaterial option to both unchecked market capitalism and militant radicalism. I say "essentially" nonmaterial because no one could contend that there was dignity in either poverty or powerlessness. Certainly the Church did not and neither do I.[39]

The more I read and listened—to both my informants and my background music—the more I was convinced that what the Butte workers wanted was dignity and respect. They did not want the dictatorship of the proletariat, they did not want to own the mines, they did not want to raise a red flag above Anaconda's corporate headquarters, as William Haywood, the grandstanding Wobbly, once demanded. They wanted a fair living, which involved a recognition of the value of the work they did. They had bargained for and won the highest wages in industrial America, but more was involved than paychecks. They also wanted some acknowledgment that they were men whose lives had merit. This the Church provided by telling them that God treasured them. I think they believed the Church, not because they were naive or deluded but because they were neither, and because—to a degree greater than that of other Catholic working people—the Irish had a historically and culturally formed predisposition to believe it. *Na muintirí* told them that their neighbors treasured them as well, and the transplanted *muintir* of Butte confirmed that important lesson.

I was always prepared for the historical record to prove me wrong. It never did—until the World War I era, after the Irish had lost control of Butte and its unions, and that is a very different story from the one I was telling. Before that time, social class did not replace religious and ethnic allegiances, at least not for sustained periods of time and never with revolutionary consequences. But why should it have? It is, of course, the case that Butte's Irish world was interclass; it included some highly placed officers of ACM as well as working miners. This is troublesome only for those who insist on the inevitability of class conflict. I want to quote Charles Tilly again: "Revolutionary class consciousness," he wrote, "is to labor history as frictionless motion is to elementary mechanics: *Neither has ever existed,* but both underlie vast theoretical constructions and wide-ranging empirical inquiries." I think that Tilly is right. Worker and capitalist came to know one another, perhaps even to like and esteem one another. The idea that only the hard edge of worker class consciousness was dulled in the process is inaccurate. It either insults working people by implying that they were dumber than capitalists or idealizes them by implying that they were sweeter and more tolerant. My perception of historical reality rebels at both possibilities. So does common sense.[40]

But Tilly goes on. Physicists at least have the "good sense" not to look for frictionless motion or, "worse yet," to investigate why it does not explain the physical world. Labor historians, however, "generally lack that good sense," seeking constantly to explain why revolutionary class consciousness was not a part of this or that event in labor history. Since militancy was assumed to be the natural condition of workers, almost in the sense of being genetically programmed, Catholicism, by definition, becomes unnatural and deviant. For me, it is enough simply to point out the obvious: The Catholic Church is not a mutant aspect of some superstructure and hence not responsible for the absence of frictionless motion and can claim no more than partial credit or—for those who insist—blame for the absence of revolutionary class consciousness.[41]

After listening to these Irish miners as intently as I could, after asking them as many questions—Catholic and otherwise—as a limited imagination could devise, I came away convinced that they did not live in a world organized on some ideological binary scale and that being Catholic and being Irish were more important to them than being working class. Their Catholicism was not an opiate. It did not dull their sensibilities; it defined them and sanctified their lives. The same must be said of their Irishness. They spent more time being Irish and Catholic than they did being Worker. They shared more of their treasure with the Church and the "old rock" than with their labor union. That is the way it was. When the big strike finally came in 1917, the old-time Irish miners of Butte walked out—not as workers in protest of the capitalist system but as Catholic Irishmen in solemn defiance of the American declaration of war against Germany, revolutionary Ireland's "gallant ally." They understood themselves and their relationships on the basis of ethnicity and faith. In sum, they did not try to overthrow the capitalist system because they did not need to. The meaningful parts of their lives were not lived within that system.[42]

Let me return to Albert Borgmann. His point was never that my hermeneutic was the only one that might have worked, or even that it had worked better than any other might have. He was saying only that it had given me access to specific parts of the lives of the Butte Irish. He had the source of my empathy wrong, but I think he was right about its usefulness. Butte's Irish were a complicated people. The component parts of their lives could not have been disaggregated and parceled out on the basis of any historical predisposition. The point, however, is that if I did in fact enter into parts of the worlds of Butte's Irish and make even partial sense of them, it was because—after many fits and starts on my part—they and I came to share a religious faith and the traditions, the cultural memories, it contains. There may be some who would contend that such feelings, bordering as they do on the emotional and poetic, are disqualifying for historians. Obviously, I am not of that mind, preferring to take seriously and literally Dening's warning to be "wary of the history that claims to be separate from the circumstances of its telling. . . . The past you uncover will never be separated from the occasion and the mode of your discovering it." Certainly that was the case with me. I discovered the past from halfway up a sycamore tree. The Butte Irish past was part of the making of my present.[43]

The soul and substance of Butte were not to be found in its corporate boardrooms or its union halls or even in its deep mines. The marrow of the place and its animating spirit came from the Catholic Church. Catholicism sustained and guided the people of Butte; it sustains and guides me. It bids me to be hospitable—which involves considerably more than hospitality—and it taught them the same. It sets me apart from some fundamental American values, as it did them. The answers Catholicism provides me formed the questions I asked them. Those question were my entry into their social worlds where I had no choice but to take the bad with the good and to learn and try to teach from both. As this became clearer to me, so did the meaning of "affectionate." Butte's Irish offered me lessons in *how* to act toward neighbors—with kindness and generosity. They had an entirely too restrictive view of *who* their neighbors were, of how far the neighborhood extended, but I liked the Butte Irish—most of them, at least, and most of the time—despite their inability or unwillingness to meet the demands for Catholic inclusivity and universalism. But the point is that the ethnocentrism and intolerance of the Butte Irish were also familiar to me. I felt no affection in the sense of respect or admiration for their narrowness, but that is not what "affection" means here. It means that this narrowness was a part of my vernacular too, secondary and ugly chords in my background music. Knowing that is also a part of my effort—and it requires one—to be a Catholic historian.[44]

I am supported in this effort by St. Thomas Aquinas's prayer Ante Studium. It supplies the lyrics for my background music and I have placed a copy of it in such a way that I cannot avoid seeing it without turning my back on the work to be done that day. It is there to nag me and keep me at my task. I am drawn to this particular prayer because it is for me a cautionary tale as much as a prayerful petition—a methodological as well as a spiritual guide. Thomas importuned the "ineffable Creator" to

Pour forth a ray of your brightness
into the darkened places of my mind;
disperse from my soul
the two-fold darkness
into which I was born:
Sin and ignorance.

Later in his prayer, St. Thomas's supplications became more specific. He asked God to "grant to me keenness of mind, capacity of remembering, skill in learning, subtlety in interpreting. . . ."[45]

Interestingly, he did not ask the ineffable Creator to give him an attentive ear or certainty of purpose, but the former was implied, and the latter was not an issue. He knew his purpose. I cannot be as confident as St. Thomas, but the purpose of my work is as ready-made as the questions I pose. Both derive from my home place and from the actuating spirit that was both cause and effect of my return to it. As to that attentive ear, it is the instrument of historical memory and understanding, of Thomas's "capacity of remembering [and] subtlety of interpreting." After all, "our stories," and I borrow from Greg Dening again, "are as much about us as about something else." *The Butte Irish* is as much about me as it is about them. As I stated at the beginning: I was not certain what a hermeneutic was and quite unaware that I had one. I know more now. My hermeneutic was not only of affection; it was also of faith, of Catholicism. Affection did not define it. Affection was the result of it. I am comfortable with that. After all, what else would a Catholic or any other hermeneutic be for but understanding and being understood—for remembering and being remembered?[46]

Notes

1. David Emmons, *The Butte Irish: Class and Ethnicity in an American Mining Town, 1875–1925* (Urbana: University of Illinois Press, 1989).

2. I am deeply indebted to University of Montana professor of religion Paul Dietrich for walking me through the hermeneutics of suspicion and affection and for explaining how each term is used. The "analogical imagination" is from David Tracy, *The Analogical Imagination* (New York: Crossroads, 1982). See also Andrew Greeley, *The Catholic Myth: The Behavior and Beliefs of American Catholics* (New York: Macmillan, 1990), 35, 45; and Greeley, *The Catholic Imagination* (Berkeley: University of California Press, 2000). Both of Greeley's books were dedicated to Tracy.

3. On Republican anti-Catholicism, see William Gienapp, *The Origins of the Republican Party, 1852–1856* (New York: Oxford University Press, 1987), 106, 193, 234, 289, 365–67, 414–27; Tyler Anbinder, *Nativism and Slavery: The Northern Know-Nothings and the Politics of the 1850s* (New York: Oxford University

Press, 1992); and Michael Holt, *The Political Crisis of the 1850s* (New York: W. W. Norton, 1978), 159–64, 176–80, 215–16. For a different interpretation, see Eric Foner, *Free Soil, Free Labor, Free Men: The Ideology of the Republican Party before the Civil War* (New York: Oxford University Press, 1970).

4. The fact of Irish dominance of the American Church is too well established to require documentation. For Irish devotionalism, see Emmet Larkin, "The Devotional Revolution in Ireland, 1850–1875," in *The Historical Dimension of Irish Catholicism* (Washington, D.C.: Catholic University of America Press, 1984), 57–90.

5. Wordsworth's quote is from Greg Dening, *The Death of William Gooch: A History's Anthropology,* 2nd ed. (Honolulu: University of Hawaii Press, 1995), 83.

6. Dening, *Death of William Gooch,* and Greg Dening *Performances* (Chicago: University of Chicago Press, 1996). See also Allistair MacIntyre, *Three Rival Versions of Moral Enquiry: Encyclopædia, Genealogy, and Tradition* (Notre Dame, Ind.: University of Notre Dame Press, 1990), and Allistair MacIntyre, *After Virtue: A Study in Moral Theory,* 2nd ed. (Notre Dame, Ind.: University of Notre Dame Press, 1984). MacIntyre is at times impossibly difficult to understand, and at other times impossible to agree with when understood. I am indebted to Ken Lockridge for bringing Dening to my attention and to Chris Shannon for doing likewise with MacIntyre. Eamon Duffy's *Faith of Our Fathers: Reflections on Catholic Tradition* (London: Continuum, 2004) and Robert Orsi's *Between Heaven and Earth: The Religious Worlds People Make and the Scholars Who Study Them* (Princeton, N.J.: Princeton University Press, 2005) came out to late for me to use. But I can't wait to read them.

7. Denver's story is not appreciably different from those of other northern cities; see John T. McGreevy, *Parish Boundaries: The Catholic Encounter with Race in the Twentieth-Century Urban North* (Chicago: University of Chicago Press, 1996).

8. Wendell Berry, *Collected Poems, 1957–1982* (New York: Farrar, Strauss, and Giroux, 1984), 108.

9. Charles Tilly, "Retrieving European Lives," in *Reliving the Past: The Worlds of Social History,* ed. Olivier Zunz (Chapel Hill: University of North Carolina Press, 1985), 11.

10. Dening discusses similar issues in *Performances,* 40.

11. On the Church and Communism, see James Hennesey, S.J., *American Catholics: A History of the Roman Catholic Community in the United States* (New York: Oxford University Press, 1981), 280–306; Charles R. Morris, *American Catholic: The Saints and Sinners Who Built America's Most Powerful Church* (New York: Vintage, 1997), 228–54; and Donald J. Crosby, S.J., *God, Church, and Flag: Senator Joseph McCarthy and the Catholic Church, 1950–1957* (Chapel Hill: University of North Carolina Press, 1978).

12. On Harrington, see, among other sources, his memoir *Fragments of the Century* (New York: E. P. Dutton, 1973).

13. Jack Kerouac once told the story of a time that he walked though Denver's "colored section, wishing [he] were a Negro. . . ." But what Kerouac envied was not so much the black sense of community—of being racial brothers and sisters to one another. He envied them their music, "joys, kicks, darkness. . . ." I admit

that there was something subcultural about that, too, but that is not what we (or at least I) were looking for in the late 1960s. See Jackson T. Lears, *No Place of Grace: Antimodernism and the Transformation of American Culture, 1880–1920* (New York: Pantheon Books, 1981), 306.

14. James R. Barrett and David Roediger, "Inbetween Peoples: Race, Nationality, and the 'New Immigrant' Working Class," *Journal of American Ethnic History* 16 (Spring 1997): 3–44. For anti-Catholicism generally, see Ray Allen Billington, *The Protestant Crusade: A Study of the Origins of American Nativism* (New York: Rinehart, 1938), and John Higham, *Strangers in the Land: Patterns of American Nativism, 1860–1925* (New York: Atheneum, 1981). Martin Marty, *Righteous Empire: The Protestant Experience in America* (New York: Harper & Row, 1970).

15. Robert Darnton's insistence that historians seek "points of entry" into the interior worlds of past generations has long seemed to me wise and fair. Darnton, *The Great Cat Massacre and Other Episodes in French Cultural History* (New York: Basic Books, 1984), 7. MacIntyre agues that "membership in a particular type of moral community" rather than being "neutral or disinterested" is "*required*" if that entry is to be gained. MacIntyre, *Three Rival Versions,* 60 (my emphasis); see also 64–69.

16. On these and related points, see MacIntyre, *After Virtue,* 220–25.

17. Cf. Robert Putnam, *Bowling Alone: The Collapse and Revival of American Community* (New York: Touchstone, 2001).

18. On *an muintir,* see Cyril Ceirin, introduction to *My Story: Reminiscences of a Life in Ireland from the Great Hunger to the Gaelic League,* by Peter O'Leary (1915; repr., New York: Oxford University Press, 1987), 11–13. *Irish-English/English-Irish Dictionary* (Boulder, Colo.: Roberts Rinehart, 1998), 181–82.

19. Patrick O'Farrell, *Ireland's English Question: Anglo-Irish Relations, 1534–1970* (New York: Schocken Books, 1971), 31–37, and Emmet Larkin, "Myths, Revisionism, and the Writing of Irish History," *New Hibernia Review* 2 (Summer 1998): 64–65.

20. Dening has a wonderful discussion of the Jesuits in *Performances,* 17–20.

21. Luke 19:1–10. MacIntyre deals with some of this in *Three Rival Versions,* 196–98.

22. For a wise and sympathetic account of the Spiritual Exercises, see Dening, *Performances,* 12–24.

23. For Merton, see his classic, *The Seven Storey Mountain* (New York: Harcourt, Brace, 1948); for Day, *The Long Loneliness* (New York: Curtis Books, 1972); for Percy, *Lost in the Cosmos: The Last Self-Help Book* (New York: Noonday Press, 1983); see also Bertram Wyatt-Brown, *The House of Percy: Honor, Melancholy, and Imagination in a Southern Family* (New York: Oxford University Press, 1994), esp. 289–355.

24. As it happened, the priest who started the social justice committee at St. Francis Xavier left the Jesuits, the priesthood, and the Church—a not uncommon occurrence. But his flame burned brightly while it lasted!

25. On the radical orthodoxy movement, see John Milbank, Catherine Pickstock, and Graham Ward, eds., *Radical Orthodoxy* (London: Routledge, 1999), and Michael Budde and Robert Brimlow, eds., *The Church as Counterculture* (Albany: SUNY Press, 2000). I learned of these and other titles from Eugene McCarraher, "Theology at the Barricades," *Commonweal,* July 13, 2001.

26. On liberals and Catholics, see John T. McGreevy, "Thinking on One's Own: Catholicism in the American Intellectual Imagination, 1928–1960," *The Journal of American History* 84 (June 1997): 97–131.

27. Paul Messbarger contends that "the all-American Catholic boy comes very close to being schizophrenic." Messbarger, *Fiction with a Parochial Purpose: Social Uses of American Catholic Literature, 1884–1900* (Boston: Boston University Press, 1971), 96. See also Stanley Hauerwas, *With the Grain of the Universe: The Church's Witness and Natural Theology* (New York: Brazos Press, 2001). See also the comments by Michael Baxter, C.S.C., in "Writing History in a World without Ends: An Evangelical Catholic Critique of U.S. Catholic History," *Pro Ecclesia* 4 (Fall 1996): 440–69, and MacIntyre, *After Virtue,* 114, 220–25. Jay Dolan's new book on these and related issues was only hastily read; Dolan, *In Search of an American Catholicism: A History of Religion and Culture in Tension* (New York: Oxford University Press, 2002).

28. John W. O'Malley, S.J., "The Council of Trent: Myths, Misunderstandings, and Misinformation," in *Spirit, Style, Story: Essays Honoring John W. Padberg, S.J.,* ed. Thomas M. Lucas, S.J. (Chicago: Loyola Press, 2003), 205–23, 212.

29. MacIntyre, *After Virtue,* 216–22; Dening, *Death of William Gooch,* 53–87; Dening, *Performances,* xiv–xvi. The O'Connor quote is from Robert Fitzgerald, introduction to *Everything That Rises Must Converge,* by Flannery O'Connor (New York: Noonday, 1973), xiii.

30. George Marsden, *The Outrageous Idea of Christian Scholarship* (New York: Oxford University Press, 1997). See also the summary of James Turner's remarks on the issue of "Sunday knowledge and Everyday knowledge" from University of Notre Dame, Cushwa Center, "American Catholic Studies Newsletter," no. 24 (Spring 1997): 4–5. Dening, *Performances,* 126.

31. The Keats quote is from Peter Novick, *That Noble Dream: The "Objectivity Question" and the American Historical Profession* (Cambridge: Cambridge University Press, 1988), 274–75.

32. For an overly strong statement of the Catholic idea of society as sacrament, see Andrew Greeley, *The Catholic Myth: The Behavior and Beliefs of American Catholics* (New York: Macmillan, 1990), 45. Thomas à Kempis, *The Imitation of Christ,* trans. Leo Sherley-Price (New York: Dorset Press, 1952).

33. This is not quite what he meant by the phrase "without a history," but see Eric R. Wolf, *Europe and the People without History* (Berkeley: University of California Press, 1982).

34. Bernard Bailyn, *Voyagers to the West: A Passage in the Peopling of America on the Eve of the Revolution* (New York: Knopf, 1986), xix–xx.

35. Quote from Emmons, *Butte Irish,* 282. The Butte material in this and the following paragraphs is taken from that book.

36. The "community of memory" quote is from Robert Bellah, et al., *Habits of the Heart: Individualism and Commitment in American Life* (Berkeley: University of California Press, 1985), 333. The Chesterton quote is from Bellah, "Religion and the Shape of National Culture," *America,* July 31–August 7, 1999, 10.

37. The "fair living" quote is from Kerby Miller, *Emigrants and Exiles: Ireland and the Irish Exodus to North America* (New York: Oxford University Press, 1985), 359. For an account of the communalism of another Irish Catholic enclave,

see Timothy J. Meagher, *Inventing Irish America: Generation, Class, and Ethnic Identity in a New England City, 1880–1928* (Notre Dame, Ind.: University of Notre Dame Press, 2001), 50–96.

38. The Joe Shannon quote is from Emmons, *Butte Irish,* 265. James Carroll, "On Not Skipping the Sermon," *Commonweal,* April 14, 1984.

39. The two papal encyclicals on the rights of labor, *Rerum Novarum* (1891) and *Quadragesimo Anno* (1931), are obviously relevant here. I think the best discussion of the Third Way can be found in the works of Monsignor John A. Ryan; see, for example, his *The Church and Labor* (New York: Macmillan, 1924); see also Francis L. Broderick, *Right Reverend New Dealer: John A. Ryan* (New York: Collier-Macmillan, 1962). MacIntyre deals with this "Third Way" (without identifying it as such) in *After Virtue,* 218–25. See Aileen Kraditor's *The Radical Persuasion: Aspects of the Intellectual History and Historiography of Three American Radical Organizations* (Baton Rouge: Louisiana State University Press, 1981) for an extended discussion of how often radical organizations appealed to the workers' "manliness"—or lack of same.

40. Charles Tilly, review of *Urban Workers in the Early Industrial Revolution,* by Robert Glen, *Labor History* 32 (Summer 1991): 467–69. My emphasis.

41. Ibid.

42. Germany was identified as revolutionary Ireland's "gallant ally" in the 1916 Proclamation of the Irish Republic. On the other question, as an Irishman in Worcester, Massachusetts, put it, "We cannot hope to reorganize the industrial system, but we can refuse to permit [it] to reorganize our . . . life." Meagher, *Inventing Irish America,* 48–49.

43. Dening, *Death of William Gooch,* 30, 64.

44. As Dening writes, "we history-makers must know ourselves. We must have an ethnographic sense of our cultural persons"; Dening, *Performances,* 30.

45. Aquinas's prayer was reprinted in *First Things,* May 1998.

46. Dening, *Performances,* 34.

MARIO T. GARCÍA

4 *In Search of Chicano Catholic Identity and History*

I

While I was a college student at the University of Texas at El Paso, every Sunday morning I drove my grandmother, whom we called Nama, to 6:30 Mass. This was from 1962 to 1966, years that coincided with Vatican II but before its liturgical reforms became very evident. It was a quiet Mass with not many in attendance, but always the same people. We sat in the same pew at St. Patrick's Cathedral on Arizona Avenue about a mile from our rented house, which was also on the same street on what was referred to as the Golden Hill with its sweeping vista of El Paso and Ciudad Juárez to the south. We literally looked south at the border and to Mexico where Nama had come from many years before during the Mexican Revolution of 1910.

It was a silent Mass with only the drone of the priest's prayers in Latin. Because it was the early Mass, no homily was preached and we were out by 7:00 A.M. We walked to the car—not mine but my mother's—and before driving home we always stopped at the Mexican bakery on Nevada Street, just a couple of blocks from St. Patrick's. We always ordered the same Mexican bread whose colorful names I never learned as an acculturated Mexican American. But the teenage girl behind the counter, whom I liked and who was the daughter of the owner, always gave us one extra piece of bread—a *pilón* as Nama called it—for free. We then drove home where my aunt, Tanaca, had breakfast ready, way before my mother and my other siblings had yet awoken. This consisted of fresh flour tortillas that Nama and Tanaca had already prepared even before we went to Mass. Hot tortillas with butter, eggs over easy, a beef patty, hot coffee, and an orange drink called Tang that you mixed with water made up my big Sunday breakfast. After this, in the still-cool of the morning in summertime or in the bright glare of the winter sun, I retired to devour the Sunday *El Paso Times.*

Religion, specifically Catholicism, was always with me. There wasn't a day in my conscious coming-of-age years when I wasn't aware of this. It was a Catholicism planted in the Southwest first by Spanish Franciscan friars and over time influenced by both Mexican and Anglo-American (in reality Irish American) sources in a border context. But I wasn't yet aware of all of these historical influences. This would come later and, in fact, I'm still learning about this.

My family was Catholic but not in an extreme way. This would not be fitting for a family on my mother's side that saw itself as *gente decente,* or properly brought up and from the better classes that had escaped from the Mexican Revolution. My great-grandfather of the Araiza family in northern Chihuahua was a well-to-do landowner and partner to American mining companies. His fate was sealed as a supporter of Francisco Madero, the "Apostle" of Mexican democracy who raised his banner against the long-standing dictator Porfirio Díaz. My great-grandfather was executed and his family fled to the border and crossed into El Paso. The family left everything behind but its honor and middle-class Catholic values. I inherited that honor and those values.

We were Catholics but not barrio Catholics; we had escaped the barrio experience. My mother, born and raised in El Paso, grew up not in the big immigrant barrio *El Segundo Barrio,* or south El Paso, but in west and central El Paso. This is where the middle-class political refugees from Mexico had settled—apart from the lower-class immigrants and workers, and with their own kind. They built the Catholic church of *La Sagrada Familia,* or Holy Family Church, in the westside Sunset Heights area where my mother was married to a man from the state of Durango, thus bridging the Mexican American experience with the Mexican experience, and especially with the *norteno* one, the northern Mexican region where most of our families were from.

We were always on the move but always north of the tracks where the more aspiring Mexican Americans resided: first on Missouri Street where I was born, then Yandell Boulevard, then Wyoming Street, and then finally to Arizona Avenue, all in the central part of El Paso.

As a kid, I don't remember particular Catholic images in our different rented homes. We must have had a crucifix and some holy pictures, but they don't stand out in my memory. I think it's because we didn't have too many of these images. My family was religious, but it was a religious style that complemented our sense of ourselves as a cultured family and that would have worked against the appearance of too many religious home icons more associated with poorer Mexican immigrants. I think too that even though Nama and Tanaca lived with us all of these years, my mother—a bilingual and bicultural Mexican American—set the tone at home, at least in terms of appearance. My mother was proud of her ethnic heritage, but she also aspired to American mobility and hence probably did not want a household that was too "Mexican" or "Catholic Mexican" in appearance.

I do remember the elaborate home altar at the home of my friend and classmate, Frank de la Torre. Actually, I don't remember if this was Frank's house on Yandell or his grandmother's, but I remember being there with several other neighborhood kids and being awed by the elaborate nature of the home altar. I don't remember specific images, but just the clutter of items on it. It was like a separate chapel in the house, situated in its own room. I now am more aware that home altars—*altarcitos*—big and small, elaborate or simple, are very much a part of Mexican Catholic culture along the border and in the Southwest. Some installation artists such as Amalia Mesa-Bains today have elevated home altars to new artistic heights.

I also associate border Catholic culture with older women wearing black. Neither Nama and Tanaca wore black, nor did my mother, but I recall many other women, especially in *El Segundo Barrio* and around the Catholic churches there such as *El Sagrado Corazón* (Sacred Heart Church), always wearing black, including black shawls and always with rosaries in their hands. This darkness always had a air of mystery for me and made those southside churches, with their ornate icons including darker and more bloody crucified Christ figures, more scary and even threatening to me.

Border and southwestern Catholic culture also meant attending parochial schools. My mother insisted that we attend Catholic schools. She herself was a product of public schools but believed, and correctly so at that time, that the parochial schools provided a better education and thus we were enrolled in St. Patrick's Elementary School. I have distinct memories of the images of the Sisters of Loretto who operated and taught in the school. Every class, with one or two exceptions, was taught by a nun in a classic black habit with only a small amount of white garment around the rim of the head habit and a bit into the bodice. The habits seemed heavy and hot, especially for the warm El Paso climate that had but a few cold winter weeks. I can still smell the odor of the habits when I would need to come close to one of the nuns. I don't know whether it was the habit or the nun herself, but it smelled of old cloth or an old gunnysack.

I have no idea whether any of these nuns—sisters they're now called—was Mexican American. I suspect one or two were. The rest were Anglos, most likely of Irish backgrounds. I remember some of their names: Sister Charatina, Sister Eugene Marie. They seemed old to me but probably were not; here and there were a few young and even pretty faces, which was all we could see of them.

But it was a good education, as far as I knew at the time. There was a good spirit to the school. It was also a mixed school; many of us were Mexican Americans, but there were also a good number of Anglos (again probably Irish Americans). This was the usual pattern for the parochial schools north of the tracks. South El Paso and east El Paso parishes such as Sacred Heart, St. Ignatius, and Guardian Angel had all Mexican Americans in their schools.

Many of the Mexican American kids, like me, knew mostly Spanish when we entered kindergarten, but we quickly picked up English. There was no bilingual education at St. Patrick's in the 1950s when I attended, but, unlike what seemed to be a pattern in the public schools, you were not punished or made to feel bad about speaking Spanish. The sisters were strict—quite strict in some cases—but they seemed to genuinely care about us.

St. Patrick's, which was under the administration of Monsignor Caffrey with his full head of white hair, was not a "Mexican" parish, even though many Mexican Americans attended the church. It was, of course, the official church of Bishop Sidney Metzger who reigned, it seemed, for years and years. St. Patrick's and the other north-of-the-tracks Catholic churches were different from the "Mexican" churches south of the tracks. Our church was more "Anglo." It seemed more airy and roomier in comparison to the few times I would go to Sacred Heart, for example, which seemed more crowded and stifling. Our homilies were in English whereas those at Sacred Heart were in Spanish. St. Patrick's was more middle class while Sacred Heart was poor and immigrant.

But our whole culture while growing up was very much Catholic. Our education was Catholic; our friends were Catholics; our sports activities were all centered around the Catholic Youth Organization (CYO); and our social events, such as dances, were all connected to our Catholic school. We lived in a Catholic culture that I am more cognizant now as representing a border and southwestern Catholic culture. The metaphor of the border is appropriate to signify this culture because, like real borders, it was an intersection of different influences. For those of us in a school such as St. Patrick's, it was an intersection of our family Mexican American culture with that of what I now recognize as largely Irish American culture. St. Patrick may have been an Irish saint but he was our saint as well—and not as *San Patricio* but as *St. Patrick.* We wore the green and white in our school athletic uniforms.

Later, when I attended the local Catholic high school, Cathedral High School, located just up the street from St. Patrick's, I identified with the school's nickname, "the Irish." Our colors were blue and gold, patterned after the University of Notre Dame, and our school song was the Notre Dame fight song. I'll never forget attending with our basketball team the Texas Catholic High School Basketball Tournament in San Antonio in 1961. Before one of our games, an older Anglo gentleman came up to us and asked us why we called ourselves "Irish" since clearly all of us were Mexican Americans. We couldn't really answer him in this pre–Chicano Movement era; all we could say was that it was our nickname.

Catholic high school only extended the pervasiveness of Catholic culture in our lives. The boys—the majority being Mexican Americans—attended Cathedral, which was run by the Christian Brothers, and the girls, including my own sister, attended Loretto High School, which was run by the Sisters of Loretto. Because there were kids from south El Paso at Cathedral, I was introduced to Chicano barrio culture that made me more aware of ethnicity. It wasn't that ethnic identity was not part of our growing up; it was. We knew that we were of Mexican descent—how could we not? We could only speak Spanish to Nama and Tanaca, who knew very little or no English—and they didn't really need to since El Paso was such a predominantly Spanish-speaking city with even more Mexicans across the border in Juárez. Yet we saw ourselves as middle-class Mexican Americans.

It was at Cathedral that I learned more about barrio culture from my south El Paso classmates. This is where I first heard the term "Chicano" and it was used as a term of identity by the barrio students. I didn't identify fully with "Chicano," but still I was fascinated by the swagger and what seemed to be pride in identifying as Chicano. I recall being impressed by the Elvis-like ducktail hairstyle the Chicanos employed, wearing it almost as a crown. I tried in a modest way to comb my hair into a ducktail with varying degrees of success. I liked these kids; although I didn't run around with them, I did play sports with some of them. I think that this connection and even fascination with the barrio students provided an unconscious base for my later work as a historian, such as my history of Mexican immigrant El Paso that focused on the southside and the ancestors of many of the Chicanos I went to school with at Cathedral. By later studying and writing about this history, I came to appreciate what I didn't as a high-school-age, more middle-class Mexican American on the "right side of the tracks."

Catholicism in El Paso was not only a matter of family and school; it also had its more public manifestations. I particularly recall the large processions on the feast day of Corpus Christi each June. It would begin later in the day around 5:00 P.M. in order to avoid the hot June weather that at this time of the year is always close to 100 degrees. I remember marching in a procession while in high school. The assembly point was the front of St. Patrick's Cathedral. People covered the front steps and spilled onto Arizona Avenue and Mesa Boulevard. I remember the richly colored robes of the clergy, including those of the bishop. I was especially attracted to the elaborate outfits of the Knights of Columbus with their white plumed hats and their black and red capes—it was all so impressive and awesome. The large assembly would proceed down Mesa into the downtown area, stopping at several points where prayers were said at what resembled decorated stations of the cross or makeshift altars. People came from all of the parishes so that some recited the rosary in English and some in Spanish. The procession wound through the streets of the city, stopping all traffic. Later, the large antiwar marches of the 1960s reminded me of these processions. The procession would snake its way into south El Paso where it seemed to take on an even more Mexican character. The final destination was Sacred Heart in *El Segundo Barrio.* By the time it reached the church, evening was approaching, which gave the ceremony within the already-somber church an even more dark appearance. By now, everything was in Spanish and this was now a clearly Mexican event.

I also remember occasionally going with my family, including my father, to Cristo Rey. This was a hill—and not a very small one—overlooking the El Paso smelter on one side of the Rio Grande and Juárez on the other. On top of the hill was a large cross of the crucified Jesus that was dedicated to Christ the King or *Cristo Rey.* At different times of the year, but I mostly remember summertime, people would make pilgrimages up the hill. It was a winding road and I have visions of mostly dark-shawled Mexican women praying the rosary ascending the hill. Like the Corpus Christi procession, this one was also impressive.

Visits to the Evergreen cemetery, going over the bridge to Juárez to visit the cathedral on that side of the border, going with Nama to take my little sister, Alma María, to offer flowers to the Virgin Mary at a small church on the border of the barrio—all of these and more remain memories of what Catholicism meant to me growing up in El Paso, along the U.S.–Mexico border, and in the Southwest.

There is no question but that my Catholic faith was very much a part of a particular region. Yes, it may have shared—and still shares—elements with other regions, but it also had a particular southwestern touch. It is only recently that I have been studying more about just what this regionalism means to southwestern Catholicism, but, in a way, my earlier work as a historian of the Chicano experience was already leading me in this direction.

II

By the time I was in graduate school in the early 1970s at the University of California, San Diego, I was not as Catholic in faith as I was growing up in El Paso. By now I had become in a political sense a "Chicano" as a result of my involvement with the Chicano Movement when I came to California in 1969. "Chicanismo" in a sense replaced Catholicism as my faith. Nevertheless, I was still culturally a Catholic. One could not escape such a Catholic upbringing.

As I look back on this very politicized period in my life, I have to believe that my concern for issues of social justice, civil rights, human rights, and respect for people of all backgrounds had its origins in my Catholic background. I didn't become a "Chicano" out of thin air. My progressive political views came in part from my Catholic faith taught to me by the sisters and brothers. I can't pinpoint any particular doctrine or biblical teachings that constitute this influence. I think it was just a general sense that we were all people of God and that God did not support such things as racism and discrimination. I grew up during the civil rights era and there was a sense in my high school that what that movement stood for was the right thing and that as Catholics we should support it.

I can remember watching as a sophomore in college at Texas Western College (which became the University of Texas at El Paso) Dr. Martin Luther King's "I Have a Dream" speech at the March on Washington in 1963 and being moved by his stirring words. Now I think that this reaction also had to do with my own ethnic background as a Mexican American. In the early 1960s, I certainly wasn't politically conscious in ethnic terms, but I believe that part of my positive response to the black civil rights movement had to do with identifying with the underdogs. In my town, Mexican Americans were the underdogs. Growing up along the border, you couldn't help but distinguish between Anglos and Mexican Americans. Even though we had a Mexican American mayor, Raymond Telles, whose biography I would later write, as I was growing up, most of the faces in the newspapers and on television, especially representing business, civics, and social circles, were still predominantly Anglos. I remember being aware of how every year the Sun Carnival Pageant during the Christmas holidays always had an Anglo queen and mostly Anglo princesses with the exception being the representative from Juárez across the border. I always thought this a bit strange since Anglos were in the minority of El Paso's population.

I think that whatever political and even intellectual bearings I had then were shaped by my Catholicism and by being Mexican American in a border context. The Mexican part was a more intuitive and emotional reaction. The Catholic part was the more cerebral and intellectual. These two combined to provide the foundation for my more conscious politics when I became part of the Chicano Movement in the late 1960s after I moved from El Paso to California.

This move ignited my ethnic identity as a Chicano—a term that I now embraced. I became absorbed in rethinking my identity and in taking on a more radical and militant position. But, as I reflect on this conversion to Chicanismo, I don't think that it was as big a leap perhaps as I might have considered it to be at the time. During much of the 1960s, I saw myself as a liberal Democrat. I supported not only civil rights but also liberal reforms such as the War on Poverty, and I gradually became more skeptical of the Vietnam War. In retrospect, I don't think it was such a huge change to go from liberalism to radical Chicano Movement politics that stood for Chicanos not being ashamed of their ethnic background and for pushing more militantly for civil rights and equal opportunities.

As I became more of a Chicano radical, however, I became less of a practicing Catholic. Chicanismo, or what was called "cultural nationalism," became of greater intensity and interest to me. I remember in the fall of 1969, shortly after arriving in California after being hired as an instructor of history at San Jose State College (later University), attending Mass in a downtown San Jose church and thinking how irrelevant the priest's homily was after being stirred by Movement rhetoric and the excitement of participating in marches and demonstrations. My public Catholicism began to wane. During the next two decades, I only attended Mass and other religious services occasionally. These were my radical and Marxist years when I combined being a Chicano—in a political sense—with being a Marxist and joining the Trotskyist Socialist Workers Party.

I wasn't a public Catholic but I have to believe that my earlier Catholic ideals were still there and in fact complementing my new secular ones. I think too, from a certain cultural and psychological perspective, that my Catholic school formation was still very much a part of me. This would include a sense of discipline, respect for others, and a certain proper behavior (which often conflicted with radical politics)—all of this was still there. And it's not that I completely abandoned the Church. I suppose if asked then what my religion was, I would have still answered "Catholic." When I got married in 1979, I knew that I wanted a Catholic ceremony. What may be strange and interesting is that my wife, whom I met in graduate school, is also Catholic, although of Irish-Italian background. It's possible that we found much in common because of our similar Catholic upbringing, including both of us attending parochial schools. Indeed, my wife had done one better than me; she attended a Catholic college and graduated from Santa Clara University, a Jesuit institution. Because of her Santa Clara affiliation, we were married in the beautiful Santa Clara Mission. I had no problem with this. I was still a Catholic.

But what does all of this have to do with my career as a historian? As with other historians, we bring a whole baggage of cultural, social, political, and ideological formation. What we choose to study is more than an intellectual and scholarly interest. We study in part based on who we are. History for us is also autobiographical. This doesn't mean that as a historian of Catholic background, I chose to work only on Catholic subjects although, in my case, I am now doing this. But it does mean that our personal experiences have a lot to do with our research endeavors. The historian is a product of his or her own history.

In my case, I think that the combination of my Catholic liberalism, which included accepting the new progressive winds of change brought on by Vatican II (1962–65), and my political radicalism, which was a result of my involvement with the Chicano Movement, directly and indirectly affected my research and intellectual interests. I chose to work on Chicano history, but it was a history that, in retrospect, was a liberating history. I wasn't conscious of liberation theology as it was developing in Latin America that endorsed social change and even revolutionary changes and that called on the Church to have a "preferential option for the poor." However, as I embarked on my dissertation research, which in 1981 became my book *Desert Immigrants: The Mexicans of El Paso, 1880–1920,* I chose to focus on poor Mexican immigrants workers. This was, in a way, accepting a preferential option for the poor. It was and is a history that although in a scholarly sense is aimed at uncovering the role of Chicanos in U.S. history, at another level is also aimed at how discovering or rediscovering that history (I was in fact rediscovering my own history in El Paso) could likewise be liberating for Chicanos. A significant part of Chicanismo was knowing oneself through a rediscovering of one's roots in pre-Columbian history, in Mexico, and as a Chicano. The truth, or in this case history, would set us free. Chicano history and those of us who researched and wrote it were both scholars and, in a sense, "theologians." Our history had dual purposes: although certainly written in a professional academic style, they were not done solely for a professional audience, but also for the Movement, for Chicanos, for our communities, and for advocating *La Causa*—the cause of freedom and social justice.

This theological involvement with history—this liberating aspect to my writing of Chicano history—was not only, I believe, the result of secular politics. It was part of my Catholic soul. It was my unconscious reflection on the Passion, the crucifixion of Jesus, carrying my cross, and the resurrection that would follow. I may have come from a more middle-class Mexican American Catholic background, but my Catholic sensibility, my ethnic border position, and my later radical politics did not divorce me from the oppression of the poor. Indeed, it not only made me sympathetic to researching about the Mexican immigrant poor, but also about the Mexican American middle class (see my book *Mexican Americans: Leadership, Ideology and Identity, 1930–1960*) because I knew, having been raised in a struggling middle-class household, that to be "middle class" and Mexican American also meant experiencing different degrees of discrimination, injustice, exclusion, and being treated as a "stranger." When I chose to write about the civil rights and labor rights struggles of what I called the Mexican American Generation between the 1930s and 1960s, I again was continuing that liberationist tendency. To be a Catholic, a Chicano Catholic, along the U.S.–Mexican border and in the Southwest is to be an underdog—what the great novelist of the Mexican Revolution of 1910, Mariano Azuela, referred to as *los de abajo.*

This emphasis on liberation extends to some of my other works. In my oral history or *testimonio* of Bert Corona, a major Chicano labor and civil rights leader (*Memories of Chicano History: The Life and Narrative of Bert Corona*), I focused on Corona's long history of giving his life, almost in a sacrificial way, to empowering the poor and oppressed Chicanos. In my edited volume on Ruben Salazar, a leading Mexican American journalist who championed the rights of Mexican Americans (with Ruben Salazar, *Border Correspondent: Selected Writings, 1955–1970*), I stressed not only Salazar's writings on the impact of discrimination and exclusion on Mexican Americans, but also how Salazar supported the Chicano

Movement for liberation. And in my book coauthored with Frances Esquibel Tywoniak—a coming-of-age story of a young Mexican American girl in the 1940s in the San Joaquin Valley (*Migrant Daughter: Coming of Age as a Mexican American Woman*), we highlighted a daughter of migrant parents who struggled to make something of herself through education and who went on to dedicate herself—almost in a missionary sense—to teach the children of poor Latino families.

All of these different texts have to do with the concept of liberation. They don't ostensibly focus on Catholic themes; however, they are guided, in my opinion, by my ingrained Catholic faith and sensitivity to the marginalized. Not all of this has to do, of course, with just Catholicism. The Chicano Movement resonates in my research as well. But the liberationist character of these studies is the product of more than sectarian political concerns. I believe that there is also a certain spiritual aspect to them that speaks to my own faith background.

Yes, I know that some will say "he's really straining here to make the Catholic connection and he's reading back what might have not been there at all." This is a reasonable response; I *am* reading back. But in so doing, I truly believe that there is a religious and certainly moral influence in my early work as a historian that in part has to do with my Catholic background.

III

However, how do I now explain that a good portion of my current research during the past ten years or so has direct connections with Catholicism and, in particular, Chicano Catholicism in the Southwest? Like other Catholics who at certain points have not been active in the Church but who as part of their midlife crisis return, I've undergone some of this journey. Part of this return has to do with having children. When my daughter Giuliana was born in 1986 and then my son Carlo in 1987, I began to renew my participation in the Church, not all at once but gradually. We baptized both of them at the Santa Clara Mission. When old enough, they were enrolled in catechism classes at our parish church. There they began to learn about their religion and also prepare for their First Communion. To support them in their religious education, my wife and I both started to attend Sunday Mass again with our kids. Was this hypocritical? Perhaps. But in all honesty, I think I was ready to once again become a practicing Catholic. Having a family and children, wanting to be role models for them, and feeling that they had to grow up with certain moral values all seemed to lead me to returning to the

Church. I don't think that I had ever left the Church, but being a parent as well as approaching fifty seemed to make becoming an active Catholic once again the right thing to do. I don't regret this and while I don't agree with the Church's position on all issues and am as shocked by the sexual scandals as anyone, I still feel that the Church is comforting for me and that my faith is something I can look to for a sense of security and support in those difficult moments.

But it wasn't just being a parent that renewed my interest and involvement in the Church. It also was affected by certain professional connections. I cite two in particular. In the mid-1990s, I agreed to work with a graduate student, Gaston Espinosa, who came to University of California at Santa Barbara (UCSB) to work with me in Chicano history. Gaston wanted to write a dissertation on the origins of Latino Pentecostalism in the United States, an original and much-needed study. In addition, two other graduate students in the Department of Religious Studies, Luis Leon and Darell Caterine, also wanted to work on Latino religion themes and also sought me out to work with them on Chicano history. Working with these students stimulated in me a new interest in Chicano religion research. This interest increased when Gaston suggested that we co-organize a conference at UCSB on Chicano religion. We labored several months to prepare it and it was quite successful. We invited many other faculty and graduate students from our campus as well as other campuses.

Because I wanted to also read a paper at the conference and not just serve as an organizer, I decided to do a paper on a Chicano Catholic youth group during the period of the Chicano Movement called *Católicos por la Raza.* I had known of *Católicos,* but learned more about the group as a result of an oral history project that I was doing on the Chicano Movement in Los Angeles. One of the activists whom I interviewed for this study was Raul Ruiz, who was involved in a number of Movement activities including *Católicos.* As editor of *La Raza,* a key Movement publication, Raul had published stories about *Católicos.* I interviewed other former *Católicos* members as well as discovering additional sources for my paper.

It was an exciting experience because I identified with *Católicos.* Like me, they were Chicano Catholics but also, like me, disaffected ones who became involved in the Chicano Movement. However, as Catholics, they chose to confront the Church in Los Angeles as part of the establishment and to raise questions as to why the Church was not doing more for Chicanos. Not getting any response from the demands they made to Cardinal McIntyre in the fall of 1969, *Católicos* staged a large and confrontational protest on Christmas Eve that year with the aim of disrupting the cardinal's midnight Mass, or the *misa de gallo* in Spanish. Their strategy was to enter the newly built $3 million St. Basil's Church on Wilshire Boulevard that to *Católicos* symbolized the Church's greater concern with building edifices rather than assisting the poor and to read their demands to the assembled congregation. However, they encountered resistance by police officers disguised as ushers. While the Mass went on, the battle between *Católicos* and the reinforced police took place in the vestibule and outside the church. A number of protestors were arrested and, a few weeks later, some were charged with various indictments.

Católicos didn't last very long; activists went off to work on other Movement actions such as the Chicano anti–Vietnam War effort. Yet in a short time, they made a significant impact that led to the Church becoming more sensitive to the Chicano Movement and to the needs of its extensive Latino parishioners.

Writing my paper on *Católicos* was an important scholarly and personal turning point for me. It reinforced to an extent my being back as a practicing Catholic and it opened up a whole new research field for me. It stimulated what Fr. Andrew Greeley calls "the Catholic imagination" or, in my case, my Chicano Catholic imagination. This new direction was thus rooted in both my own personal family circumstances plus my professional associations.

The second important influence that steered me into what I call Chicano Catholic studies was my meeting Fr. Virgilio Elizondo. Inspired by our Chicano religion conference, I proposed bringing Fr. Elizondo, the foremost theologian and scholar concerning Latino Catholicism in the United States, to UCSB as a distinguished Regents' Lecturer for two weeks. I felt that his presence would further contribute to our effort to stress the importance of studying Chicano/Latino religion. By now, my interest in this subject had expanded to include the curriculum in our Department of Chicano Studies where I hold an appointment along with one in history. My growing involvement in religious studies made me cognizant that we did not offer a single course on Chicano/Latino religion in Chicano Studies. How could this be? This represented an enormous gap in our offerings. This omission, in my opinion, had resulted from the fact that Chicano Studies as a discipline had emerged out of the Chicano Movement, which had been antagonistic to all establishment institutions, including religious ones, especially the Catholic Church as exemplified by the actions of *Católicos por la Raza.* Seeing organized religion as opposed to the interests of the people and, in Marxist terms, as the "opiate of the people," early organizers of Chicano Studies programs excluded courses on religion. Some faculty, of course, addressed religion in other courses, especially popular religiosity; however, the specific study of Chicano religion was not part of the curriculum. Even today, it is difficult to find such classes in Chicano Studies programs.

Yet religion, as in other cultures, is fundamental to understanding the Chicano/Latino experience. This is as true for popular religiosity as it is for the role of the churches in these communities. Fr. Elizondo's lectures on liberation theology and on the relationship of religion and culture were marvelous. He certainly made an impression on me. As his host, I got to know him well, and this laid the foundation for what is now a very strong friendship. As important, I learned much from him that further stimulated my interest in studying Chicano religion.

In part inspired by my initial engagement with Chicano religious studies and my encounter with Fr. Elizondo, some of my current research has come to focus even more on Chicano Catholic religion. I say "in part" because this research also reflects my resumed identity as a Chicano Catholic. It is, in a way, a resumption of my earlier Catholic education. Through my research, I am adding to the knowledge about my religion that the nuns and brothers initially taught me. It has also been a way of being inspired by my faith as I confront it now in more than midlife.

I think, as I reflect on them, that these ongoing projects also convey some of the religious dimensions that I now discern in my earlier work. One is the role of leadership and social justice that has been a strong current in so much of my scholarship. But in this case, it has now turned to religious leadership and the influence of Catholic social doctrine and liberation theology. All of my recent projects involve these themes. One has to do with the biography of Fray Angélico Chávez that I am coauthoring with my wife, Professor Ellen McCracken. A New Mexican Franciscan, Fray Angélico was the first native-born Hispanic Franciscan. His life spanned much of the twentieth century and his leadership was both in his ministry among Hispanics and Native Americans as well as in his role as a leading intellectual. A second project is a book of interviews with Chicano Catholic priests such as Fr. Elizondo and how they have exercised leadership as Catholic priests among Mexican Americans. A third concerns the life and times of Fr. Luis Olivares, who in the 1980s spearheaded the sanctuary movement in Los Angeles to provide refuge and support to both Central American refugees fleeing the civil wars in that region and undocumented Mexican immigrants fleeing poverty in their country. I am further assembling a book on the spirituality of César Chávez as reflected in his own words. Finally, I have collected and revised some of my more recent conference papers on Chicano religious topics that I have assembled into a book that reflects my main concerns about Chicano Catholicism in the twentieth century.

The linkage of leadership and Catholic faith in my current research is likewise a reflection of myself. As noted, there is no question in my mind that much of my own political and social values, beliefs, principles, and actions are rooted in my Catholic upbringing and faith. Catholicism is at the root of how I have come to view the world. It is the beginning of my own journey as a historical subject. Other influences have affected me along the way, but my Catholic values have always been there. In my own way, I have tried to exercise my own form of Catholic leadership in the political issues I have been involved in over the years concerning the Chicano Movement, social justice issues, the fight against racism, and opposition to the disastrous affects of imperialism and globalization. It has also influenced my leadership with respect to my students and my teaching and how I try to convey certain moral issues in how we examine history. I don't preach in my classes (or at least I hope I don't), but I certainly convey a sense of justice, especially in the teaching of Chicano history. By examining Catholic religious leadership in my research, I perhaps am also examining myself. Like the subjects I am researching, I too have a ministry and a vocation. I see myself, especially now in my later years, as conveying my own sense of the Word, not in a strict religious sense, but hopefully in the sense of awakening my students to the continuing injustices of the world and how they must address these and combat them. I don't know how successful I am in this mission, but it is a mission that I have come to and will continue for the rest of my life.

IV

I feel as if I've come full circle—a non-Western view of history. My deep involvement today with Chicano Catholic studies is a return to my own embrace of my Catholic faith when I was younger. Even as a college undergraduate, I attended Mass regularly; I always carried a rosary; I prayed at night; I made visits to church during the week. I think that by attending a public undergraduate school, I became even more conscious of my Catholic identity. I then went through those alienated years of the Chicano Movement with respect to the Church. But now I'm back. I don't have the same fervor as a Catholic that I did earlier; I've lived too long and experienced too many things to be that idealistic. However, from a more subdued religious and spiritual perspective, and certainly from a cultural—a Chicano Catholic culture, that is—and intellectual point of view, I am once again comfortable being a Catholic. It is not only part of my personal life but of my professional one as well. Perhaps in a way, I've never stopped driving Nama to Sunday Mass.

References

García, Mario T. *Desert Immigrants: The Mexicans of El Paso, 1880–1920.* New Haven, Conn.: Yale University Press, 1981.
García, Mario T. *The Making of a Mexican American Mayor: Raymond L. Telles of El Paso.* El Paso: Texas Western Press, 1998.
García, Mario T. *Mexican Americans: Leadership, Ideology and Identity, 1930–1960.* New Haven, Conn.: Yale University Press, 1989.
García, Mario T. *Memories of Chicano History: The Life and Narrative of Bert Corona.* Berkeley and Los Angeles: University of California Press, 1994.
García, Mario T., ed., and Ruben Salazar. *Border Correspondent: Selected Writings, 1955–1970.* Berkeley and Los Angeles: University of California Press, 1995.
Tywoniak, Frances Esquibel, and Mario T. García. *Migrant Daughter: Coming of Age as a Mexican American Woman.* Berkeley and Los Angeles: University of California Press, 2000.

NICK SALVATORE

5 *Deeply Within: Catholicism, Faith, and History*

> I'm not a churchgoer, but I realized, as time passed, that my music is filled with Catholic imagery. It's not a negative thing. There was a powerful world of potent imagery that became alive and vital and vibrant, and was both very frightening and held out the promise of ecstasies and paradise. There was this incredible internal landscape that they created in you. As I got older, I got less and less defensive about it. I thought, I've inherited this particular landscape and I can build it into something of my own.
>
> —Bruce Springsteen, 2005

I find myself in Detroit, Michigan, on any one of many Sundays between 1998 and 2004. I get off the Lodge Freeway, take a right on West Grand, past Ford Hospital, past Hitsville, Motown's original home, and on past some badly run-down houses, to Linwood. A right on Linwood takes me past the Shrine of the Black Madonna, the still-operating site of the Reverend Albert Cleage's Black Christian Nationalist movement. Shortly beyond this church, Linwood becomes C. L. Franklin Boulevard, and I make a left into the parking lot, leave the car, and walk across the boulevard to New Bethel Baptist Church. It's about 10:30 A.M., and the congregation is gathering for the eleven o'clock service. This is Reverend Franklin's former church, the physical space he regularly transcended in the powerful sermons he preached here between 1946 and 1979, the church that made him one of the most influential preachers of his generation. It is also the space where two of his three children whom

I met, daughters Erma and Aretha, immersed themselves in the Baptist tradition and established the foundations of their sense of self. New Bethel Baptist Church is ground zero for so much of modern American religious experience and popular culture, and I am writing a biography of Reverend Franklin. As I approach the wooden doors, a member of the congregation acknowledges me, welcomes me with a warm smile, and holds open the door.

But who am I as I enter? In part, of course, I am the social historian and biographer, and that is a role that feels comfortable at this stage in my career. But it has become very clear to me in past visits that I am here more than as the historian. I have shown myself enough in the church beyond the need to make contacts for interviews, and even given three talks from the pulpit on different occasions. No, some part of me I don't know (but is anything but foreign nonetheless) is asking my travel agent to book my return flights home in a way that usually enables me to attend services. Over time, other things have happened to me as well in that church, with that congregation. Gradually I stopped sitting in the visitor's section (although I am still occasionally placed there by the ushers) but rather sit among the worshippers. Then too I found myself voluntarily going forward with most of the congregation for a prayer service in the well of the sanctuary—two hundred or more people, whose joined hands form a bond the strength of which I marvel at, praying as Deacon Milton Hall chants an ancient spiritual in tones that still echo his Arkansas upbringing. But praying? I feel so self-conscious, stymied—how do you do this praying thing? And yet I sense a calmness as well, not quite of belonging, but more akin to coming closer to an internal home. Later, during Altar Call, when Pastor Robert Smith seeks those who would accept Jesus Christ, two young junior deacons, one of whom I know, approach me. I respond with an informal, "Ahm, but you know who I am. I live in upstate New York." The man I know—his seriousness cuts right through: "You are in this church enough to be a member regardless of where you live. When will you make the jump?" Reading his seriousness, I dismiss the glib retorts that had leapt to mind. I think: "But I'm a Catholic." My vocal cords cannot pronounce those words. Instead, I startle myself as I blurt out, "Not yet."

What does this mean? I ask myself for the rest of the day heading home. I don't think I will become an Afro-Baptist (although it is already clear that the congregation would welcome me as they would any believer). I try, in another approach, to be the social scientist, consoling myself that there are library shelves full of anthropological and sociological literature that warn about "overidentification" by investigators with their subjects. True enough, but the "loss" of scholarly objectivity is far distant from the powerful feelings I experience. Over time I began to realize that what pulled me back to that church, well beyond the needs of the research itself, was the palpable, complex expression of faith that encased me in that building. These men and women helped me to name at least part of what was absent in my life. This was no mean feat, as the only thing more rigid than the faith of a recent convert is the persistent denial of that very possibility by one scarred by earlier engagements with other communities of faith. It was becoming clear to me that this book project was going to be very complicated indeed.

I was baptized into the Roman Catholic faith, shortly after my birth in November 1943, at St. Saviour's church in Brooklyn, New York. That parish influenced my early years in many ways. When my father died fourteen months after my birth, it was the parish that supported my mother and her three sons until my younger brother was old enough so that my mother could go to work. All three of us boys went to the parish parochial school, staffed by the Sisters of Notre Dame, through eighth grade. It was in this parish that I made the sacrament of First Communion and celebrated the rite of confirmation, and it was here too that I served as an altar boy for some five years. As I look back on that time now, I am struck by the absence of a recognizable spiritual dimension in so much of that experience. I remember repeated warnings from various nuns that the Russians were poisoning the drinking water; the obsession with sin, especially of a sexual nature, even at an age when most of us had no idea what the attraction was; and the preoccupation with guilt in the dour Sunday sermons preached by generally uninspired men. I think now that the greatest tragedy lay in the fact that the authorities in both parish and school had the wisdom to ask the central question, Who is God? and the audacity to instruct that one had but to memorize the answer. In this atmosphere, I later came to see, this narrowed perception obscured even the possibility of an engagement with faith beyond belief.

Yet there were other influences too. As an altar boy I was touched by the liturgical cycle as prayed in the traditional Latin: the higher the Mass the more layered the ritual, as the sanctuary overflowed with priests, altar boys, candles, and incense. But even Low Mass had an affecting influence, as the near-daily participation in a ritual celebration of a power far beyond oneself almost transcended the imperative to reduce this mystery to a matter of memorization. That desire to be connected to such a ritual, and its uplifting possibility, would remain a part of my life even when I turned from Catholicism. In other ways as well these early years at St. Saviour's framed the person I would become. From church, school, and home came the repeated emphasis on the centrality of a moral law in human existence. One was not a free agent, bound solely by personal desire or, as I would later comprehend, social and political goals. Rather, in fulfilling one's commitment to God, one acknowledged a force beyond oneself and discovered, not insignificantly, a responsibility to other human beings as well. The God we worshipped at St. Saviour's was not a providential God as in the Afro-Baptist tradition, whose interventions in human affairs have as an ultimate goal the liberation of his chosen people in this world as in the next. Yet the Catholicism of my childhood did allow for a sense of the shared worth of all human beings. As important as that was, it was also a somewhat quiescent belief in parish life during the 1950s. Too often, the absence of any other vision suggested, a believer fulfilled the responsibility to both God and man by staying on the correct side of the narrow morality those guilt-inducing sermons emphasized. In the process, a broader understanding of moral law contracted, and individual avoidance of sin became of primary concern. But I nonetheless had some inkling, however ill-formed, that faith might reach beyond those limits.

There was as well another quality that deeply touched me in those formative years, one that has remained surprisingly consistent even as my perspective has revolved around it thoroughly in the intervening years. What I understood of original sin as a child was indistinguishable from the sermonic hectoring that, at its worst, left me at a loss as how to justify any feeling of competence or self-worth. But, I would come to see, the concept of original sin—the inherent fallibility of all human endeavor, the humanness of the frailty that circumscribed thought and deed—remained essential to my being. Years later, when Leonard Cohen sang of being "Like a bird on the wire / like a drunk in a midnight choir / I have tried in my way to be free," I found a power in those melancholy lyrics that brought joy.[1] Cohen's secular voice with its deep spiritual vision encompassed human limitations, and I found in it an exultant relief from the arrogance of thinking that I, or indeed we, actually directed in toto this existence we inhabited. This understanding of my humanness, then, led me to a (re)embrace of the concept of original sin well before I first read Reinhold Niebuhr—and with a spirit so fundamentally different from my first encounter. This sensibility informed my historical writing from the very beginning and proved to be as well a critical bridge in the rediscovery of the spiritual in my life.

My years in parochial school left me with at least one other trait, a love of history. I won the history medal upon graduation, and I still remember the excitement when I realized that "New York" meant there was an "Old York," and that there was some connection between the two. Although more contemporary events than historical at the time, the Hungarian Revolution of 1956 fueled this interest further. The fate of Josef Cardinal Mindszenty was uppermost in the minds of the parish religious leaders, but I was also intrigued by how one group (i.e., the Communists) took over a nation such as Hungary. Partly fueled by the wild speculation about Communist subversion of America in this decade of McCarthyism, I had stumbled on possible links between two seemingly disparate entities. A very early, rough appreciation of historical causality even then appeared on my horizon, although I would never have had the words to express it at that time.

The four years at Brooklyn Prep High School (1957–61) were quite a different experience from grammar school. The Jesuits were demanding teachers who, within careful limits, tested our minds and emerging belief systems. A history teacher in sophomore year offered another intriguing linkage: How, he asked, could nineteenth-century philosophical liberals become twentieth-century philosophical conservatives? That kept me engaged even through the last two years of high school history taught by the football coach, where I learned more about 4-3 defenses than I did about anything else. It was also in high school that I became sharply conscious of class issues. As a financial aid student (the $300 yearly tuition in 1957 was beyond my mother's staunchest effort), I met others my age with money for the first time in a sustained way, and at an age when it counted. Not surprisingly, I deeply wanted to belong (wearing daily, for a year, as my obligatory jacket a classmate's hand-me-down passed on through the parish can have that effect); yet I always felt a beat off. But "the Prep," as we all called it as if there were no other, had its strongest immediate impact on the development of my religious beliefs.

While I cannot now remember any religious class that made an impression, something must have happened in those classes during those years, for I know that my understanding of faith grew enormously by the time I graduated in 1961. In part, to be sure, this is not an unusual adolescent experience, and it was intimately interconnected with an emerging sexuality and the need for self-definition. Indeed, the Jesuits encouraged us to attend weekend retreats (two days of meditation, prayer, and spiritual talks) in the last years of high school at least as much to inculcate a stern sexual morality as to further a deeper sense of faith. The Jesuits also could taper the meaning of faith to fit a narrowed morality. But in addition to all of that, something else also happened to me. I found myself grappling with the question of God; specifically, whether I could have direct contact with him and what the nature of that would be. Although I did not understand it at the time, this was my first sustained engagement with the possibility of faith beyond a set of memorized beliefs. I struggled with these questions, talked with Jesuits at school about them, and never felt satisfied that I had approached the underlying meaning I sensed. In part this is not surprising, given the depth of the issue I was raising. But I also felt, I recall now, that I lacked both the conception and the inner language necessary to pursue these disturbances in my soul. In 1964 (when I was in a very different place), I wrote to my uncle, a Jesuit missionary in the Caroline–Marshall Islands in the Pacific, and told him, essentially, that I had lost any "personal contact with God" during my senior year retreat. He doubted that, and indeed he was right, for I continued to struggle with the possibility that I might have a relationship with God. My sense of faith was then dominated by an easily grasped set of beliefs, and I could not see beyond the barrier those beliefs created. Yet the strong urge, however inchoate at the moment, to continue this journey intensified and I applied and was accepted into the Society of Jesus, the Jesuit order, in July 1961.

The two-page personal statement I wrote in January 1961 as part of my application to enter the Jesuit order vividly reflected my understandings at that time. (My mother, in her wisdom, kept a copy and I found it among her papers following her death.) I began, perhaps oddly for the occasion, with my father's death when I was fourteen months old. This I termed the day my life began but, rather than exploring the psychological dimensions of that experience (the search for definition in an order of religious men had deep roots in my familial and religious history), I immediately tied it to my family's economic life. Work had been a necessity from grammar school on—delivering packages at supermarkets, delivering newspapers after school, doing odd jobs for neighbors, and the like. But along with the need for work and for the money it provided within a family context, I wrote, work also "educated me. It taught me the ways of people." My seventeen-year-old self then continued: "You may ask—how does this facet of my life enter into my decision to become a Jesuit? Well, I delivered papers for two years, at a very impressionable age, to very poor people in horrible neighborhoods. It just seemed to me that no one was trying to help these people, and I thought that something should be done, although at the time I didn't know what."

The tone of this paragraph amuses me now. How American is it for the product of a rather poor working family such as mine to look with an assumed superiority at others who were, in fact, so much like oneself?

But it was also evident that, even at this early age, my understanding of faith had a strong social component—this was, after all, an application for the priesthood. I then suggested that a priest, by addressing the troubled spiritual dimensions of people's lives, might indeed alleviate the pain. I sensed, and remember saying to a friend at about the same time, that the priest might be a bridge between the worlds of the church and social problems. But I remained innocently unaware then of the degrees of complexity at the center of that commingling.

I did attempt to recognize the dimension of faith beyond simple belief, in however limited a fashion. Contact with the Jesuits at my high school, I explained, had "offered me a chance to find God—not merely through memorizing catechism questions—but finding Him through extra spiritual activities." I noted the availability of the sacraments and the counseling by the Jesuits as a particularly valuable aspect of my school experience. And that was it. A few more concluding words—and I was done. Part of me laughs now and wonders what the Jesuits saw in this statement that possessed them to accept me. The very essence of my search for God, that near arithmetical search through "extra spiritual activities," left but little room for a faith within. That I was engaged in some kind of searching, I can now see; but as I had no inner sensibility (or confidence I should have one) to recognize it, I knew but a far narrower understanding. But I also recognize both the prominence and the relative length of my discussion of social issues as a catalyst for, and a projected sustaining element of, my vocation. This concern with life around me, and the instinctive effort to span the distance between that world and "knowing God," reflected the core meaning of my youthful Catholic yearning. The explicit duality of that formulation as I experienced it, drilled into me as it was throughout my school years, ill-prepared me as a Catholic for the decade to come, one that would be dominated by the transformations that accompanied Vatican II. Indeed, by the time these stirrings reach my awareness, I had long rejected Catholicism. I experienced Vatican II through my rearview mirror. Yet, oddly, as I changed over time, the desire to span that distance, understood now in a different manner, to be sure, remained a central concern of my work as a historian.

The year I spent at St. Andrew's-on-Hudson, the magnificent 700-acre Jesuit novitiate along the Hudson River just outside Poughkeepsie, New York (now the site of the Culinary Institute of America), proved to be a foundational year in my life. I entered in July 1961 relatively innocent of the person I was, and left a year later sharply self-conscious of exactly how complex a journey I was on. The vehicles of this developmental transformation were multiple: daily meditation early in the morning, followed by Mass, and self-reflection during the long periods of silence during the day. But the central experience was making the "Long Retreat," the thirty days of silence and meditation under the direction of a spiritual advisor that was first devised by St. Ignatius Loyola, the founder of the Jesuit order. Formally known as the Spiritual Exercises, the intensity of this experience transformed me in the years that followed in complex and often contradictory ways. At the time, however, I had other feelings.

During that long October of 1961, I never found a way to meditate that brought me closer to a sense of the Divine. Meditations for me became these painful interior monologues that inevitably circled back on myself no matter where I started. I felt profoundly inadequate. I found myself unable to envision a God beyond the rigid structure of beliefs I had absorbed as a youth. God was this external umpire, an arbiter of rules with whom only truly sainted people might relate. In a sense, I waited for an apparition during the Long Retreat, a condition guaranteed to produce the inadequacy I experienced. My earlier training had presented the idea of "knowing God" in such a removed manner, uninvolved in my life but for the role as the omnipresent "judge" in this ongoing neo-Jansenist trial, that I had little sense of where my "I" became relevant. (The reduction of the central mystery of faith to so mundane a concept that it could be memorized was critical here.) Not surprisingly, I sensed even during that month that my call to the priesthood was not viable; however, I lacked the confidence to act on it. I am glad that the Master of Novices did not intervene and counsel me to leave the seminary. It would take another eight months to decide on my own, but that time of decision proved to be of central importance for my future.

As I have come to understand this experience over the intervening years, I see two different aspects to it. The first looks backward, toward the religious training in my youth, and realizes now how ill-prepared both by experience and training I was for the seminary. At seventeen and a half years old, I had at best a rudimentary sense of self, and the narrowed understanding of the moral and spiritual aspects of my life left me with few resources. There was no place I could identify within my Catholic experience that transcended the circumscribed dimensions of the avid catechist. As that power diminished, so did my identification with Catholic practice that was so intimately intertwined with it. Others (some fellow seminarians, individuals such as Dorothy Day, Thomas Merton, Daniel Berrigan, and others whom I would read later) felt differently, and at times in the years to come I envied them. But that was not my experience.

The other impact of the seminary experience was quite different. The central power of the Spiritual Exercises for me was the discovery of self. The ensuing eight months of self-examination that focused on the viability of my vocation was, in secular terms, a growing into a consciousness of self that formed the basis of my adult life. I had to decide how I would live that life; I began to question the meaning of the inadequacy I had so sharply felt; and in the process I became more conscious of that responsibility to self than ever before. It may be ironic that in the process I left the seminary and, ultimately, Catholicism. But there is even a greater irony as well: I struggled with that decision in those eight months as in the years that immediately followed from within a recognizable Catholic framework. My concern was with the relationship of this emerging self to my responsibility to God, and if over time that sense of God became less identifiable than the God of my Catholic youth, I remained profoundly influenced by moral and religious sensibilities forged deeply within the Catholic experience. Michael Harrington was by no means the only one raised in the Catholic tradition who could say, more than three decades after leaving the Church, that he remained culturally and, in a certain way, intellectually as well, a Catholic nonetheless. Perhaps the greatest irony of all is that this search, experienced through political activity as through my work as a historian, would bring me, not to Catholicism, but to a sense of the power of faith beyond belief in my life.

In this sense, the struggle to discover myself, to better understand me in my place in the world as found, and to consciously begin that lifelong process of defining the parameters of spiritual and moral life, proved to be the most important meaning I took from the Long Retreat. I say this now not with any intent to be sacrilegious toward that Catholic experience but rather with the realization that this would be, in fact, my path toward an understanding of the spiritual dimension in my life. Not surprisingly, given the tone of my application to the Jesuits, a concern with social and political affairs would be prominent.

I returned from St. Andrew's in the summer of 1962 more pained than ever before at the abyss that lay so enormously between my emerging awareness and the possibility of faith in my life. This tension continued over the following two years as I moved in and out of college (a classics major at Fordham University, into which the Jesuits got me immediately upon leaving the seminary), worked the night shift as a messenger at a printing firm in Manhattan, and then, in the fall of 1963, became a full-time worker at the Railway Express Company and a member of

Local 808 of the Teamsters union. Simultaneously, I became active in the civil rights movement, participating in a sit-in at New York's City Hall and at a construction site in Brooklyn, where I was arrested for the first time—both actions protesting the systematic exclusion of black and Hispanic working people from the building trades. That by 1964 I resolved my inner tension by declaring faith, or at least the Catholic faith I knew, irrelevant is not, in retrospect, surprising. As my political activity continued (and fueled for the first time in me an avaricious hunger to read everything), I worked on citywide school boycotts, helped staff a summer leadership camp for young activists from Harlem, and became involved in the anti–Vietnam War movement. Faith seemed to me ever more distant from my concerns. Harshly I dismissed it, quick to point out the hypocrisy I perceived in attitudes and actions by Catholics leaders, and all the while remained consciously oblivious to the profound religious grounding that in fact motivated so many civil rights activists in New York as across the nation. At this point, a different faith dominated, a faith marked by Marxist shibboleths (Marx's writings, beyond *The Communist Manifesto,* lay largely unread) and an insistence that revolutionary transformation was essential if the nation was to survive into the next decade. I can now see that, understood as an expression of faith, my more secular, political formulations shared much with the narrowness that in my youth mistook arid beliefs for faith. To have suggested that much in 1966, however, would have evoked from me only dismissive scorn.

In a manner that was terribly unclear for a long time, my path toward the realm of faith would partially unfold through an intellectual process. My particular experience with Catholicism all but demanded it. The God of my imagination elicited belief, and in time disbelief as well, but the idea that faith rather than belief was at the core of spiritual life was then foreign to me. This recitation of memorized tenets was also a poor substitute for serious intellectual engagement. Conflating as I did then belief and faith, I dismissed both in one swipe (or so I thought) and sought to feed an intellectual hunger that then had no name. This eventually brought me back to complete my undergraduate degree at Hunter College in the Bronx and, in the fall of 1968, to the graduate program in American history at the University of California at Berkeley. Political and social life were my concerns, and I thought that I had left behind on the East Coast any troubling questions of faith.

Berkeley was then an enormously exciting place, full of intellectual ferment, political activity, and, in cycles, a fierce engagement with the world. For all its excesses, it was a wonderful atmosphere in which to grow. Before I had left New York I had already begun to question the simplistic analysis that framed my political activity, and that process continued in Berkeley. The quick dismissal of patriotism among both black and white working people that was so prevalent in the antiwar movement caused me to rethink my own experiences: How viable was a politics that separated me, seemingly permanently, from the men and women I grew up with? The point, I came to see, was not to support the war but rather to resist the caricature of these complex lives caused by a blind political belief. Indeed, my favorite quip during these years was to the effect that, having "won" my mind from Catholicism, I damn sure wasn't giving it over to some pseudo-Marxist idiocy!

In this way, then, to study history was to create a space to explore issues fundamental to my world through the experience of others. I did not envision this space as apolitical, but neither did I see it as being driven by immediate political concerns. That type of history, one that would use the past to directly influence the present, I rejected as puerile even in graduate school—a stance that ensured many a heated discussion in seminar or over coffee in the graduate lounge. History's "lessons," I was beginning to understand, were really more complicated, and to reduce humans to categorical groups whose motivations and interests could be neatly determined was profoundly dangerous. It was in this mood, then, in 1969 or 1970, that I decided to do my outside field for the degree with Robert N. Bellah in the sociology of religion.

I remember my explicit motivation clearly. In part, I knew from experience that religion was an important part of many people's lives and its near exclusion in the social history I was reading was disturbing. But the major catalyst at the time for my approaching Bob Bellah (whose career and reputation I was blissfully unaware of at first!) was in fact far more personal. It was coming on a decade since I had entered the novitiate and I thought it was time to resolve my relationship with Catholicism. I had not, it turned out, left these questions behind. As motivation for graduate work, the intensely personal clearly outweighed at that moment the emerging scholarly interest. As I started this journey, I recall feeling an almost detached curiosity about where it might take me and a certain relief that I was approaching an issue that I had finally acknowledged was important to my life. I did not envision a return to Catholicism, nor did I particularly desire that. Rather, I knew that the blanket dismissal of my Catholic experience harmed me in at least two ways: It detached me from the potentially rich emotional and cultural seedbed that formed me; as long as that blockade existed within me, I separated myself from continuing my own understanding of faith. For the reality was, I finally acknowledged, that I had not been able to dismiss this issue of faith as I had once blithely imagined. From the vantage point of three decades later, another theme strikes me as well: I simply assumed that through my intellect I could address, if not resolve, questions of faith. Unwittingly, I began to explore a theme that would play a major role in my future personal and professional life.

My work with Bob Bellah was wonderful, opening up as it did new vistas to explore. In readings with Bellah and in talks with other faculty and graduate students interested in "things religious," I was able to lift the giant weight I had carried for nearly a decade: I no longer had to hide my Catholic past, and my failure with it, in a rush of political/historical intellectualizing. I was beginning to understand that faith, as opposed to the narrowed belief system experienced in youth, came in a grand variety of ways to human beings precisely because as humans we are indeed spiritual animals. Not insignificantly, I felt the joy of bridging, however hesitantly at first, the chasm I had perceived between intellectual and spiritual concerns. Importantly, more than a decade after my first efforts, I returned with very different eyes to the vision I had tried to articulate in my application to the seminary, where in the fullness of my seventeen-plus years I had lurched toward the possible interplay between religious faith and social life. It was during these years in Berkeley that I first read Dorothy Day, Daniel Berrigan, Thomas Merton, Dietrich Bonhoeffer, and other socially conscious people of faith. In short, I began anew thinking about faith, with one central difference from the past. I began to see more thoroughly than in 1961 that religious faith not only lived within an individual but lived within the individual in the community one inhabited as well. The "I" who passively waited for the unimaginable God to reveal himself now claimed a place in both the worlds of faith and of human concerns, and reveled in their commingling. Recognizing spiritual strivings in this fashion went far to free me from the dualities that had so dominated my earlier experiences. As Bellah frequently noted of a far broader process than just my own, it was, in a way, the Protestantization of American Catholicism.

Ironically, despite the very real epiphany I experienced, I still conceived of these intellectual and spiritual dimensions as largely separate. Or so I thought, at least. Through a certain process of trial and error, I entered into a dissertation, a biography of the American socialist leader Eugene Victor Debs, consciously conceiving the project primarily as the intellectual/political "compartment" of my newly expanded sense of self. This was important to me, of course, as I sought to explore in all its strengths and weaknesses the meaning of an American dissenting tradition through a biographical study of one of the nation's preeminent dissenters. But almost against my will the issue of faith interjected itself. Early in my dissertation research, I presented a paper to a discussion group at Berkeley's Graduate School of Theology on Debs and American religion; at roughly the same time, I remember talking with a member of the history faculty about understanding Debs's life from within the concentric circles of Christian suffering and redemption. Both approaches were heavy-handed, but they announced loudly and clearly, even if I did not always hear, a deeper theme that would not go away. I remained fascinated, for example, by the heavily evangelical socialists of the American Southwest whose revival-style organizing proved influential for a moment before World War I.

The very issue of faith, I can now see, attracted me to Debs in the first place. He was a vehicle for me to explore that dissenting tradition, to gain perspective on my personal and generational experience with dissent as well, and perhaps contribute to a rethinking of the old dictum that history is nothing more than past politics updated. But, in the language of the distinctions I was now sensitive to, Debs was a man of faith rather than of narrow belief. He rejected both the triumphal understandings of American life embraced by those in power and the narrow, materialist-base class proclamations of the Marxist minority. Rather, Debs grasped the promise of American life in a fashion that would have made both Horatio Alger and Communist leader William Z. Foster blanch. Debs's faith lay grounded in the possibility of American democracy, in the potential that resided in the heart of the national experiment if only the people would grasp it. Romantic at times, to be sure, yet the Debs who thrilled and inspired me was the one who repeatedly told audiences that "I do not want you to follow me or anyone else; if you are looking for a Moses to lead you out of this capitalist wilderness, you will stay right where you are. I would not lead you into the promised land if I could, because if I could lead you in, some one else would lead you out. *You must use your heads as well as your hands,* and get yourself out of your present condition." Here was the fundamental Debs, the socialist leader who understood the centrality of the individual in the crowd before him, who recognized the bonds between that individual and the larger collectivity, and who preached the need for that individual's soul to soar beyond the limitations triumphalists of any belief might impose. He was a man of faith who persisted against great odds while bearing serious personal faults that also affected his public role. It was this Debs, moreover, who chose the one picture that adorned his cell at Atlanta Federal Penitentiary during his last incarceration after World War I: the contorted visage, crowned with thorns, of the crucified Christ.[2]

In the decade I spent living with Gene Debs, I thought much about faith's relation to intellect, especially in the political realm. It was not just that a socialist in capitalist America needed faith but rather that Debs's very vision of America's promise was itself a profound act of faith. But with the exception of the last chapter, which I titled, "A Species of Purging," following a phrase in one of Debs's prison letters, overt discussion of any religious sensibility was largely sotto voce, echoes of a private dialogue with myself. Pleased as I was with the book when finished, I also knew I needed to return to this issue of religion. For I had done enough reading by 1982 to realize that no serious history of American people could be written that did not take into account the religious sensibilities of the individual or group under discussion. But rather than engage that idea directly, I promptly ran from it, polishing in the process a series of feints and spins as I worked out how I might continue as both a biographer and a social historian. Despite this complicated avoidance strategy, I would soon discover that my next biographical companion would insist that I explore anew this issue of faith.[3]

Amos Webber was many things—a black man born free in Pennsylvania in 1826; a janitor and messenger; a Civil War veteran; a husband and father; and a community activist in both Philadelphia and Worcester, Massachusetts, whose political and social activities helped to provide structure and direction for other black Americans. But above all he was a chronicler, a man whose faith in the meaning of his own experience propelled him to maintain a chronicle for exactly half a century before his death in 1904. As I got to know Amos Webber, that fact alone stunned me. But over the course of researching and writing the book, the power of Webber's faith in two additional ways equally impressed me. His commitment to democracy, to the possible that might yet supplant the actual, was as profound an act of faith as any I have ever encountered. Sharply aware of lived social reality, Webber devoted much of his life to building and strengthening institutions and organizations within black America that both gave expression to black creativity and culture and simultaneously insisted on the right for full inclusion as American citizens. As I wrote in the book's epilogue: "Belittled as a porter, a janitor, and a messenger in the eyes of so many whites, he was in fact a man who could make an act of faith in the future and work intensely for its fulfillment."[4]

As I grew more sensitive to the currents in Webber's life, I became intrigued with the sources within him that allowed for that public expression of both faith and hope. Prior to his war experience, Webber regularly attended black churches in Philadelphia and Worcester. Indeed, Webber begins his chronicle in 1854 with a discussion of a religious revival in Philadelphia, and throughout commented on religious matters. But church records also suggest that he was active in a variety of church affairs, including as an organist. His fraternal associations only reinforced this religious-based foundation. Both the Grand United Order of Odd Fellows and the Prince Hall Masons, created in the face of segregated policies by white cofraternalists, were deeply embedded in the black religious experience. But in the almost four decades following his mustering out of the service in 1865, his political, fraternal, and social activities remained as before, but he never mentioned his own involvement with a church. Further, when he did discuss revivals and other religious matters in these postwar decades, he almost always stressed how the intensity of the faith expressed had in fact declined since the prewar years. This may be simply the reactions of an aging, not-so-graceful curmudgeon but, although there is no evidence, I began to think otherwise. The war had done something to Amos Webber's faith; it altered it, or at least its expression, in subtle but critical ways. Perhaps, in the face of the carnage that was the Peninsula campaign of 1864 in Virginia, he questioned the very existence of God. Perhaps it was another experience, or even the totality of his wartime service. What impressed me was the evocation of his prior faith in his criticism of postwar religious expression, coupled with his continued affirmation of faith in his political, cultural, and indeed spiritual involvements across the latter part of the nineteenth century. Webber remained too guarded a chronicler to allow me to grasp its sources, but his ability to reach beyond experience to faith deeply touched me.

As I finished *We All Got History* in the spring of 1995, I sensed that the issues I had approached in that book still left many coiled strings yet to unravel. But in contrast to the period following *Citizen and Socialist,* I did not run from them, although I had no idea precisely where they might take me. I knew I wanted to write about race again: I had gone to Berkeley to study with Leon Litwack precisely because I saw racial issues as the central prism through which to gauge the meaning of American democracy. (Debs, in this sense, was an excursion away from my original intent.) I also knew that I was particularly interested in examining religious commitments, and their relationship to political life and the development of social consciousness, more directly than ever before; I was already listening to tapes of some C. L. Franklin sermons. My original instinct was to complicate this by writing a multiple biography of three working pastors in Detroit, what my editor at Little, Brown, Geoff Shandler, referred to as my "Detroit Trilogy": Reinhold Niebuhr, pastor of a Lutheran church in the 1920s; Father Charles Coughlin, nationally known anti-Semitic Catholic pastor of the Shrine of the Little Flower; and Franklin. The more I read, and the more I listened to his sermons, the more Franklin occupied my consciousness. Despite the generational, cultural, and occupational differences that exist between us, I came to see that his understanding of faith's relation to social life unwittingly addressed my own awkward formulations nearly four decades earlier. That Franklin embraced his faith seriously, even as he moved into the world with it, was important to me; even more, however, was the nature of that faith as I began to understand it. As was generally true throughout the Afro-Baptist community, Franklin's God was transcendent, yet dwelled within the world as found; was immanent as well; and promised a salvation to his people that was simultaneously personal and collective, in this world as in the next. The gap between that God and the believer's "I," so broad in my own experience of Catholicism, all but disappeared in Franklin's sermons without, paradoxically, ever equating the two. Franklin's faith, as I continue to understand it, impresses with its depth and complexity (he never felt compelled to reject his intellect), but most of all with its *availability.* Mystery abounds, but faith and hope ground the individual in their God's promise of deliverance within as without. An emphasis on the tenets of belief pales before the power of this immanence in people's lives.[5]

In ways that I never could have predicted, my understanding of faith in my own life has deepened in the years since I began this book. To a large extent, the congregation at New Bethel has played an important part in this, as I noted at the beginning of this essay. But I have also done more than sixty interviews with people throughout the country and the issue of faith has usually been an important component of their relationship to C. L. Franklin. This too has propelled me further on my own journey. In Memphis, for example, in 1999, I listened while the Reverend Benjamin L. Hooks, the Baptist minister who led the NAACP during the 1970s, explained how his liberal politics and his fundamentalist profession of faith were anything but contradictory despite the prominence of the contemporary Christian right; and he shared his understanding of similar processes in his friend and fellow Detroit minister, C. L. Franklin. Some days later in the Mississippi Delta, in a small, primly neat house, an eighty-three-year-old Mrs. Cleo Myles talked of her knowledge of Franklin and so much more. She shared the same baptismal class with her more famous friend, and they were baptized together with other youths in the Sunflower River on the last Sunday of August 1929. As important as her discussion of Franklin was for me the biographer, her expression of the centrality of her faith—she has remained in the same church in Cleveland, Mississippi, since 1929—struck me personally as well as professionally. Throughout this journey of research that was, in reality, so much more, my engagement with people such as Mrs. Myles or Deacon Milton Hall drawing out the palpable faith of the New Bethel congregants, Sister Rosetta Tharpe's words called out to me more times than I can remember:

> There's something within me
> More than I can explain.
> All I can say, Praise God
> There's something within.[6]

One Sunday in September 2003 I entered the pulpit in Cornell's Sage Chapel to give the homily. I had done this before, at Sage and at New Bethel, but for the first time I moved beyond the protective covering of a straight historical account. In a presentation I entitled "Son of Man," I followed Franklin's famous sermon, "Dry Bones in the Valley," and took my text from Ezekiel 37:1–4. In preparing my text, I had marveled anew at the complex, intertwined layers of meaning embedded in Franklin's sermon. There was the theme of the liberation of his people, always important in his sermons, and a reassertion of the power still vital in the prophetic tradition. But there was something else as well. As Ezekiel considered biblical Israel's problems in the midst of its Babylonian captivity, he experienced a vision in which those difficulties, visualized as "a valley of dry bones," weighed down his spirit. Pressed by his Lord with the demand, "Son of man, can these bones live?" a paralyzed Ezekiel stood inert, overwhelmed by the desolation that filled his soul. As Franklin preached his message, for the prophet to overcome this isolation and despair would require a deeper commitment in faith, one that might reach beyond the limits of human knowledge, the boundary of human finiteness. Teaching by familiar analogy, Franklin instructed that Ezekiel, with all of humanity's knowledge, could at best but diagnose the evil before him; he could not "write a prescription" that would cleanse. It was only when an Ezekiel, tested to his very limits, touched the faith beyond reason and uttered in awe and hope, "Lord, thou knoweth," that he glimpsed another possibility. Yet, in the short run, his despondency intensified, but Ezekiel persisted and then, "one morning, the valley began to rumble." Franklin's Ezekiel chanted through faith the skeletal bones back toward completeness as the foot sought out an ankle, which in turn found the leg, and on until from a fractured hopelessness the prophet, in his Lord, created the possibility of human wholeness.[7]

In the pulpit that morning, I stunned myself. Although I largely relied on C. L. Franklin's words, the emotional affect I gave them as I delivered my text had everything to do with me. It was not that I tried to mimic Franklin (which would have been a travesty), but I claimed his words for myself as I became aware of new understandings of inner tensions that had long been forming during my immersion in Franklin's world. Faith and reason were not, as I had once thought, inexorably opposites or, as I later thought, separate entities each in its own air-locked cubicle. Reason might not actually bring you to faith—that, Franklin's Ezekiel suggested, would require something else—but it was not necessarily an obstacle either. The finiteness of human existence, that reverberation of the original sin of my youth, was actually a release from an impossible burden precisely because it remained a sign of fundamental limitations. New doors to my own interior opened.

There is no simple ending possible for this essay. There is no question but that my intellectual work has led me to new understandings professionally and personally on this matter of faith, and that I have grown in complex ways during the course of my career as a historian. This is a joy. Catholicism itself, however, remains as distant as before. Although I have not been in a Catholic church as a worshipper for almost four decades, my occasional forays over the years into services for a variety of reasons have usually left me with the disturbing feeling, as Yogi Berra brilliantly framed it, of "déjà vu all over again." Sermons more often than not are as narrow as I remember them, and the weight of my memory might color those that are not. Despite the changes since Vatican II, I am still struck by what I experience there as the profound distance between one's God and one's "I." I do not see Catholicism in my near future, yet I still feel its influence deeply within. Embedded in this mingled, arabesque pattern is a journey with no announced destination, with no ending one might term final. I have sought to identify one or two of the pattern's major threads, but the central weave is beyond my ability to name, and certainly to direct.

Notes

I would like to thank Maria Cristina Garcia, Joseph McCartin, Robert Orsi, Albert Raboteau, Ann Sullivan, and Leslie Tentler Woodcock for their sensitive and demanding readings of earlier drafts of this essay. The Springsteen quote that opens this essay is from Jon Pareles, "Bruce Almighty: Having Lost His Bet on John Kerry, the Boss Turns to a Higher Authority," *New York Times,* April 24, 2005, Section 2, 1, 24.

1. Leonard Cohen, "Bird on the Wire," *Songs from a Room,* CBS 63587. Some years before this 1969 release, a song by Bob Dylan struck me and stayed with me, but I was not then able to think about his words in relation to my experience with faith. Dylan sang: "Ah, my friends from the prison, they ask unto me, / 'How good, how good, does it feel to be free?' / And I answer them most mysteriously, / 'Are birds free from the chains of the skyway?'" Bob Dylan, "Ballad in Plain D," *Another Side of Bob Dylan,* Columbia CL 2193/CS 8993, released August 1964.
2. Nick Salvatore, *Eugene V. Debs: Citizen and Socialist* (Urbana, 1982).
3. For a brief account of how I came to write about Amos Webber, see the preface to my book, *We All Got History: The Memory Books of Amos Webber* (New York, 1996).
4. Salvatore, *We All Got History,* 320–21.
5. Nick Salvatore, *Singing in a Strange Land: C. L. Franklin, the Black Church, and the Transformation of America* (New York, 2005).
6. Sister Rosetta Tharpe, "There Is Something Within Me," *Shout Sister Shout* (Proper Records Ltd P1301), disc 1 of the 4–disc set, *Sister Rosetta Tharpe: The Original Soul Sister* (Proper Records Ltd Properbox 51).
7. For a more complete discussion of this sermon, see Salvatore, *Singing in a Strange Land,* 158–63.

JAMES R. BARRETT

6 The Blessed Virgin Made Me a Socialist: An Experiment in Catholic Autobiography and the Historical Understanding of Race and Class

> Protestants, it seems to me, tend to have dramatic conversions. They are "born again" and do not look back. Catholics—and though I have been an atheist for many years, I am culturally and psychologically a Catholic—are forever backsliding, deconverting, returning to their previously sinful life.
>
> —Michael Harrington, *The Long Distance Runner: An Autobiography*

As Renee Remond has observed, historians are taught "to be on their guard against subjectivity, their own as much as others'. They know from experience the precariousness of recollection, the unreliability of first-person testimony. . . . Everyone has an unconscious tendency to introduce a factitious coherence into the path of his [sic] life. They have no reason to think that they have any better chance to avoid the tricks of memory that they have learned to spy out in others."[1] Is there a reason we might be interested in the details of any given historian's life for their own sake?

Here I am most interested in understanding the relationship between a particular religious background and the historical scholarship I have made my life's work. As Remond suggests, there is a danger here of reading more coherence and intellectual development into one's background than was actually there and, in the process, missing the broader dimensions. For many, it seems, the essence of Catholicism involved guilt, fear, and sexual repression. Many Catholic women locate the essence of their own experiences in the Church's everyday patriarchy. I recognize both the validity of these observations and the diversity of Catholic lives. Mine is a recollection of a particular place and time, shaped by all those influences that I emphasize in analyzing the lives of my historical subjects—class, race, gender, and ethnicity.[2]

Aside from funerals and family celebrations, I have not attended Mass for over three decades. Thus, in considering the Catholic roots of my own historical interests, I am a little surprised to find how positive my recollections are—whether because of, or in spite of, my distance from the Church. My identity is deeply imbued with Catholicism, which has fundamentally shaped my political perspective and my approach to history. It is the *place* I came from—my old neighborhood with my parish at its center; the *community, family* and other people who nurtured me; the *worldview* that shaped my values. At its best, it is a promise that invests human life with the dignity it deserves. Growing up Catholic, Michael Harrington recalled, "meant, above all, that I accepted the idea that life was a trust to be used for a good purpose and accounted for when it was over. . . . In this fundamental conception of the meaning of existence I am as Catholic as the day on which I made my first communion." Long after leaving, Harrington continued to find the Church, "in its highest expressions, profound and beautiful. My only problem," he concluded, "was that I did not believe in it."[3] I could not forget my Catholic background if I wished to; it is an important part of who I am. I choose not to forget it.

It has taken a long time for me to realize the degree to which Catholicism has shaped the questions I am interested in as a historian and led me to view them a bit differently from many of my colleagues. Given the secular character of scholarly life, indeed the materialist bias in my own field of working-class history, the delayed recognition is hardly surprising. I want to explore several questions here: How did growing up in an ethnic, blue-collar, inner-city parish and coming to social and political awareness *through* the Church provide me with many of the concerns and ideas that have remained with me, particularly my interests in race, ethnicity, and class? How have these influences shaped my scholarship on such historical issues? Why have my "Catholic sensibilities" about these issues remained submerged for so long?

Incense and Miracles

My early memories of the Church are mostly sensual. I remember not only the visual images—the flickering red altar lamp in a dark church, ornate religious paintings on the vaulted ceilings, gilded banners with inscriptions in Latin and Slovak, sun streaming through stained glass, and the bloody stations of the cross, but also the sounds and smells—the call and response of the litanies in Latin, the altar bells, the candle wax and incense. All of this I found very attractive. Part of the church's aesthetic attraction probably derived from its juxtaposition with the outside world. My neighborhood was by no means a slum, but it was surrounded by factories and rail yards and filled with two-flats and drab apartment buildings—quite a contrast with the crafted beauty of the sanctuary. When you opened the large doors of the church and stepped inside, you left the clamor, noise, and dirt of the city and you entered a world of grace and beauty. One aspect of working-class life I understood, then, as a result of growing up Catholic, was simply that amid the squalor and struggle embraced by working-class historians, many of these people also found great joy and beauty in their religious lives.

There was also a strong emotional bond that is more difficult to describe. American Catholicism in its 1950s high tide was, as Charles Morris noted, "highly formal, even mechanistic . . . enshrouded in bewitching mysteries and ritual, combining a remarkable degree of theological rigor and a high degree of abstraction with a practical religion that was intensely personal and emotional." I believed that the spiritual part of my life was much more important than its other dimensions, and I took more interest in it, I think, than most kids. Being a part of the Mass gave me a strong sense of security and belonging as well as a sense of beauty. "For a trembling moment every week," Morris wrote, "or every day if they chose, ordinary people reached out and touched the Divine."[4]

The Church's theological rigor provided what I think of as an active intellectual life—even if, until recently, intellectual historians would not have recognized it as such. Catholic thinking about God and her/his relationship to man was universal in many respects. It provided a unified worldview and explained why things worked as they did, or did not. I came eventually to question the pat answers we memorized from *Father McGuire's New Baltimore Catechism No. 2*, but at the time, I was glad to have them.[5]

On one level, ours was a quintessential "parochial" life, bounded physically by railroad overpasses and factory doors and spiritually by the boundaries of our parish and the teachings of the Church. Most of what gave my early life meaning occurred within a few blocks of my house and my church. This issue of parochialism is important. It helps to explain the social intolerance I noted eventually in my surroundings and the intellectual intolerance that sometimes characterized the Church as an institution. Yet by the standards of a small parish on the West Side of Chicago, we were also taught to think "globally," a perspective that derived from the Church's universal character and claims. Its "apostolic" history and continuing mission activities took my imagination well beyond my parish and city to other parts of the world. I knew that Catholics in Asia and Africa were quite different from us in many respects, but I also knew that we shared with them that which was most important. Discussions of mission work often sent me to the storeroom in our basement. Here I consulted an old edition of *Compton's Pictured Encyclopedia* where I could find various maps and descriptions of nations and peoples. A vivid photo diagram lined up "Races of Mankind" in order of the shapes of their skulls and included photos of a Watusi warrior, a Native American chief in full headdress, a small Chinese guy, and, inexplicably, Benjamin Franklin.[6] Whatever my sources lacked in the way of subtlety with regard to race, the Church's reach did spark my interests in other peoples and cultures. I do not project later scholarly interests back onto these early forays, but in this limited sense at least, the Church introduced me to the broader world.

My first taste for history and politics came through the peculiarly Catholic approach in our texts, which seemed not only to organize the whole narrative around the development of the Church in various parts of the world, but also explained most historical change in terms of famous Catholics. *Treasure Chest,* a Catholic children's magazine that arrived twice monthly in comic book format, included a series on the discovery of the New World, the Revolutionary War, and the opening of the West, with a special emphasis on Catholic heroes.[7]

My introduction to the Cold War came not from the usual popular culture sources cited now in historical works on the subject (though I did follow events in *Life* magazine), but from *Treasure Chest.* Here or in other Catholic children's publications I encountered China and communism through the tragic fates of our missionaries. I admired Tom Dooley long before I ever heard of his classmate Michael Harrington. For us, the problem with the Chinese revolution was not that it suppressed capitalism—I don't think the term ever came up—but rather that it suppressed Catholicism. An elaborate series, "This Godless Communism," introduced by no less than J. Edgar Hoover, ran throughout the 1961–62 academic year (in the midst of the Cuban missile crisis). *Treasure Chest* also graphically laid out what the Communist invasion of the United States would look like if we ever let our guard down. I saw Russian tanks rolling down a city street that looked a lot like Michigan Avenue and the statue of a boy who had denounced his Catholic parents because they persisted in their lives of prayer (as always, it seemed, the Catholics had it the roughest). The new Communist regime made mothers go to work in factories and placed their children in communal child-care centers. (I recall confusion on this score. Even without "Communist authorities," many of my friends' mothers already worked in factories. It was true, however, that we had no communal day care; immigrant grandparents cared for most of the kids.)[8]

Catholic anomalies surfaced in the midst of all these Cold War fears. Our nuns first welcomed Fidel Castro, and not simply because of his Jesuit education (they were School Sisters of St. Francis and clearly irritated by what they probably saw as Jesuit chauvinism in many of our texts). They objected to the lurid casino life in Havana and also to the poverty in which many Cubans lived. Any enthusiasm for Fidel faded, of course, as the stories of Catholic suffering began to filter from Catholics in Florida to Catholics in Chicago, but it was our fellow communicants we worried about, not U.S. investments.

My lifelong interests in ethnicity and race started early, beginning with what I might term an "urban curiosity." My father fueled this with his stories of the city, but so did my own experiences amid the striking diversity that characterized Chicago's neighborhoods. My father (1912–94) joined the Chicago Police Department during the Great Depression because he needed a job. He was the kind of person social historians need to think more about if they hope to understand American workers—precisely because his life reflects elements of working-class experience often ignored by labor historians. Raised by a fireman and his strong-willed, second-generation Irish wife, he was a good Irish Catholic boy. It seems that my grandparents, whom I remember only dimly, were both class-conscious and devout. Like many union workers in early twentieth-century Chicago, my grandfather wore only union suits and shoes and smoked only union cigarettes. He helped to organize the fire department engineers and claimed that the "bosses" transferred him from one firehouse to another around the city. Intended as punishment, this actually facilitated the organizing. One of my father's earliest memories was sitting with his sister in a double stroller as my grandmother pushed them through city streets, distributing union literature. The union was strong enough to launch an effective strike against the city in the midst of the great 1919 labor upheavals. My grandfather's engineers' strike was one of dozens that erupted, along with a great race riot, in the summer of 1919.[9]

But if strikes and unions were very much a part of my grandparents' life, the Church was its center. The family started out on the old West Side, just south of Hull House and west of the old Jewish ghetto in Holy Family parish (established in 1857), which historian James Sanders called "the single great Irish Workingman's parish." Father Damen, the original pastor, refused more attractive locations and instead built the city's most impressive Catholic church and its premier men's and women's schools in a "desolate and uninviting locality" amid the shanties of Irish squatters accused of frequent "riots and ructions." The largely poor immigrants responded with lavish support for the church that became "the undisputed symbol of Catholic confidence and respectability." My father attended St. Ignatius, still one of the top Jesuit high schools in the country. Although we had little awareness that these roots placed us near the center of the ethnic working-class history in Chicago, what little sense we had of history was tied to Holy Family. Aside from school texts, the only history book I can recall seeing around our house in my early childhood was a history of this parish.[10]

Just before World War I, my grandparents moved to an ethnically mixed neighborhood much further out on the West Side, the neighborhood where my father and all of his children grew up. They joined another huge parish, Our Lady of the Angels (OLA) which was tucked between two more middle-class neighborhoods of second settlement, Humboldt Park and Garfield Park. Until the 1950s, both these neighborhoods contained significant Jewish populations transplanted from the old West Side ghetto. By the time I was growing up in the late 1950s and early 1960s, however, both were changing, the latter quickly emerging as one of the city's largest black ghettoes, and the former as its most important Puerto Rican barrio. In North Lawndale, two miles south of our church, the white population dropped from 87,000 in 1950 to 11,000 by 1960 and *none* of the forty-eight synagogues active in the previous decade still remained in the latter. While Jewish and Protestant congregations "fled," however, my own neighbors assumed the beleaguered parochial mentality John McGreevy has described so well: they dug in to "defend" their parish neighborhoods against "invasion."[11] Ours had long been considered a rough neighborhood. As the ghetto moved closer during the 1960s, however, my neighbors took on an embattled mentality and, some of them, a more militant kind of racism than I had seen earlier in my life.

In the year I was born (1950), West Humboldt Park had a steadily declining population of 39,000, including only twenty-three blacks. Most residents were native-born from immigrant families, with Italians and Poles predominating. Most were wage earners, almost half working in plants scattered throughout the neighborhoods—candy and toy factories, small metalworking shops, electrical manufacturing plants—and others in the skilled trades or lower-level white-collar jobs. My own census tract, about one mile west of OLA, was entirely white but quite mixed ethnically, with large numbers of Poles and Slovaks in our immediate area and greater numbers of Italians to the east, closer to the parish church. Ten years later, small numbers of Puerto Rican families had moved into some parts of West Humboldt Park; otherwise, little had changed. Originally dominated by the Irish, OLA parish was about 60 percent Italian and 30 percent Irish in the late fifties, the remainder largely Polish. By 1965, however, the population of West Garfield Park, directly south of my own neighborhood, was between 65 and 85 percent African American. By 1970, shortly after my family left the neighborhood, West Humboldt Park was over 20 percent nonwhite; by 1980, it was over 85 percent nonwhite.[12] I did not need the census figures to tell me that the neighborhood was changing while I lived there as a teenager; my neighbors were obsessed with the changes.

This age of racial transition on the West Side coincided with the golden age of American Catholicism, though I did not realize it as I was growing up. The number of Catholics in the country doubled between 1940 and 1960, and much of this growth came during the fifties through intermarriage, conversion, or immigration, but above all through high birth rates. At the time of John Kennedy's election in 1960, a critical moment of ethnoreligious and political awakening for many in my generation, Catholics were growing at a rate twice that of the rest of the population. Between 1949 and 1959, parochial school enrollments more than doubled from 2.6 to 5.6 million, while more than 24 million subscribers read (or failed to read) a dense network of 580 Catholic publications.[13] The huge numbers, especially in the nation's older industrial cities, and the resources loyally provided by a largely working-class constituency produced an elaborate parallel institutional structure and culture that was distinct from the WASP mainstream, though deeply patriotic. Nowhere was this dramatic growth more apparent than in Chicago. It is remarkable enough that half the city's population was Catholic in 1956, but I was surprised to find the figure was so low. Growing up on the West Side, I thought of Chicago as a Catholic city where one could walk for miles without encountering a Protestant or a Republican.[14] I was aware of but seldom considered other faiths. My parish, one of the largest ethnically mixed "territorial" parishes in the city, contained 4,500 registered families, a mixture of Italians, Irish, Poles, and other nationalities, spread out over 150 city blocks. Every school morning found me standing on Iowa Street in front of Our Lady of the Angels along with some 1,400 other uniformed children, lined up along with our priests and nuns, to pray and salute the flag.[15] Not surprisingly, I always assumed the power and the pervasive presence of the Church.

Although OLA was a territorial parish, as late as 1950, nearly half (at least 128) of Chicago's 281 parishes were instead ethically homogeneous "national" parishes. Having created their own fairly isolated ethnoreligious cultures based on their parishes, often at great sacrifice, these congregations were the most determined to remain. Here the defensive mentality settled in most deeply. Laypeople were determined to "preserve" their neighborhoods (that is, to preserve their racially segregated character) and pastors often cooperated in the project, at least until the early 1960s. Even among the more tolerant people, one found the slide that John McGreevy has noted from the deeply embedded tradition of distinct national parishes to overt racial segregation: "We have our churches (and schools and stores) and they have theirs." Studying Catholicism and race relations in Chicago in the 1960s, William Osborne and his colleagues found that the line of defense between white and black neighborhoods was most often a national parish like the one we moved to in the fall of 1958.[16]

For me, American Catholicism's golden age was one of miracles. In September 1958, after my sister was stricken with a mysterious paralysis that made it increasingly difficult for her to walk the mile to OLA, my parents transferred us to Sts. Cyril and Methodius, a Slovak parish. This was a typically closed national parish with its parishioners jealously guarding their own ethnic subculture, hardly the place for a bunch of Irish kids. The pastor reluctantly accepted us as a hard-luck case, perhaps with encouragement from the archdiocese. My interests in immigration and ethnicity probably derive in part from my grade school years at St. Cyril's, where I was steeped in an ethnic culture that was not my own. We learned our prayers and songs in Slovak, while the kids down the street learned theirs in Polish. Refugees from Czechoslovakia and Hungary occasionally joined my classmates, their first-generation parents and their immigrant grandparents reinforcing the Old World atmosphere of the place. More than it had been at the ethnically mixed OLA, ethnic culture was promoted and palpable throughout my new parish. One could attend Mass and receive the sacraments, buy groceries or a beer, and read the day's news or listen to it on the radio—all with no recourse whatsoever to English.

The first miracle came on December 1, 1958, "the day Chicago wept," when a fire swept through the main building at OLA, killing ninety-two schoolchildren and three nuns and devastating a once-vibrant neighborhood around the school.[17] Arriving on the scene at the end of our own school day, we could still see many of the bodies under blankets. My sister's large seventh-grade class on the second floor of the school had been virtually wiped out. The illness that seemed to be destroying her muscles had saved her life. Another miracle followed within a year. After a series of novenas and prayers to Blessed Julie Billart and Our Lady of Fatima, my sister's paralysis left as quickly as it had come. The prayers took place in my living room, often with a group of neighbors and sometimes with a large statue of Our Lady of Fatima, which toured homes throughout the 1950s and early 1960s.[18] Doctors had considered my sister a lost cause, but she recovered completely.

It is easy enough for me today to dismiss my mother's claim that the unexpected recovery was the product of Julie's and the Virgin's intercession; at the time, it only increased my faith, a gift from my family and community. It probably also intensified my feeling that I was supposed to give something back for all of these gifts. I was delighted by my sister's recovery and our survival, but I was not shocked. Miracles, it seemed, were well within the realm of the possible. Yet the experience might also have set the stage for an eventual decline in faith. My development beyond the coming decade left little room for miracles.

By the 1960s, the kind of ethnic segregation among white Catholics that had characterized the older national parishes like St. Cyril's was clearly breaking down. My own and other ethnic neighborhoods were actually quite diverse, with street gangs and other characteristic forms of social organization reflecting a range of nationalities and individuals two or three generations removed from the immigrant experience. In the context of the massive in-migration of blacks to the West Side in the 1950s and 1960s, race rather than ethnicity became the dominant source of identity. In the wake of the tragedy at OLA, "block-busting" real estate agents moved into the neighborhoods south and east of ours. Throughout these years, the arrival of these black families produced racial confrontations and we learned a new word, "ghetto." We still recognized one another by our parents' and grandparents' nationalities, but there was no mistaking who "we" were, and "they" were either black or Puerto Rican.[19]

Confronting Race

My confrontation with race and my efforts to understand it suggest the kind of influence Catholicism had in this environment and its transformation from the highly ritualized, isolated parish life of the fifties to the more cosmopolitan and liberal atmosphere of the sixties. I saw black people often as they went to work in the numerous factories, dairies, and rail yards around the neighborhood, but they were clearly outsiders—automatically suspect, watched rather closely. To be fair, this was generally quite a closed neighborhood, laced with street gangs who occasionally pounced on strangers thought to represent some kind of a challenge. Most outsiders who met this fate, as we did occasionally when we wandered away from our own turf, were white, not black.[20] I noticed, however, that blacks, who had reason to be going through the neighborhood on their way to work, never entered "our" stores or playgrounds or lingered anywhere to talk. If they did, what my mother called "a scene" would soon develop.

When I encountered a black person—a construction worker in front of my house or a black cop sitting with my father in our living room—this was an unusual event. I took advantage of the situation to investigate. If I asked my father about these friendly episodes afterward, in light of the racism I heard and saw all about me, I received no satisfactory answer except, "He's okay." Were some other blacks also okay? I became not only aware but also interested in race quite early. Why?

My father knew the city extremely well, from tough police precincts up and down the riverfront and a variety of other work sites he frequented on his days off for extra pay. He was at once attracted and repelled by the drama he saw every day as cop. He kept a good deal of this out of our house and I only realized how much his job had scarred him emotionally when he came to the end of his life. But he was a wonderful storyteller and he carried the less grisly stories home with him. These were marked by a cynicism and intolerance shaped by having often seen people at their worst, but also by a genuine fascination with the complicated cultures people created amid such diversity. His mental map of the city, like that of most Chicagoans, was organized around race and ethnicity. Class was something taken for granted; less significant, it seemed, for sorting out the stories. He described our own neighbors as "the Polack (or Dago, or Bohunk) down the street." His worldview is suggested by the fact he also used a derogatory term to refer to the Irish, who were "Turkeys" in his urban lexicon. Yet these people were our friends and neighbors in a much deeper sense than the terms connote today.

My dad sometimes took me with him on errands to more distant neighborhoods. A Chinese hand laundry where he took his uniform shirts became familiar but remained exotic by my standards. The proprietor's little daughter seemed different—and fascinating. I was particularly struck by the Garfield Park ghetto, physically close to my own parish, but socially distant and mysterious—precisely because it was out of bounds. Except in retail stores, many of them still maintained by Jewish merchants, there were few white people here. It seemed to me like a parallel world with all of its own institutions, comparable to but different from ours. At least some of the mystery of the ghetto also rubbed off on my friends. At a time when one's musical tastes said it all, our gang listened only to rhythm and blues on the black radio station WVON, never to the Beatles, and we shopped for clothes in stores on Madison and Pulaski that catered to young black men. There was something here, then, besides all the racism. Young black guys provided a male model of bravado and style, and they were known to be tough. They might not have been welcomed in our neighborhood, but they were cool. Certainly part of this had to do with gender roles and symbolism, but I do not pretend to understand this attitude any better now than I did then.

I think what intrigued me about race from an early age was this combination of the frequent appearance of people of color, especially African Americans, and the almost total lack of personal contact or understanding. Racial difference was clearly important, judging from the amount of time people spent worrying about it and the energy they employed to enforce the various boundaries between races. Yet no one around me really seemed to understand blacks. In part, then, I was just curious. The widespread racism deeply embedded in my surroundings made me fear black kids a bit when I did encounter them . . . but I was still interested. Were their lives like ours? Were they like me, did they wonder about the white kids? The curiosity evolved as I moved out of my neighborhood into the broader city, and out of the city into the broader world. It became more theorized and hopefully more directed, but it remains.

The fact that such encounters produced more interest than fear or hatred was due in part to the Church and in part to my mother. If the daily routine and occasional surprises of inner-city life sparked an urban curiosity about such difference, Catholicism provided a framework within which to make sense of all this. Part of the Church's universal quality was that Catholics came in all races and nationalities.[21] Such teachings were not irrelevant. Notwithstanding conventional liberal wisdom, survey data from the 1940s through the 1960s suggested that ethnic Catholics in northern cities were consistently more tolerant on issues of race and more supportive of civil rights than other white groups.[22] This did not mean that laypeople or religious were free from racism and other forms of intolerance that surrounded us daily. What it seems to suggest is that urban Catholics were deeply conflicted over these issues. For me, the obvious disjuncture between the Church's formal teachings and the daily reality of racism, sometimes within the Church itself, was the source of great interest and many questions. Our pastor might worry about the neighborhood "changing," but the Church taught us that all people were brothers and sisters. And, like my reading of the *Baltimore Catechism,* I was inclined to accept the Church at its word. About the time I might have begun to question it, a new kind of Catholicism began to emerge. As the Church itself changed in the course of the 1960s, there seemed to be more room and even some encouragement for my questions.

Perhaps because she was more sheltered than my father was, my mother (1913–2005) was more open, social, and tolerant in various respects, including in terms of racial and ethnic difference. From early on in her life, she had slightly more exposure to blacks than my father had and, while she shared many of the fears common to my neighborhood, she taught us to treat all people with respect. She conveyed to her children the joy she found in meeting different sorts of people. If my father's stories displayed an urban panorama of people from diverse backgrounds, my mother's example taught us to value such diversity. She also taught us charity and the Church's "preference for the poor" at our own front door. She could be uncharacteristically rude with Jehovah's Witnesses, but she never turned away the people my father called "bums." If I asked her why she gave the guy a quarter or a can of soup, she simply said, "Because he was hungry." This was another face of Catholicism, a face I knew well and loved. I have no way to measure her influence on me; I have no doubt that it has been enormous.

Vatican II Arrives on the West Side

I would like to say that I gave up my original intention of joining the priesthood as I entered my teens for complex or idealistic reasons. In fact, the decision can be explained in one word: girls. I listened to visiting priests' descriptions of their seminaries with great interest, but I realized eventually that something was missing in the slides of bowling alleys and swimming pools. Once the recognition set in, I decided I could contribute to the Church in other ways, and I remained deeply involved in parish activities.

It is autobiographically convenient when a vital development in world history resonates with one's personal story. The source for a lot of my own social and intellectual development, even if I did not always recognize it, was the Second Vatican Council (1962–65), which displayed what Philip Gleason has called "the Church in eruption."[23] I welcomed the council's more relaxed, understandable liturgy and its socially oriented practice. Naturally, my experience of this big transformation came locally and, like most other important changes in twentieth-century Chicago, this one involved race.

The eruption arrived in my own parish in the person of a new assistant pastor, Father John Spitscovsky—Slovak to be sure, but young, energetic, and full of passion for Vatican II. Our little parish had never had an assistant pastor before. I now realize that Vatican II's social implications were emerging at the same time that the Chicago archdiocese was implementing its own mission of creating peaceful integration. Father John was probably there not only to carry the message of the former, but also to begin advancing the latter. He arrived shortly after the Council got going and quickly set about organizing a teen club and aiming to "drag religion into everyday life."[24]

A major turning point came in the summer of 1963 when Father John hatched a plan with the assistant at Our Lady of Sorrows basilica, in the heart of the West Side ghetto. The idea was deceptively simple—a joint religious retreat with the teen clubs of the two parishes. It is difficult to appreciate the revolutionary quality of this plan without understanding the breadth of the racial divide between these two neighborhoods on Chicago's West Side at this moment in their histories. The ghetto around Our Lady of Sorrows exploded soon after in the first of several major riots that claimed lives and wrecked large parts of the black neighborhoods. Newspapers were filled with lurid stories of black street gangs, and crime in the area was, in fact, rising.[25] These events greatly increased the fear in my own neighborhood and this fear bred racism. Our retreat, which occurred amid all these racial tensions, was my first sustained encounter with young black people. I was uncomfortable at first, but my contacts with black kids at the retreat began to undermine whatever stereotypes I had embraced up to that point. The parish groups slept in different rooms of the same dormitory. A small group of the black guys came to our room in the middle of the night with the plan for a raid on the girls' dormitory. The fact that it was gender harassment that provided the basis for this tentative interracial overture was probably significant, but lost on me at the time. I thought this was a great idea. Most of the tough guys from my neighborhood demurred, though I am not sure whether they were more afraid of a bunch of black guys in their room in the middle of the night or what the priests would do to us. I was one of only two from our parish who joined the raid. We ran screaming through the girls' dorm, and retreated to a secluded spot on the grounds. I remember talking there for a long time in the dark. Miraculously, the priests made no issue of it the next morning.

In the following year I paid more attention to the civil rights movement, in the city and nationally. In the years since my birth, Chicago had become the focal point for both Catholic civil rights activism—through the Catholic Interracial Council (CIC) and the archdiocesan Office of Urban Affairs under Father John Egan (a renowned liberal on civil rights and other matters who lived at OLA during my early school years)—and also some of the era's most violent racial confrontations. These occurred in parishes very much like my own. Each summer brought considerable racial tension, as in Visitation Parish just south of the stockyards where white teenagers attacked blacks moving into the neighborhood or simply passing through. I considered such attacks on blacks wrong; *why* I considered them wrong had more to do with Catholicism than with 1960s liberalism. "Time after time," William Osborne wrote in the mid-sixties, "Negroes, in their efforts to break out of the ghetto, have encountered the resolute opposition of the city's white Catholics." At the same time, "In the interval between 1951 and 1965, the leadership of the Catholic interracial movement shifted from New York to Chicago."[26]

My own role in all of this was extremely modest, but it suggests the distance I traveled with regard to race and the route I took to get where I was going. As president of the parish teen club, I helped my assistant pastor plan a workshop with volunteers from the Catholic Interracial Council. I remember singing a lot of folk songs and planning the liturgy for the first "guitar Mass" I had ever seen, but the weekend also involved a hair-raising trip through the neighborhood to interview "typical teens" about their racial attitudes. We ran into a gang from the next playground with whom we had fought only recently. I was saved only by my partner, a beautiful (and fearless) young woman from the *Catholic Worker* who attracted the attention of the various guys we encountered and actually got some of them to answer the questions (their answers were not very encouraging). Through this work, I became involved in the Young Christian Students (YCS) movement and had more contact with the CIC and the *Catholic Worker.* I remember few of the details. It is revealing, perhaps, that I clearly recall that the gatherings were racially mixed, including black kids from the West Side. These meetings were at once strange and gratifying.

My adherence to civil rights and later to the antiwar movement brought me into frequent conflict with my father during the late sixties, but now a new kind of Catholicism provided me with some authority. I always reminded him of the Catholic support for these movements (though I clearly exaggerated in both cases) and used this, rather unfairly, to justify my own ideas and actions. My father was extremely proud of his education with the BVMs (Sisters of Charity of the Blessed Virgin Mary, an old Irish immigrant order) and the Jesuits. When I asked the old cop when he would join the movement, he always said he would be there as soon as he could see a Jesuit priest on one side of him and a BVM nun on the other. The inevitable moment came with a July 1963 *Chicago Daily News* photo that I displayed proudly on the kitchen table. Staring at the photo of nuns and priests in a July 1, 1963, civil rights demonstration to desegregate a Catholic facility, my father looked confused and hurt. He never showed up at any demonstrations. By the late 1960s, dinner conversations often revolved around race relations and peace demonstrations with me talking about my involvement and him talking about locking people up.[27]

Generational divisions within the Church over civil rights come alive in the letters to Father Daniel Mallette during the early to mid-sixties. Mallette served a black parish on the West Side and was one of the clergy frequently involved in civil disobedience in Chicago, Selma, and elsewhere. I cannot recall how aware I was of his particular activities, but he was the sort of priest who provided a role model for young Catholics becoming active in the movement. High school student Maria Romano tutored in an inner-city school, contributed her allowance to a civil rights organization, and explained to her classmates that the Church did not, in fact, condemn interracial marriage. Mallette's actions encouraged her to persist in her own commitment. "As long as there are Catholics like you in the world," she wrote, "I shall do my best to be a good Christian. Thanks a million." She enclosed five dollars. Mallette's correspondence is full of such letters, most of them from young people, sometimes from middle-aged Catholics, enclosing money, offering prayers, or proposing to join him working on the West Side. But there was another sort of letter, almost as frequent, usually from older Catholics. A person who signed only as "Irish Catholic" wrote in the wake of Mallette's Selma march, "When I think when I was a kid the respect we had for a priest or nun. . . . Take off the collar." The deep divide that McGreevy has noted in the Church from the mid-sixties between liberals and parish traditionalists, exacerbated by the escalation of the war in Vietnam, continued to be fought every night over our dinner table.[28]

My brush with the Catholic interracial movement underscores the conflicted Catholic attitudes about race that John McGreevy develops in *Parish Boundaries.* He describes the emerging chasm in the sixties between Catholic liberals and ethnic blue-collar parishioners, but my own experience suggests that the two categories sometimes overlapped. One might identify the CIC leadership, for example, as middle class, distinct from blue-collar ethnics, particularly if one classifies clergy as middle class and educated. It is difficult to assess the Catholic interracial movement's rank and file, however, without a good deal more research. What is compelling to me in the story of the Catholic Interracial Council, however, is not that most inner-city parishioners opposed its efforts, but rather that some defended them. There were civil rights supporters out in the parishes where it must have been difficult to take such a stand, and at least some of the movement's leaders came from backgrounds similar to my own.[29] It would be easy and wrong to romanticize the church's mixed record on race. My point is not that working-class ethnic Catholics supported civil rights and integration, though some clearly did, but rather that the tension McGreevy finds between the liberal leadership and conservative flock could run through local parishes congregations as well.

Us and Them

Given my later preoccupation with class, it is ironic that it had little role in my early consciousness. I certainly saw differences in wealth even within my own neighborhood, but none of these were very striking. I lived my life in a sea of blue collars and never thought much about it. Industrial unions and periodic strikes were taken for granted. We always sided with labor, but reflexively, not because of any well-developed ideology. Any ideas and values involved more likely came from the Church than from unions or any political organization. Catholics were expected to have what came to be called a "preference for the poor" and if we saw poor neighbors all about us, then that made the preference a little easier to come by. If class was reproduced in my neighborhood (and clearly it was), this happened at some more subtle level than most labor historians seem to have in mind. St. Patrick's, my large boys' Catholic high school, provided little basis for class distinctions. With no girls present, the delicate situation of courting across class lines never came up. The girls with whom we socialized after school hours were either from Notre Dame, the girls' Catholic high school down the street or, more often, from our own parishes. Uniforms meant few if any distinctions in appearance. Even most upper classmen arrived together on the same city buses. We did everything together and any distinctions were based on issues other than wealth and family status. I remember the few black kids; I remember only one "rich kid," and he was clearly an outcast.

All of this changed when I turned sixteen, shortly after my family "fled" the West Side for a blue-collar suburb on the edge of Hillary Clinton's excellent school district. For the first time in my life, I encountered considerable wealth and active class discrimination. The small minority of black and Hispanic kids at my old school was totally absent; this was the whitest place I had ever seen. The resulting alienation was stark and deep. Overnight, I went from being a leader in both my high school and my parish, with a large group of friends in both places, to being a social outcast. The occasional breaks, like making a friend or being invited to a formal dance, always seemed to end with my feeling marginalized. When a friend dropped me off, he thought my father must be our gardener. Labor historians are trained to think of class in terms of material deprivation and the political and organizational results of such deprivation in situations of class consciousness. We think of class in strictly social terms, but at the personal level, class is also experienced emotionally. My own feelings were mostly of resentment and insecurity. I lived my life as an outsider, a feeling that has stuck with me in most academic settings. But such marginalization was not all negative; it forced me to reflect on and value my family and parish background. I gave up on any effort to blend in at the new place and retreated instead to the neighborhood my parents had just fled. I came to think of blue-collar Catholics, my people, as both victimized and superior in many ways to the teenage snobs I endured in my classes. Long before encountering social stratification theory or Marxism, I resented these people deeply. I identified closely with my old neighborhood, which soon took on mythic proportions in my imagination. Looking for a way to reconnect with all this—and to avoid the draft—I entered college in September 1968, just after the Democratic convention in Chicago.

I realize now that the University of Illinois's Chicago campus is a rather drab place by the standards of many university campuses. For me, it represented a vital liberation from my stifling suburban existence and a return to the city. The university had swallowed up a vibrant ethnic neighborhood around Hull House, but part of the old Italian community remained. I traveled to campus every day on the El and discovered parts of the city I had never known. I had a state scholarship, but like the overwhelming majority of first-generation college students on campus, I worked to pay for books and expenses. This was hardly an "ivory tower" existence. Once again, the Church gave me my bearings. A friend from the old neighborhood brought me to the Newman House and I organized much of my life around the place. Like others of my generation, I became active in the antiwar movement and went from a "peace now" position to a more elaborate critique of U.S. imperialism. Like some, this led me to an interest in Marxism and socialist politics. At Newman, we joined the United Farm Workers' (UFWA) movement, connected students with the Chicago Area Draft Resistance (CADRE), planned panels against the university's new Police Training Institute, and helped to organize antiwar demonstrations. My own evolution, however, took place within a Catholic context, facilitated by the presence of an active Catholic Left in and beyond the city. I developed critiques of particular aspects of the Church, but I lived within a progressive, interracial Catholic environment.

At the time, Newman was a politically active, diverse community with personal relationships crossing various racial and ethnic lines. The most important of these for me was my lifelong relationship with Jenny Wong Barrett. Born at St. Francis Cabrini Hospital on the old West Side just two weeks after her parents arrived in Chicago from China, she was raised in an inner-city parish and was making her own sense of race and politics and history at the time we met. We went through our changes together, creating an emotional bond that has persisted for almost forty years.

I never consciously "left" the Church, but rather drifted away. And the drifting had much less to do with specific disagreements (though I certainly had some) than with losing "the gift of faith." Such a drift, which started in college and accelerated in graduate school, was hardly peculiar to me. Marxism taught me to analyze problems in materialist terms, but I never developed the kind of faith in it as a universal theory that I once had for Catholicism. Socialism did not displace but rather grew out of religious values and sensibilities. My involvement in labor and socialist politics was always dictated far more by heart than by brain, and its ethical foundations remained what I still think of as "Catholic." Some of our political activities, first in the 1970s with support work for the UFWA and later, in the 1980s, organizing against U.S. intervention in Central America, provided links between Catholic social action thought and socialist politics. Both movements were based in part on Church groups and included many other Catholics and former Catholics. I still cannot explain it, but my movement from Catholicism to socialism seemed very natural. I stopped attending Mass, but I retained contact with the culture through my family. My affinity for Catholicism continues to appear in many little ways.

Religion and Working-Class History

I encountered both working-class history and radical politics at the University of Illinois at Chicago in 1969, and the two were fused in my mind from the beginning. I sought out courses on race and ethnicity, which always had a mixed clientele, mostly blue-collar whites, but also Asians, Hispanics, and African Americans. I had no access to labor history courses, though a couple of my instructors encouraged this interest. My earliest research papers reflect the interests I have retained throughout my education and my professional life—rank and file organization and strikes among Jewish immigrant garment workers, Langston Hughes and the Harlem Renaissance, and the Abraham Lincoln Brigade volunteers—immigration and ethnicity; racial identity and race relations; work, protest, and political radicalism. I hope my approach to each of these subjects has evolved over the past thirty years, but my general scholarly concerns were clearly set by the end of my college years. Why? And what, if anything, did this have to do with Catholicism?

I have never featured religion prominently in my work, much of which looks like the rest of the "new labor history." This has a great deal to do with the theory and politics of working-class history as a research field, characteristics that I embraced. Yet I believe that my blue-collar, ethnic Catholic background, a different one than most of my colleagues, has made a difference in my approach. The subjects of my work were never abstractions. Particularly when I wrote of immigrant factory workers and their families in city neighborhoods, I thought of these people as an earlier generation in communities very much like my own. More important, perhaps, the values that shaped my life and ideas up to the time I became a professional historian were still there, beneath the language of class analysis and systematic social history. The former translated into a set of sensibilities that informed the latter.

These sensibilities can be best viewed in my doctoral dissertation on the work, family, and community lives of Chicago packinghouse workers and in related projects. At nineteen, I read *The Jungle,* Upton Sinclair's classic novel of the destruction of immigrant workers at the hands of the great "meat trust." I was moved by the novel and identified with the characters, but I was also troubled by it in ways that I could not explain at the time. This neighborhood, though poorer, was not substantially different from my own, yet I did not recognize mine in the squalor of "Packingtown" or my friends and neighbors in Sinclair's degraded and defeated characters. In real life the neighborhood was dominated by vital parishes that formed the nuclei of the various ethnic communities "back of the yards," yet he ignored religion. I sensed that these people, like my neighbors, had not only poverty and hard work in their lives, but also love and beauty. I just did not know what to do about this. When I reencountered the book in the midst of my doctoral research, I had developed an approach to labor history that helped me to place these misgivings into a broader framework and to write a history of Packingtown and its people that was at once more sympathetic and more realistic. Yet I too missed much of the life in this neighborhood.

What drew me more than anything else in the "new labor history" was the notion of human agency—the idea that workers themselves made this history through the creation of their own institutions and movements, their own cultures and ideas. I wanted to do for "new immigrants," early mass-production industry, and big city life what Edward Thompson and his American followers were already doing for artisans and others in early industrialization—to recreate the worlds that Chicago's immigrant workers made for themselves and to put them at the center of my analysis. All of this came from Thompson, Herbert Gutman, David Montgomery, and other historians, but I also had those vague misgivings about Sinclair's depiction of people I was having trouble recognizing. And those feelings derived far more from my own background than from reading the new labor history. The two influences came together for me in Pittsburgh in the late 1970s.

My central concern was certainly not religion but rather work and its effects on peoples' lives. Four books were particularly important to my formulation of the project. *Outcast London,* Gareth Stedman Jones's brilliant history of social class relations, interested me in the problem of casual labor with which families in Chicago's stockyards district struggled on a daily basis. Carter Goodrich's *The Frontier of Control,* a study of the politics of work in the British metalworking industry, led me to think about the packinghouse work process, the nation's first assembly-line operation, in terms of "work rationalization." I concluded that such "rationalization" in the slaughterhouses and packing plants was a relative, class-based concept. Changes that appeared rational in terms of the profit motive often disrupted workers' lives and left their families destitute. David Brody's *Steelworkers in America* provided a model by focusing on two distinct generations of steelworkers in the mill towns that I still saw about me in the Steel Valley around Pittsburgh and on the psychologies (what we called the "mentalities") of both workers and management. David Montgomery's essays, which eventually appeared in *Workers' Control in America,* and his courses projected the pervasiveness of class in workers' lives at work and in their communities and were by far the biggest influence.[30]

Yet none of these works successfully followed workers beyond the factory walls, into their homes and neighborhoods, and none of these scholars paid much attention to religion. I was convinced from the beginning that the real drama of this story lay in showing the impact of what Montgomery sometimes called "the long arm of the job."[31] Here I was particularly drawn by John Bodnar's argument that it was a commitment to family that motivated immigrant workers and not Montgomery's notion of workers' control. Rather than juxtapose such traditional family values and the pursuit of workplace control, however, I insisted that these workers pursued work control issues and working-class organization more generally precisely because they saw these as vital to the protection of their families and communities. In this way, I linked Bodnar's "working class realism" to Montgomery's world of shop-floor politics and class conflict.[32]

The residents of Packingtown created vibrant and deeply religious lives organized around ethnic parishes—eleven in the space of less than a square mile, each of them with an elaborate array of voluntary organizations. Yet I tended to analyze religion in organizational terms and as a general influence in the community, never as the center of these peoples' lives and as the basis of their worldviews. Another study of this same community, Robert Slayton's more ethnographic *Back of the Yards,* picked up on this part of the story. As Leslie Woodcock Tentler has noted, Slayton was too nostalgic and optimistic in his readings of these religious communities. Like the Church generally, they were conservative in many respects, particularly with regard to issues of gender, and subject to all of their own conflicts along generational and other lines. But, as Tentler notes, Slayton captured the centrality and even something of the meaning of religion "as a source of comfort and personal integrity, of social order and communal vitality" in the rather dismal setting of the stockyards and slaughterhouses. Slayton's more ethnographic and cultural approach, in contrast to my own emphasis on work and the quality of life, accounts to some degree for the centrality of religion in his evocation of the community and its one-dimensional treatment in my own. I certainly understood, however, that the mighty "meat trust" did not dominate the minds in Packingtown. These workers and their families found alternative sources for their values and ideals in their various ethnic and religious enclaves. As Tentler has observed for immigrant workers more generally, creating these cultures in the face of

WASP cultural condescension and the acquisitive logic of the giant corporation represented an "act of resistance." "Religion provided them with perhaps their richest resources for shaping the world of everyday living, and with a potent counterweight to the dominant American ideology of competitive individualism."[33]

Their religion also invested their lives with a dignity that helps to explain their desperate struggles to maintain these precious cultures in the face of very real corporate threats. The same Lithuanian laborer who swept blood and offal amid commercialized death on a vast scale on the killing floor, or the Irish or Polish girl who spent her days stuffing chipped beef into cans, each also had music and beauty in her or his life and a brush with the divine each Sunday. Like Mike Dobrejak, the central character in Thomas Bell's epic proletarian novel *Out of This Furnace*, their religious perspective was vital to their continuing struggles to protect their communities and build a better world.[34] Theirs were class struggles, but they were fundamentally shaped by their religious beliefs.

What I found most compelling in the human drama at the stockyards was *not* what riveted Sinclair—the destruction of these people by the meat trust—but rather their creation of vital family lives and rich religious cultures. I was attracted by this confirmation of the human spirit under such conditions, but this was not simply a good story. It is impossible to understand the emergence of strong social movements like the United Packinghouse Workers-CIO and the Back of the Yards Council at work and in the community without documenting the basis for this human spirit and the culture it spawned. The people "back of the yards" built these movements to protect their communities and their families, and Catholic conceptions of the sacred were at the basis of both of these concerns. Celebrated community activist Saul Alinsky concluded, "It is the Catholic Church that serves as the medium through which these people express their hopes, desires and aspirations."[35]

I never raised the obvious connections between a religious worldview and these kinds of traditional "family values," but I saw such values not as opposed to or even distinct from but rather integral to these class experiences. As Leslie Woodcock-Tentler suggests, "by preaching so conservative a version of marriage and family life, the clergy endorsed, albeit indirectly, a radical critique of existing economic arrangements." The vitality of religious values as a basis for what we analyze as class behavior is only one aspect of working-class religion that badly needs to be explored. The Back of the Yards was both a deeply religious community and the site of chronic class conflict in and outside the slaughterhouses, independent labor politics, and effective community organizing. Labor historians have largely ignored the nature of the relationship between such religious devotion and such class behavior—here and in comparable communities.[36]

The material manifestations of working-class religious devotion alone—the huge edifices built on laborers' and factory operatives' wages; the elaborate networks of schools carefully designed to shape the values and, so, the characters and personalities of the communities' children; the voluntary groups and social service agencies erected to provide support for the poorest among the poor, in part because many of them would turn only to their own in times of need—all of this suggests religion's centrality in working-class life. Yet these creations represented only the more obvious dimensions of cultures that operated as potent intellectual and moral influences vital to the worldviews we seek to understand. A careful study of religion could at least begin to give us the basis for a new kind of plebian intellectual history and, at best, suggest the cosmology of poor and anonymous people in industrial communities throughout the country. Yet we have largely ignored the vast landscape of workers' religious lives.

And this failure to investigate such a vital aspect of working-class life was my failure as well. Catholicism, so embedded in my own life and in the lives of many of my subjects, has been largely absent from my research and writing down to the present. Why? First, I had changed. The loss of religious faith paralleled the development of a materialist conception of historical change, even if many of my earlier sensibilities remained. It is impossible to separate this personal shift from my immersion in a dynamic subculture of radical labor historians. In a profession where I might otherwise have felt even more marginalized than I did, I found in radical history a group of friends and colleagues, some of them in Pittsburgh from working-class backgrounds similar to my own, who shared my interests and values. This was an enormously exciting intellectual journey that promised the opportunity to rewrite the history of the United States with common people at its very center, but it left little room for religion as a proper subject of historical inquiry.

Why have we learned so little about an influence that was clearly so important in workers' lives? Judging from Leslie Woodcock Tentler's surveys of the more general bias in U.S. social history, labor historians are in good company in ignoring the centrality of religion in general and Catholicism in particular. "Complaints about exclusion often strike a petulant tone," John McGreevy notes in a recent review of new religious history, "but it is noteworthy that historians of the most religious nation in the industrialized world understand their country's immediate past with little reference to religion."[37] Given their interest in anonymous common people, working-class historians face major source and methods problems, especially if we wish to investigate personal thoughts and beliefs as well as buildings, organizations, and activities. But social historians have long faced similar research problems. Labor historians' resistance to the analysis of religious thought and behavior derives in part at least from the strong materialist bias in much of working-class history and the political perspectives of those of us who do this research. For all of our discussion of consciousness and culture, we often embrace what William Sewell calls a "materialist common sense"—an assumption that the material precedes, shapes, and produces the cultural.[38] In a rare early foray into the significance of religion for labor history, Herbert Gutman discovered labor reformers' use of religious symbolism and language. But Gutman still tended to analyze religion in instrumental terms, as a resource rather than an elaborate worldview, and he continued to see politics as distinct from and more fundamental than religion. Some labor historians clearly believe not only that material conditions and the social relations surrounding them are causally more important than religious ideas, but also that religion is, after all, not a good thing. We often analyze it as an obstruction, a conservative influence and the source of conflict among workers from diverse backgrounds, something to be cleared away to allow for the construction of a progressive labor movement—but never as part of the very basis for class as well as ethnic identity or as an element in the motivation of workers engaged in class conflict.[39]

Much has happened in the past decade to confront me once again with the significance of religion and with the subjective dimensions of historical experience more broadly. My shift to these concerns has less to do with the "death of communism" and with the displacement of Marxism by postmodern theory and method than with personal events. My mother's and father's and other deaths among family and friends, the departure of my son for a life of his own, and my own natural process of aging have forced me to think more about those vast realms of life that the "new social history," for all of its accomplishments, has never approached. Such personal experiences have drawn me to the deceptively simple observation that our historical subjects clearly had their own emotional and spiritual lives that we have ignored at the risk of fundamentally misunderstanding them.

One result of this shift has been a tendency to simply consider the personal side of fairly traditional subjects like working-class radicalism. I began to think of radical movements like American communism not only as social movements but also in terms of the personal lives of individual activists.[40] Another result has been a renewed interest in race as a form of personal as well as social identity. Although race occupied a central place in my analysis of the rise and fall of the packinghouse workers' movement, like most labor historians of the time, I analyzed it largely as an obstacle to effective organization and struggle. I noticed, however, that most violence in the 1919 Chicago race riot had been perpetrated by second- and third-generation Irish American youth and that the more recent Slavic immigrants played little part.[41] Yet homeowners from Slavic immigrant backgrounds became central in the racist violence following World War II. This reminded me of the observation a priest had made about recent Italian immigrants in Our Lady of the Angels parish in the sixties. It was remarkable, he said, how little they understood the racial conventions of the neighborhood, how little they embraced white racism when they first moved in—and remarkable too how quickly they absorbed the dominant attitudes of the resident white population. My own background among Slavic American Catholics made it difficult for me to abstract them as "typical working-class racists." Instead, I determined to understand racism as one part of a process of immigrant acculturation within distinctly working-class environments and situations, what I termed "Americanization from the bottom up." Several of my most recent articles, including some with friend and colleague Dave Roediger, concern this problem and I continue to be interested in exploring working-class racism as part of a broader learning process rather than the "natural" product of a multiracial working-class population.[42]

My continuing interest in the racial identity and racial attitudes of recent immigrants is just one dimension, however, of a broader concern with the personal lives of working-class people. This too certainly derives both from my own background and also from more recent personal experience. Through a combination of method and perspective, social historians simply miss much of the personal, the emotional and spiritual side of life. There is little reason to think that such events were any less important in our subjects' lives than they are in our own, though surely attitudes about death and other life transitions differed from one culture to another and changed over time. Is it possible to fuse labor history's broad categories of structural and material analysis with a serious investigation of the subjective and the personal—the emotional content of life, strong personal relationships particularly within families, and various forms of personal identity and sources of motivation? Though I am still not a practicing Catholic, for me, religion generally and my Catholic background in particular are critical to such concerns. Bringing a serious consideration of religion into the study of poor and wage-earning peoples' history not only rings true with my own experience, but it also offers even those without this background an opening into a particularly important dimension of working peoples' lives.

Notes

Earlier versions of this essay were presented at the Faith in History conference at Cornell University, April 2001, and as the Father Martin Mangan Memorial Lecture, Decatur, Illinois, December 12, 2001. Portions first appeared as "Vatican II Comes to the West Side: An Experiment in Catholic Autobiography and the Historiography of Race and Class," *U.S. Catholic Historian* 23 (Fall 2005): 95–119. Many thanks to Nicki Ranganath and Adam Hodges for research help and to Nick Salvatore, Dave Roediger, Pat Simpson, Kathy Oberdeck, the University of Illinois History Workshop, and especially to Jenny Barrett and other members of the Barrett family for their encouragement and comments on the paper.

1. Renee Remond in *Essais d'Ego-Histoire* by Pierre Nora (Paris, 1987), 294, translated and quoted from the French in Jeremy Popkin, "Historians on the Autobiographical Frontier," *American Historical Review* 104 (June 1999): 726–27.

2. On the "discourse of fear" in American Catholicism through the mid-twentieth century, particularly with regard to sexuality, see Timothy Kelly and Joseph Kelly, "American Catholics and the Discourse of Fear," in *An Emotional History of the United States,* ed. Peter Stearns and Jan Lewis (New York, 1998), 259–77. The Kellys argue that this tendency was in decline by the 1950s, but it certainly sounds familiar to me. See also the early fiction of Mary Gordon and her reminiscence, "The Irish Catholic Church," in *Once a Catholic: Prominent Catholics and Ex-Catholics Reveal the Influence of the Church on Their Lives and Work,* ed. Peter Ochiogrosso (New York, 1987), 71–85.

3. Michael Harrington, *The Long Distance Runner: An Autobiography* (New York, 1988), 4, 240.

4. Charles Morris, *American Catholics: The Saints and Sinners Who Built America's Most Powerful Church* (New York, 1998), 174, 175.

5. Rev. Michael A. McGuire, *Father McGuire's New Baltimore Catechism and Mass* (New York, 1953).

6. "Races of Mankind," *Compton's Pictured Encyclopedia,* vol. 7 (Chicago, 1928), 2956–57.

7. Interestingly, historian Elizabeth McKeown, growing up in a small Montana town, isolated from the larger Catholic communities of cities like Chicago, also attributed her early understanding of a world beyond her town—and of the broader Catholic experience—to *Treasure Chest.* See Elizabeth McKeown, "Local Memories," *U.S. Catholic Historian* 21 (Spring 2003): 21–22.

8. *Treasure Chest,* 1961. On the legacies of Tom Dooley and Michael Harrington, see Maurice Isserman, *The Other American: The Life of Michael Harrington* (New York, 2000) and James Terrence Fisher, *Dr. America: The Lives of Thomas A. Dooley* (Amherst, Mass., 1997).

9. See James R. Barrett, "Ethnic and Racial Fragmentation: Toward a Reinterpretation of a Local Labor Movement," in *African American Urban Experience:*

Perspectives from the Colonial Period to the Present, ed. Joe Trotter, Earl Lewis, and Tera Hunters (New York, 2004), 294–95; Graham Taylor, "An Epidemic of Strikes at Chicago," *The Survey* 42 (August 2, 1919): 645–46.

10. James W. Sanders, *The Education of an Urban Minority: Catholics in Chicago, 1833–1965* (Chicago, 1977), 91, quoted in Eileen McMahon, *What Parish Are You From? A Chicago Irish Community and Race Relations* (Lexington, Ky., 1995), 20; Brother Thomas M. Mulerkins, S.J., *Holy Family Parish, Chicago: Priests and People* (Chicago, 1923); Ellen Skerrett, "Sacred Space: Parish and Neighborhood in Chicago," in *Catholicism, Chicago Style,* by Ellen Skerrett, Edward R. Kantowicz, and Steven M. Avella (Chicago, 1993), 143–46, quotes, 143, 145. See also Ellen Skerrett, "The Irish of Chicago's Hull House Neighborhood," in *New Perspectives on the Irish Diaspora,* ed. Charles Fanning (Carbondale, Ill., 2000), 189–222.

11. John T. McGreevy, *Parish Boundaries: The Catholic Encounter with Race in the Twentieth Century Urban North* (Chicago, 1996), 102–3, passim. On the proclivity of Catholic parishes to persist in the process of integration while Jewish and Protestant congregations tended to "flee," see Gerald Gamm, *Urban Exodus: Why the Jews Left Boston and the Catholics Stayed* (Cambridge, Mass., 1999). On the racial transformation of East and West Garfield Park, including the area around Our Lady of the Angels, see Amanda Irene Seligman, "Block by Block: Racing Decay on Chicago's West Side, 1948–1968" (Ph.D. diss., Northwestern University, 1999).

12. *Local Community Fact Book for Chicago, 1950,* ed. Evelyn M. Kitagawa and Karl E. Taeuber (Chicago, 1953), 98–101; *Local Community Fact Book for Chicago, 1960,* ed. Evelyn M. Kitagawa and Karl E. Taeuber (Chicago, 1963),60–61; *Local Community Fact Book, Chicago Metropolitan Area, Based on the 1970 and 1980 Censuses,* Chicago Fact Book Consortium (Chicago 1983), 59–61; Seligman, "Block by Block," 262.

13. Martin E. Marty, *Modern American Religion,* vol. 3, *Under God Indivisible, 1941–1960* (Chicago, 1996), 417–18; Morris, *American Catholics,* 256.

14. My conception of my world as homogeneous was not unusual. A National Opinion Research Center study in the late sixties found that about 20 percent of Catholics surveyed said they lived in a neighborhood that was "almost all Catholic"—even though this was rarely the case. The study was cited in Andrew M. Greeley, *The American Catholic: A Social Portrait* (New York, 1977), 214.

15. David Cowan and John Kuenster, *To Sleep with the Angels: The Story of a Fire* (Chicago, 1996), 8.

16. McGreevy, *Parish Boundaries,* 33–35, 109–10; William A. Osborne, *The Segregated Covenant: Race Relations and American Catholics* (New York, 1967), 206–8; Cowan and Kuenster, *To Sleep with the Angels,* 8.

17. On the fire and its effects on the children, religious, and the families in the surrounding neighborhood, see Cowan and Kuenster, *To Sleep with the Angels,* passim; Suellen Hoy, "Stunned with Sorrow," *Chicago History* 32 (Summer 2004): 4–24; Daniel Greene, "Tragedy in the Parish," *Chicago History* 29 (Spring 2001): 5–19.

18. Julie Billart (1751–1816), a French nun, was the founder and first superior-general of the Sisters of Notre Dame de Namur. Paralyzed in her lower extremities at the age of twenty-one, she was beatified in 1906 and canonized by Pope Paul

VI in 1969 on the strength of a series of documented miracles. See *The Catholic Encyclopedia*, vol. 8 (New York, 1907–12; online edition, 1999, http://newadvent.org/cathen/).

19. On the general context for this transition from ethnic Catholic to white Catholic, see McGreevy, *Parish Boundaries*, 109–10. Although there was certainly racial discrimination and gang violence against Puerto Ricans, whom we recognized as nonwhite, my neighbors made a distinction between them and African Americans. Perhaps there were many reasons for the distinction, but we were certainly aware that most Puerto Rican families were Catholic and that most African American families were not.

20. On the elaborate network of street gangs in Chicago during the interwar years and entrenched notions of "turf," both still very much alive in the fifties and sixties, see Frederic M. Thrasher, *The Gang: A Study of 1,313 Gangs in Chicago* (Chicago, 1927). On the world of the city's street gangs amid Chicago's changing racial and ethnic demographics, including at the time I was growing up, see Andrew Diamond, "Hoodlums, Rebels, and Vice Lords: Street Gangs, Youth Subcultures, and Race in Chicago, 1919–1968," forthcoming.

21. This theme was repeated often in the popular religious literature we encountered. See, for example, the racially integrated classrooms and play groups and the racially diverse Madonnas and saints from countries all over the world depicted in various issues of *Treasure Chest* as early as the mid-fifties: 12 (October 11, 1956); 12 (November 22, 1956); 12 (December 20, 1956); 12 (January 31, 1957); 12 (February 14, 1957); 12 (March 14, 1957); 13 (October 24, 1957); 13 (January 16, 1958).

22. Greeley, *American Catholic*, 112–25.

23. On the Second Vatican Council, see Philip Gleason, "Catholicism and Cultural Change in the 60's," in *America in Change: Reflections on the 60's and 70's*, ed. Ronald Weber (South Bend, Ind., 1972), 91.

24. On Alfred Cardinal Meyer's determination to implement the archdiocese's interracial mission, see Osborne, *Segregated Covenant*, 211–20; Steven M. Avella, "Cardinal Meyer and the Era of Confidence," in Skerrett, Kantowicz, and Avella, *Catholicism, Chicago Style*, 120–21; McGreevy, *Parish Boundaries*, 119–20, 136–37, 147. The last quote is from one of our parishioners who objected to the socially oriented message that arrived in the parish in the early 1960s.

25. On the August 12, 1965, West Side riot, see the *Chicago Tribune* August 13, 1965; Adam Cohen and Elizabeth Taylor, *American Pharaoh: Mayor Richard J. Daley: His Battle for Chicago and the Nation* (Boston, 2000), 348–49.

26. Osborne, *Segregated Covenant*, 203, 204. On widespread instances of racial violence in and near various ethnic blue-collar neighborhoods in Chicago during the postwar era, see the *Chicago Defender* May 12, 1964, 3, 17; the *Chicago American* August 3, 1963, 1, clippings in the papers of the Catholic Interracial Council, Box 73, Chicago Historical Society; Arnold Hirsch, *Making the Second Ghetto: Race and Housing in Chicago, 1940–1960* (New York, 1983, 2nd ed., 2000), and "Massive Resistance in the Urban North: Trumble Park, Chicago, 1953–1966," *Journal of American History* 82 (1995): 551–78. On white violence against African American homeowners on the West Side in particular, see Seligman, "Block by Block," 241–51. John McGreevy ties the events to the culture and perspective of Catholic parishioners in Chicago and elsewhere in *Parish Boundaries*, 93–101,

and provides the best treatment of the interracial movement in Chicago and elsewhere.

27. The photograph was reproduced in the September 1963 issue of *Community,* published by Friendship House, a South Side Catholic community dedicated to "the elimination of racial prejudice and discrimination." On the involvement of Chicago religious in civil rights actions in the city and beyond, see McGreevy, *Parish Boundaries,* 171–72. For the growing hostility of some laity to them as a result, see 189–90, and for the chasm that opened between the city's liberal and conservative Catholics in the wake of the summer 1966 open housing demonstrations in Gage Park and Marquette Park, see 184–92 and James R. Ralph, *Northern Protest: Martin Luther King, Jr., Chicago, and the Civil Rights Movement* (Cambridge, Mass., 1993). For a blue-collar ethnic memoir of growing up in Gage Park's St. Gaul Parish, see Douglas Bukowski, *Pictures of Home: A Memoir of Family and City* (Chicago, 2004).

28. Maria Romano to Father Mallette, November 30, 1964, box 3, folder 8; "Irish Catholic" to Daniel Mallette, [1965], Father Daniel Mallette Papers, Chicago Historical Society.

29. For the racial transformation of a South Side parish in the course of the 1960s and the tensions this produced within the parish, see McMahon, *What Parish Are You From?*

30. Gareth Stedman Jones, *Outcast London: A Study of the Relations between Social Classes* (Oxford, 1970); Carter Goodrich, *The Frontier of Control: A Study of British Workshop Politics* (New York, 1921; repr., London, 1975); David Brody, *Steelworkers in America, the Nonunion Era* (Cambridge, Mass., 1960; repr., Urbana, 1999); David Montgomery, *Workers' Control in America: Studies in the History of Work, Technology, and Labor Struggles* (Cambridge and New York, 1979). The British influences derived from a year of study at Warwick University in Coventry, England, where E. P. Thompson had established the Center for the Study of Social History. David Brody was the visiting American professor during my year of study there (1972–73), my first travel outside of the United States.

31. Montgomery was invoking a phrase employed by Robert and Helen Lynd in *Middletown* (New York, 1929).

32. John Bodnar, "Immigration, Kinship, and the Rise of Working Class Realism in Industrial America," *Journal of Social History* 14 (1980): 45–65; James R. Barrett, *Work and Community in the Jungle: Chicago's Packinghouse Workers, 1894–1922* (Urbana, Ill., 1987), 271–72; James R. Barrett, "*The Transplanted:* Workers, Class, and Labor" *Social Science History* 12 (Fall 1988): 221–31; James R. Barrett, "Women's Work, Family Economy, and Militancy: The Case of Chicago's Immigrant Packinghouse Workers, 1900–1922," in *Labor Divided: Race and Ethnicity in United States Labor Struggles, 1840–1970,* ed. Robert Asher and Charles Stephenson (Albany, N.Y., 1990). Neither Bodnar nor I noted the likely influence of the church's teachings on the sacredness of family life in relation to these problems. See Leslie Woodcock Tentler, "On the Margins: The State of American Catholic History," *American Quarterly* 45 (March 1993): 104–27.

33. Woodcock Tentler, "On the Margins," 114; Leslie Woodcock Tentler, "Present at the Creation: Working-Class Catholics in the United States," in *American Exceptionalism? U.S. Working-Class Formation in an International Context,* ed. Rick Halpern and Jonathan Morris (New York, 1997), 135, 144; Robert A. Slayton,

Back of the Yards: The Making of a Local Democracy (Chicago, 1986), 118–23 and passim.

34. Thomas Bell, *Out of This Furnace* (New York, 1941). For a fuller argument that traditional religious and other cultural values can provide the basis for radical social movements, see Craig Calhoun, "The Radicalism of Tradition: Community Strength or Venerable Disguise and Borrowed Language?" *American Journal of Sociology* 88 (1983): 886–914. I thank Kathy Oberdeck for the reference.

35. Barrett, *Work and Community in the Jungle*. My arguments regarding religion and working-class organization are advanced most directly in Upton Sinclair, *The Jungle,* with an introduction and notes by James R. Barrett (Urbana, Ill., 1988), xix–xxii. Alinsky is quoted in Slayton, *Back of the Yards,* 118.

36. Woodcock Tentler, "On the Margins," 111–12, quote on 112. Although I am speaking here of Catholicism, the argument applies to workers' religious lives more generally. There are some indications of a rise in interest among younger labor historians. See, for example, Kimberly L. Phillips, *AlabamaNorth: African-American Migrants, Community, and Working-Class Activism in Cleveland, 1915–1945* (Urbana, Ill., 1999), and Kathryn Oberdeck, *The Evangelist and the Impresario: Religion, Entertainment, and Politics in America, 1884–1914* (Baltimore, 1999).

37. John T. McGreevy, "Faith and Morals in the United States, 1865 to the Present," *Reviews in American History* 26 (March 1998): 240. Woodcock Tentler, "On the Margins." Woodcock Tentler's article is reprinted with responses from several Catholic historians in *U.S. Catholic Historian* 21 (Spring 2003): 77–126. See especially the response by labor historian Joseph McCartin (114–20).

38. William H. Sewell, "Toward a Post-Materialist Rhetoric for Labor History," in *Rethinking Labor History: Essays on Discourse and Class Analysis,* ed. Lenard Berlanstein (Urbana, 1993), 17–18. Again, historians are not alone. Gary Wills has argued that American intellectuals and social critics generally ignore the pervasive influence of religion in the United States, except when its enormous impact on American politics and culture make this impossible. See Gary Wills, *Under God: Religion and American Politics* (New York, 1990), 15–16.

39. Herbert Gutman, "Protestantism and the American Labor Movement: The Christian Spirit in the Gilded Age," in *Work, Culture, and Industrializing America: Essays in Working Class and Social History* by Herbert Gutman (New York, 1976), 79–117; Nick Salvatore, "Herbert Gutman's Narrative of the American Working-Class: A Reevaluation," *International Journal of Politics, Culture and Society* 12 (1998): 64–68. In contrast to Salvatore's rather sharp critique, I find Gutman's interest in religion here and elsewhere another sign of his remarkably sensitive approach to working-class life during the earliest stages of the "new labor history." For Gutman's treatment of religion as part of preindustrial culture, employed as a resource in class conflict, see "Work, Culture, and Society in Industrializing America, 1815–1919," in Gutman, *Work, Culture, and Industrializing America,* 4–66. We know far more about popular religion among workers in the early and mid-nineteenth than in the twentieth century, though much of this literature emphasizes religion as a source of class fragmentation. For some of the best of this work, see, for example, Bruce Laurie, *The Working People of Philadelphia, 1800–1850* (Philadelphia, 1980); David Montgomery, "The Shuttle and the Cross: Weavers and Artisans in the Kennsington Riots of 1844," *Journal*

of Social History 5 (1972): 411–47; and, for a critique, William R. Sutton, "Tied to the Whipping Post: New Labor Historians and Evangelical Artisans in the Early Republic," *Labor History* 36 (Spring 1995): 251–81. As in so much of the new labor history, E. P. Thompson's influence has been enormous. See his classic discussion of Methodism in E. P. Thompson, *The Making of the English Working Class* (New York, 1963), 350–400.

40. James R. Barrett, "Revolution and Personal Crisis: William Z. Foster and the American Communist Personal Narrative," *Labor History* 43, no. 4 (Fall 2002): 465–82; James R. Barrett, *William Z. Foster and the Tragedy of American Radicalism* (Urbana, Ill., 2000); and James R. Barrett, "*Was* the Personal Political? Reading the Autobiography of American Communism," article manuscript in progress.

41. Compare the treatment of the 1919 riot in Barrett, *Work and Community in the Jungle,* and Dominic Pacyga, "Chicago's 1919 Race Riot: Ethnicity, Class, and Urban Violence," in *The Making of Urban America,* ed. Raymond A. Mohl, 2nd ed. (Wilmington, Del., 1996) with the standard treatment in William M. Tuttle, *Race Riot: Chicago in the Red Summer of 1919* (New York, 1970).

42. James R. Barrett, "Americanization from the Bottom Up: Immigration and the Remaking of the Working Class in the United States, 1880–1930," *Journal of American History* 79 (December 1992): 996–1020; James R. Barrett and David R. Roediger, "In Between Peoples: Race, Nationality and the 'New Immigrant' Working Class," *Journal of American Ethnic History* 16 (Spring 1997): 3–44; David Roediger and James R. Barrett, "Irish Hosts and White Pan-Ethnicity; Or, Who Made the 'New Immigrants' Inbetween?" in *Not Just Black and White: Immigration and Race, Then and Now,* ed. Nancy Foner and George Fredrickson (New York, 2004); James R. Barrett and David Roediger, "The Irish and the 'Americanization' of the 'New Immigrants' in the Streets and in the Churches of the Urban United States, 1900–1930," *Journal of American Ethnic History* 24 (Summer 2005): 3–33.

MAUREEN FITZGERALD

7 *Lost at the Drive-In*

Several years ago I gave a talk at the College of William and Mary on my own struggles with subjectivity and research, especially as they pertained to my work on Irish Catholic women historically and my quite complex relation to Catholicism. At the end of the talk, a perceptive colleague asked me what should not have been a startling question; namely, "Is there a Catholic methodology?"[1] I was stymied, not least because I had spoken vehemently on my decision to refuse anymore to call myself an "ex-Catholic" in recognition of the impact of my Catholic childhood, family, and values on my work. I knew what I did not want to claim as well, which was that some measure of "truth," as decided by an institutional Church with which I was frequently at odds, determined the "truth" I found in history. I told her I needed to think about it, and have been thinking about it since.

I have come up with an answer that will not be satisfying to some, but is the only honest answer I can give. I ascribe to no overarching method, certainly not one that needs to be replicated by anyone else. But in my work, my Catholic, or more precisely Irish Catholic, background, is frequently in tension with my training as an historian. It is often a creative tension, one that helps me to question the presumptions in the fields with which I engage, or the presumptions of the historical actors about whom I write. This sometimes welcome, and often unwelcome, tension has given me a tolerance for ideological impurity that when I am at my best serves me and my work well, and when I am at my worst makes the work itself impossible to do.

I have never, even in my childhood when I was traditionally religious, felt entirely comfortable as a Catholic. Part of this had to do with my parents' discomfort at the options for worship on Long Island, where I grew up—first in Levittown from 1959 to 1965, and then in another similar suburb, Commack, until my graduation in 1977. My parents had grown up in the city, and their respective churches were central to how they defined neighborhood and community.[2] I heard a lot about what they missed. Dad had gone through Catholic schools until he dropped out of Manhattan College to enlist. Mom had lived her entire premarried life in the same apartment, next door to the parish and parish convent. Dad craved the more sophisticated Catholicism he learned from the brothers at Cardinal Hayes High School. Mom craved being able to enter sacred space at any given moment and the sense of peace she felt, not from Mass per se, but from space and time for contemplation. Neither was satisfied with the huge suburban church we attended, one that was architecturally indistinct from a gymnasium, and whose pastor seemed incapable of a sermon that focused on anything but the need to put more money in the collection plate.[3] This was the 1960s and 1970s, and as I got older I was increasingly dissatisfied with a religious experience impervious to the complexity of life outside the building. The most important lesson we learned was that we return from Communion not to the pews but to the back of the church, so that we might leave first and avoid a forty-five-minute wait to get out of the parking lot.

There were many aspects of our family life that made enjoyment or engagement with Catholic parish life very difficult. I was the oldest of five children born in six years. Mom did not drive, and so could not go to church except for Mass or confession, when Dad or some other adult could drive her. And our motley crew was often sick and/or too squirmy to sit long enough for Mom to get much out of church. She spent most of our childhood listening to Mass through a speaker in the otherwise soundproof nursery.

The nursery experience probably prepped Mom to try the most alienating of our suburban Catholic experiments, the drive-in Mass. I think I was about nine at the time, because I had made my First Communion but my siblings had not. We went a few times, pulling into the slot, hanging the intercom on the window, and trying to stay quiet in the back of the station wagon. We stopped going after I literally got lost coming back from Communion, which was given at a makeshift altar under the screen. It was easy to find the screen, but hard to differentiate the sea of station wagons a quarter mile back. When my father finally found me, we got into the car, drove off, and did not return. The absurdity and profound sense of loss in this experience was palpable. The local drive-in hardly satisfied my mother's search for peace in sacred space, and my own and my siblings' tendency toward car sickness made this mode of church-going an especially cruel barrier to my father's intellectual engagement with the metallic speaker.

But my life and that of my siblings was in many other respects not like my parents' childhoods. We did not live in an Irish Catholic neighborhood; we lived in one that was Italian Catholic, Puerto Rican, East European Jewish, and Irish Catholic. Because I went to public schools, my favorite teachers and mentors were Jewish women, the only women I knew from the neighborhood who had a college education. They encouraged my engagement with feminism, applauded my interests in history and politics, and otherwise served as support for seeking to understand the complex world of Vietnam and race riots, feminism and Watergate, and the haunting legacies of the Holocaust. As a teenager I went out with boys who were almost exclusively Italian. I liked them, but loved their families, who were warm and inviting and taught me how to cook. These families also practiced a different Catholicism than I did, one in which they might rarely go to Mass and yet installed and venerated the Madonna on the front lawn.[4] This meeting of various ethnic cultures was for me tremendously exciting and, for my parents, often worrisome. My values and passions were somehow nursed in this unstable mix, and if, in a catechism class, I was asked to judge non-Catholic values and people as less valid or believable than those that were Catholic, or even of a different Catholic type than Irish, I simply rejected such parochialism. I was a Catholic, but I was also engaged in so many other ways of thinking that Catholicism could not define me in the very central way it had my parents.

In trying to remember how it was that I made a break with Catholicism in my youth, I recall a slow process, but one punctuated by particular episodes and ideological shifts. I remember conversations with my friends about original sin and its connection to current debates about human sexuality. By my late teens at the end of the 1970s, I found it impossible to give much credence to the notion that human sexuality and reproduction, or human life itself, was so tainted by sin that our very essence and survival was inextricable from evil. I did, however, believe

OPPOSITE: *The Drive-in operation from 1955–68, at times hosting four masses each Sunday, with a maximum capacity of 260 cars for each mass.* St. Anne's Church, Brentwood, New York: A Century of Faith. *Custombook in 1995. St. Anne's of Brentwood, New York; courtesy of the Archives of the Archdiocese of Rockville Center. My thanks to archivist Jean Walsh.*

The wide, panoramic arrangement of automobile parking within the theatre makes it possible for the Priest to be seen from every section. A microphone, situated on the altar carries the prayers of the Priest to each car through its individual loud speaker. A narrator at a standing microphone near the altar gives descriptive commentary of the Mass.

ANNUAL SCHEDULE OF DRIVE - IN MASSES

Months of June through September
9:00, 10:00, 11:15, and 12:30

Months of October through May
9:00, 10:30, and 12:00

A special shelter up front at the foot of the altar, as pictured above, provides an altar rail for the reception of communion. It is suggested, therefore, that those receiving communion, park toward the front, for their own convenience especially during inclement weather.

Entrance to the St. Anne's Drive-in Masses on west side of 5th Avenue in Brentwood, L. I., is easily located by this large sign installation on which the schedule of Masses is included.

An individual loud speaker is available for each car. As a safety precaution, care should be taken to be certain that the speaker is returned to its post before driving away.

Collection envelopes are distributed to occupants of each automobile upon entering the Drive-in. At the conclusion of the Mass the donation envelopes are received from the cars as they exit. There are no collections during Mass.

that evil existed; how else to explain Hitler, war, racism, and women's oppression? Yet I did not believe that rooting out sexual pleasure and its effects was the solution to these challenges. When speaking to friends in college about these and other issues, I found hope from those Catholics who agreed with me, and happened to go to a particular church in which these or other "liberal" values were affirmed. For a time I remember searching for such a liberal Catholic community or congregation, and instead faced disappointments all too glaring to ignore, chief among them being the priest who said Mass at college but who was so obviously drunk during the service that it was not uncommon for him to stop and stare out the window for minutes at a time. I became so bored or angry on such occasions that I eventually stopped going to Mass. This kind of religious experience was simply not conducive to spiritual contemplation or renewal. Even when I went to church at home, looking again for the comfort of the midnight Mass, I became so passionately enraged at the male God-talk that I came to believe walking into the church was itself an occasion of sin.

At the same time, and on an intellectual level, I began to disavow Catholicism explicitly. In my first semester at Dickinson College, I took a course on early Christianity, and the simple Catholicism of my childhood crumpled in its midst. Claims to unchanging, transcendent truths looked pitiful next to a historical account of the codification of the New Testament in the fourth century. Two historical figures are at odds, one of them wins, and we therefore reiterate belief in his version of the gospel sixteen hundred years later. The more history, including religious history, that I studied, the more ridiculous the arrogance of the "one true church" seemed. The more I studied women and religion, the more egregious the mind/body dualism of ascetic Catholicism seemed to me, and the more central Catholicism's culpability in the rise of patriarchy. These intellectual and experiential interchanges with Catholicism finally made walking through church doors difficult or impossible. I was now an ex-Catholic.

And yet I never imagined myself to be a "lapsed Catholic" or one who had "lost faith" in large part because these expressions suggest passivity, and I was never passive in this journey. To suggest I was "lapsed," for instance, cannot account for the times in which I was enraged. And the rage per se, rather than indifference, is important to assess. I think that because I was a religious kid, the sense of betrayal and disgust was that much greater. I took Catholicism very seriously, and had tried to live my life according to its values. Beyond all else, the most important lesson I learned was about kindness and our moral responsibility to be kind, and to love, even when it proved personally difficult. I remember, for instance, a confession I made when I was in fifth grade. Rather than the usual litany detailing fights with my brothers and sister, I spoke of ridiculing a girl in our class who was easy to ridicule. She had no friends to speak of, no peace from incessant teasing. I left the confessional with a pledge to help her through this. Whether she noticed my efforts or not was never clear, and that was not the point. The right thing to do was clear, and I had a responsibility to do it. I expected a great deal from myself and, for a time, Catholicism gave me a supportive structure through which to do so.

Perhaps because Catholicism was not an all-encompassing influence on my early life, my rage at Catholicism was not a rage at God or religion itself. Certainly, recognition of Church misogyny, imperialist oppression, and racism was deeply painful. If kindness and love and doing the right thing was the appropriate responsibility of individual Catholics, how could I not feel betrayed by an institutional Church that systematically fostered intolerance and bigotry? But it was also in this period that I began to explore religious thought in complicated ways. I literally remember the places and times in which I read Paul Tillich's *Dynamics of Faith*, Mary Daly's "After the Death of God the Father," and Dietrich Bonhoeffer's notes from the Nazi prison in which he was to die. I was thrilled by these works, engaged in deep and unrelenting ways, and it's to this reading and contemplation that I owe my lifelong fascination with religions of any type. I took my disappointments and anger with Catholicism per se and channeled my religious energies elsewhere.

One place to do so was in my studies and research in American women's history. In graduate school at the University of Wisconsin–Madison, I found religion understudied, or underemphasized, in analyses of women's political consciousness historically. It seemed to me glaringly obvious that women, perhaps especially because of their exclusion from formal political institutions, had historically used religious language and institutions in complex ways, and that this complexity was often overlooked by historians. The presumption that women were victims of religion only seemed plainly ridiculous, and even those historians who did recognize "religion's" importance in the nineteenth-century women's movement, for instance, seemed merely to have touched the surface. I seriously began what has thus far been my life's work: an interrogation of the connections between what we call politics and what we call religion. In a master's essay on Elizabeth Cady Stanton, I traced the religious influence critical to Stanton's articulation of feminist consciousness and politics. I began delighting in excavating her shift from evangelical Protestantism to an eclectic mix of Quaker, Unitarian, and freethinker influences. Until the end of her life, she was a profoundly religious person, although quite antagonistic to those she termed Christian orthodox. In no small way, I identified with her quest to know and understand God, and therefore to have a radical politics, that, as she was prone to say, "made God, and not imperfect man, the object of worship."[5]

Stanton and her cohorts in the women's movement appealed to me in other ways. Stanton and Matilda Joslyn Gage, for instance, tried very hard over the course of their lifetimes to embrace religions more in keeping with their politics, and politics more in keeping with their religion. In either deliberate or unthinking ways, they were made uncomfortable by the dissonance caused by a lack of fit between politics and religion, and thus changed religious affiliation frequently. Their quest for perfection was constant and often rigorous, thereby necessitating that they remain on guard for corruption, rigidity, and compromise. They also took great risks in their lives to articulate publicly their beliefs, both about religion and women's oppression. They took daily sustenance from the abolitionist slogan "Resistance to tyranny is obedience to God," a comfort made necessary by activities such as Stanton's publication of *The Woman's Bible* at the end of her life, an act that prompted official censure by the bulk of the woman's movement she had helped create.

Yet Stanton irritated me in other ways. She was best at analyzing the oppressions of women with comparable class and racial standing, but hideous in understanding women of nonelite backgrounds. Her activism was made possible through the hard labor of a succession of Irish domestic servants, whom she did not ridicule explicitly; it just never occurred to her that they were women. When pushed, Stanton could also appeal to her various audiences' bigotries and prejudices in order to make her case for elite women's formal inclusion in the polity. In one speech, for instance, she reminded the audience that "Patrick and Sambo and Hans and Yung Tung"[6] had the right to vote, making it imperative that women of her stature be afforded the vote as a safeguard against them.

When it came to my dissertation, therefore, I wanted to understand working-class women of the period. I decided to focus on Irish Catholic nuns for many reasons. Reading the literature of African American religious and cultural resistance had opened up a new world for me, indicating again how important the connections between religious and political consciousness were, and how complex and awesome the articulation of religious standpoint could be, even in the more dire circumstances. Herbert Gutman's mandate that we understand working-class culture as resistance also influenced me, as did my work on Ireland in the nineteenth century, in which I glimpsed an enormously complex and fractured community only nominally brought together under the rubric "Irish Catholic."

It was not until I set out to complete a dissertation, and then a book, on the work of Irish Catholic nuns in nineteenth-century charities in New York City that I began again to grapple with Catholicism in a complex way. From the start of this work, the feeling of nakedness in seeing my very ethnic name attached to a project about the Irish prompted me to explain defensively that this dissertation would not degenerate into what I would call "rah-rah!" ethnic history—an uncritical tribute to the Irish. When I began, I told myself and others, I was approaching the study of Irish Catholicism for intellectual reasons only; it had nothing at all to do with my ethnic background. Calling myself an "ex-Catholic," moreover, elicited expressions of palpable relief from my academic advisors, who seemed afraid that my search for Catholic women's agency as historical actors might lead me to ignore the literature on Catholic control of women sexually. As one advisor put it, "everything we know about feminism *starts* with a critique of Catholic sexism." I tried to explain to this person who was never Catholic that only an ex-Catholic feminist like myself could begin to know the anger the Church's sexism and homophobia has generated.

Subjectivity, however, had launched me into this project, whether I wanted to acknowledge it or not. Perhaps principally because of my subjective standpoint as a woman raised as an Irish Catholic New Yorker, I was convinced that a distinctively "Irish Catholic" subculture managed to survive elite Protestant efforts at assimilation. In the neighborhood in which I grew up, for instance, I knew almost no Protestant kids. By the age of twelve, I had conjured up my own theory that simultaneously explained the nervousness of adults when hearing of a "mixed marriage," meaning one between a Catholic and Jew, and the lesson I learned in history class, that this was a "Protestant nation." Where did all these Protestants come from, I wondered? My answer was that they were the children of a Catholic-Jewish marriage, their continual proliferation threatening to dominate the country and making the adults very nervous. Although my mother finally convinced me that I had it all wrong, the idea that Irish Catholics, or Jews, or Italians, simply "melted" into the larger pot was so at odds with my early life that I could not accept without question the assumption in American historiography that Protestant hegemony was won, or that it was won without resistance.

Subjectivity also helped me understand that Catholic sisters were powerful women who certainly lost power over the course of the twentieth century, but played historical roles that were not as yet recognized by historians of American women. In my family, as well as those of my Catholic friends, aunts or great-aunts who were nuns were usually the only female relatives who had college educations, sometimes doctorates, were high school principals, or ran substantial charitable organizations. We might not want that life for ourselves, and indeed had opportunities to exercise power outside the Church and without submitting to ecclesiastical oversight. We might like or dislike these women intensely, but it would not occur to us to deem these women powerless.

I realized from the very beginning of this work, although perhaps only partially, that the subjectivities of other scholars had dictated an absence of work on Irish Catholic nuns. Irish Catholics formed the bulk of the late-nineteenth century working-class in the northeastern United States. I had studied the public activism of many prominent middle-class and elite Protestant women of the period who moved into the public sphere during the nineteenth century, emerging at the century's end as social reform leaders active in radical and mainstream activities. Their charitable work with women and children, and in the welfare state, form much of the backbone for what we think we know about "women's" public activism in the nineteenth and early twentieth centuries. Irish Catholic nuns, however, constructed and ran their own charities for women and children in the same places and time periods, and not studying them seemed a glaring insufficiency in the literature.[7]

I assumed that Irish Catholic nuns' activism would be distinct from, and perhaps even antagonistic to, that of Protestant elite women, especially because the majority of nuns in America hailed from poor and working-class backgrounds and worked with women and children of their own religious and ethnic culture. Knowing almost nothing about nuns historically prior to starting the project, I wanted to know whether, and then how and why, nuns played a role in resisting the assimilationist onslaught presumed to have been directed against the Irish Catholic community since the mid-nineteenth century.

As I realized within months of serious research, nuns' absence in U.S. women's history was not dictated by a lack of sources; nuns are and were scrupulous about saving anything and everything, from balls of string to the most detailed accounts of their daily work among famine migrants. Granted, combing through their basements for something I could use made me terribly envious of my friends who sat at proper desks at the National Archives and handed material to others to copy. But finding as-yet-unseen records from the nineteenth century was also terribly exciting. On one early trip to the Sisters of Mercy outside New York, for instance,

I stayed in their convent for a week, as daily transportation would have been onerous. After three days of reading pamphlets written by a member of the order about their jubilees and other anniversaries, I asked the sister for the twentieth time how I could find out more about the personal backgrounds of the sisters. For the first three days, she had responded to my inquiries by handing me another pamphlet, knowing full well that it would not serve my interests. Finally, exasperated by my persistence, she let it slip that they had full applications from all women who joined the order from the 1850s onward. After shameless begging, the sister allowed me to read them. Each included the place of birth of the applicants and their parents, the jobs and level of education each sister had upon entrance to the convent, their reasons for joining, and the amount of money, or more often lack thereof, that sisters could contribute to their dowry upon entrance. Other records allowed me to trace the kind of work each did over the course of their adult lives in the order, the reasons for some sisters' expulsions, and the reasons given by some who chose to leave. For a social historian, and a women's historian used to finding the barest evidence pertaining to working-class women, that convent proved a gold mine. And it was only one of many I was to find.

Nor was the work that nineteenth-century nuns did of limited proportion or significance in the field of U.S. women's history. In the course of study, I found more evidence of active and deliberate cultural resistance to Protestant assimilation efforts than I dreamed possible, and overwhelming evidence pointing to Catholic sisters' agency in shaping not only the larger Irish Catholic community, but also the American welfare state itself.

I also began to address the way their Catholicism, not just their Irishness, played a role in all this. Irish Catholic nuns used the language and institutional apparatuses of Catholicism to further their own self-interests as well as the interests of Irish Catholics as a group and the city's poor more generally. These nuns did not organize themselves as "working-class" per se, but rather manipulated particular traditions in Catholicism to support the poor and resist internalization of middle-class ideology that blamed the poor for poverty. Disparate ideological premises in Catholicism and Protestantism allowed Catholic nuns to support the poor in ways that Protestant Scientific Charity reformers could not. The famine Irish as a group were hardly likely to accept the premise that the famine and their desperate poverty in New York City were the results of moral failings. Rather, they were more likely to blame English colonialism and the emerging capitalist economy for the relentless poverty of the immigrant communities; the poor, in other words, were not the cause of poverty. Nuns organized their work according to medieval notions about duty to the poor. To deny charity was therefore cruel and "un-Christian," not the hearty tonic Protestant reformers believed necessary to compel the poor to change their moral habits and behavior. While Catholics supported the expansion of the welfare state, regardless of the "causes" of individual misfortune, Protestants as a group feared that, like Catholicism itself, a large welfare state would breed dependence and laziness.

In short, there were sources on which to depend, and there were reasons the study might prove significant. And yet constructing an analytical framework that enabled me to understand and elucidate the extent, and limits, of nuns' historical public power proved endlessly difficult. At issue were two problems: I neither wanted to write that "rah-rah!" history, nor did I want to write something indicative of my being an "ex-Catholic" and therefore angry at "the Church" as a whole. Keeping myself and my work between these two poles, however, proved easier said than done. So when I found myself engaged in tortuous psychological battles in researching and writing this history, I could not identify the source of my affliction without embarrassment. The intellectual and political security I had found in regularly pronouncing myself an "ex-Catholic" withered as I studied a Church and community in constant overt political conflict over issues about which I cared passionately. I became deeply identified with those I studied who brought the moral foundations of Catholicism to their struggles against gender, racial, and class oppression while sharing their anger at those who steered the politics of the Catholic community toward conservatism and reaction.

I also no longer wanted to make non-Catholic people comfortable by disowning my Catholic background. At issue was my growing realization that there was a difference between my criticisms of the Church from a feminist and leftist perspective and the derivative form of anti-Catholicism still powerful in America and certainly in the academy. And because I realized that I had internalized a great deal of anti-Catholicism myself, it became harder at this point to use the label "ex-Catholic"—not because I was going to Mass, but because other academics were too comforted by it. Although the rules were tacit, they were powerful: Only if I was an "ex" could I rightfully claim "objectivity" or legitimacy in doing this study.

And yet I was often unsuccessful in mustering clarity, in part because my emotional response to the material or research experience was so strong, and reasonably so. Consider, for instance, the following: I had been working in the archives of the Archdiocese of New York at Dunwoodie for three weeks and was exhausted. The research itself was tedious but necessary; it involved going through sixty years of uncatalogued microfilmed bishops' papers, but the finds, hidden between thousands of unrelated handwritten letters, were critical to understanding nuns' relationships with men of the Church. The atmosphere of the place, however, was much more enervating than the research. The archives are housed in the Archdiocesan male seminary, and I was one of three women on its prodigious grounds, besides the archivist (a nun) and librarian. There is no hallway leading from the lobby to the archives at the rear of the building, and so I had to walk each day through a series of rooms in which I was likely to meet a young and startled robed seminarian unused to encountering women in such a place. I have never been quite so aware of existing in female form, and so conscious of how disturbing a female body can be. Everyone was polite, as was the pianist whom I encountered one day; the sounds of his concerto drew me eagerly to the source of a little joy in a usually joyless routine. He heard the door open, looked back perfunctorily, then looked back again and stopped playing. I apologized for being there. Once in the archives, I became more stressed. Only one researcher at a time was allowed inside; the archivist's desk abutted and faced my own, and her job, as she saw it, was to watch me—all day, every day, every minute—to be sure I was handling the microfilm correctly. I tried to lose myself in the material but was not always successful, sometimes prompting an effort toward small talk that usually ended with "Yes, Sister," an expression that was quickly becoming a mantra, prompting my regression toward my six-year-old, good little Irish Catholic–girl persona. I finished the work for the day and with great relief headed toward the lobby, where I encountered another joyful sight, a big black lab snoozing in the vestibule. I love dogs, and missed my own, and so initiated the careful approach, giving him my hand to show that I was friendly and that it was up to him to convey one of the standard responses of indifference, enthusiasm, or hostility. Instead, he smelled my hand, then scampered backward, whimpering. Seeing my obvious confusion and hurt, the seminarian nearby assured me that I "should not take it personally; it's just that he's afraid of women." Unable to respond, I exited the lobby, thinking, "My God, they've done it to a dog." I could not make myself return during the following weeks, and the delay was really messing up my research schedule. For the next month, I interpreted all Catholic documents as emanating from the one true source of virulent misogyny in western civilization.

I spent a good portion of the following months wondering what, exactly, I was doing, and whether I wasn't somehow underemphasizing the part of this story that had conjured up in me feelings that were not easily assuaged by rational argument. Everyone in that seminary was kind, and yet most were afraid of me. Fear and hatred, especially that made manifest in men's struggle against sexual temptation, have been too closely linked for me to understand this experience as simply an arbitrary encounter. I regaled Catholic and non-Catholic friends with such stories. The non-Catholics seemed surprised by my surprise or trauma, as though such an experience was all that I should expect. I made pains to explain how on another day of research I could chat animatedly with my favorite sister archivist, whose desk was dwarfed by an enormous poster declaring her office a "nuclear-free zone."

Studying American anti-Catholicism in the nineteenth century helped me to understand some of these reactions. Anti-Catholicism is a hard nut to crack, precisely because those at the head of the institutional Church are often extremely conservative historically, and it is always easy to find at least some who embrace authoritarian and antidemocratic structures and ideologies. American liberal Protestants and secular thinkers have generally not been implicated in the most nasty and virulent strains of anti-Catholicism for which Know Nothings and the Klan take most credit. And yet liberal anti-Catholicism has nonetheless had a definite shape, with underlying premises, including the assumptions that Catholics are a monolith; that the words and actions of its most conservative leaders are equivalent to the ideas of all of those who call themselves Catholic; that there are no divisions within Catholicism, either ideological, theological, racial, gendered, or classed; and that all who aren't leaders are victims, so that women or nondominant racial groups who call themselves Catholic are characterized as having so thoroughly lost their capacity for rational thought that they are not worth studying. That they maintain allegiance to Catholicism suggests a personal or collective flaw so serious or inscrutable that we should ignore the allegiance in those we like, or use it in those we don't to explain or further document their contrariness.

I realized that the presumption of a monolithic political and religious consciousness among Catholics was particularly hard to swallow. Unlike the perfectionist Protestant women I had studied, few Irish Catholics joined other religions in order to more clearly weave a coherent and uncorrupted ideological or theological outlook. Even those gravitating toward "lace curtain" parishes were mercilessly pilloried by the majority, who found it difficult to differentiate between a "Catholic" identity and a demand for social justice in America as well as Ireland. Becoming Protestant was inseparable from support of British imperialism, and thus staying "Catholic" was the choice of the overwhelming majority, despite the label's irrelevance in denoting much more than group solidarity against colonialism. This was certainly the link between religion and politics that I loved to interrogate, and yet it proved much messier than tracing an individual's movement from Presbyterian to Unitarian to freethinker, a nice consistent path in which divine immanence was more and more clear. With no denominational structures or divisions, the Catholic laity generally did not, as did Protestants and Jews, differentiate themselves within the larger Catholic rubric. Profoundly conservative and revolutionary Catholics went to the same parishes, many rarely went to church at all, some were prone to follow devotedly the leadership of some priests, and others were likely to despise such priests or people. Add to this the ethnic and racial diversity of national churches at the turn of the century, and I was at a loss for what precisely defined Catholicism, except its contrast to Protestantism.

It was this contrast between anti-Catholics' presumption of monolithic obeisance, and the seemingly infinite diversity of Catholic communities historically, that proved important in understanding the culture in which I grew up and its impact on my life and work. I had grown up in this messy mix and had learned later to see its contradictions as hypocrisy and corruption; and, to degrees, I still do. Yet there is another story here, one in which tolerance for cultural and religious diversity is quite extraordinary. On my more cynical days, I see the institutional Church's tolerance for cultural diversity to be the main resource it has utilized in imperialist activities. Sure, they would initially encourage a syncretic integration between the religious cultures of those they converted, but in several generations that culture existed only as a relatively meaningless throwback. On other days, I see tremendous independence of thought among Catholics, so that what an individual priest says is always mediated by what one actually believes. This was a lesson I learned from my father early on: that individual conscience must always serve as a balance against doctrine, that one cannot commit a sin if one does not believe it's a sin. In the American media, for instance, a big deal was made during a visit of Pope John Paul of the fact that, in one poll, 90 percent of Catholics surveyed disagreed with the pope's position on birth control and abortion, and yet remained Catholics. This is hardly a revelation, except to non-Catholics. Catholics are constantly negotiating between the Church's stated values and what they themselves believe is right. If they live in one area of town, they might go to a parish with an archconservative who defines Catholicism as a top-down communication with God in which docility is expected. Or they may have a groovy priest who plays the guitar and wears Birkenstocks. One needs to develop a capacity for critical thinking given the relatively arbitrary ways in which people decide that they will worship in this or the other group.

Corruption, moreover, is quite a relative term. One could easily argue, for instance, that the nuns I study were corrupt, especially because they depended for their charitable work primarily on enormously generous funding through Tammany Hall. With that funding, they changed the political meanings of charitable work without ever claiming to do so. At first I wanted them to claim and celebrate their power, as Protestant women did, instead of writing hideously obsequious notes to archbishops whom they simultaneously manipulated with aplomb. My teleological impulses conditioned me to think, sure they got what they wanted then, but the same obsequious behavior allowed bishops eventually to gain control over their orders and steer their work elsewhere. On the other hand, Protestant women did not manage to get annual public appropriations of millions of nineteenth-century dollars to provide direct services for the poor, and there's ample reason to believe that had nuns been more forthcoming about what they did and for whom resources were provided, they would not have been able to continue the work. Ideological purity would have had very high costs, both for nuns and the people they helped. Of course, these sisters were thereafter demonized as corrupt by Progressive-era Protestant reformers, as were their Tammany Hall cohorts. The reformers tried instead to institute a system of charities that at every level produced ideologically consistent policy, and they trumpeted the virtues and careers of those few Catholics and Jews, and only those few Catholics and Jews, who agreed with them. Thus, the assumption that the poor were morally responsible for their plight, and must be made to reform accordingly, became the underlying premise of most of our welfare systems today.

I also became in this period increasingly able to worship as a Catholic when I kept all of these inconsistencies somehow balanced in my head and heart. My sister, for instance, asked me to be godmother to her first child several years ago. My partner of ten years came with us all to the baptism, her first foray into a Catholic Mass. The priest was particularly zealous; as my aunt drolly noted, he was likely "fresh out of seminary," code words for "he hasn't a clue, but let's be kind." My partner took seriously his stern and impassioned differentiation between those lukewarm Christians who understand Communion as merely metaphoric, as opposed to us Catholics who knew it is the *actual* body and blood of Christ. Thus she became a bit concerned when I nonetheless marched up to the altar and promised to guide MacKenzie in a Catholic life, then renounced "Satan" repeatedly. This priest's view of Satan, my partner realized, was perilously close to people like us, so what, exactly, was I doing? "Satan, for me, is the right wing; it's hatred and intolerance." I felt entirely comfortable disavowing Satan, but I did not assuage my partner's unease.

And that is reasonable. Indeed, it is sometimes entirely impossible for me to balance or to even grapple with a Church that simultaneously is the center of Opus Dei and liberation theology, of compassion for the poor and unrelenting disparagement of women who are not sexually chaste. My decision to live with my partner as a lesbian, for instance, has only increased my sense of the ideological messiness of Catholicism. My parents are conservatives; they do not aspire to liberalism. Yet they and my siblings chose love and charity over ideological purity when they decided to work hard to understand my choices and love and support my partner and me. My parents have only gotten more religious as they age, but the Church's position on gays and lesbians was never repeated to me as the reason for any of their thinking. If anything, their Catholicism, I think, helped them search for grace in understanding and responding to a situation that challenged them profoundly. Generosity of spirit, very well-developed senses of humor, and a tolerance for the vicissitudes of life, not dogma, shaped their responses and amazed me. And yet there are congregations and Catholics everywhere who might believe that I can only *be* a Catholic if I leave my partner and renounce a sexual life. Depending on the day, I find this either ridiculous or horrifying. The church does influence culture and politics, and so such a viewpoint is not only one I must ignore to feel comfortable in this space; it is also one I must work to make less influential in our culture.

And so I am caught betwixt and between, not searching for a perfect church, but for a way to understand the imperfect people I study and the imperfect institutions they inhabit. I've also been thinking a lot lately about the costs of perfectionism, or more accurately the privileges of those who think they can attain it, and the arrogance of those who think they have. I instead delight in watching Carmela Soprano yell at her son when she finds him smoking pot on his confirmation day. In frustration she screams, "Be a good Catholic for fifteen fucking minutes!"[8] Sometimes I can, and sometimes I'm just lost at the drive-in.

Notes

I want to thank the contributors to this anthology, especially Nick Salvatore, as well as Steve Rosswurm and others who participated in the April 2001 conference at Cornell University. I would also like to thank my parents, Joan and Thomas Fitzgerald, who read and commented on the essay, and my partner, Leisa Meyer, who did the same.

1. This was Christie Burns of the College of William and Mary.
2. Hearing about this sense of community in an urban parish gives me no small admiration for John McGreevy's *Parish Boundaries: The Catholic Encounter with Race in the Twentieth-Century Urban North* (Chicago: University of Chicago Press, 1997).
3. The parish was Christ the King.
4. Again, another work by a Catholic historian, Robert Orsi, has helped me to understand the split between Irish and Italian Catholics more clearly. See Robert Orsi, *The Madonna of 115th Street: Faith and Community in Italian Harlem, 1880–1950* (New Haven, Conn.: Yale University Press, 1985).
5. Maureen Anne Fitzgerald, "Religion and Feminism in Elizabeth Cady Stanton's Life and Thought" (master's thesis, University of Wisconsin–Madison, 1985); Maureen Fitzgerald, "The Religious Is Personal Is Political," introduction to Elizabeth Cady Stanton, *The Woman's Bible* (Boston: Northeastern University Press, 1993).
6. Elizabeth Cady Stanton, "Speech to the 'Opening Convention of the National Woman's Suffrage Association, January 19 and 20, 1869,'" Elizabeth Cady Stanton Collection, Library of Congress, Washington, D.C.
7. Maureen Fitzgerald, "Irish-Catholic Nuns and the Development of New York City's Welfare System, 1840–1900" (Ph.D. diss., University of Wisconsin–Madison, 1992).
8. "D Girl," episode no. 7, second season, *The Sopranos* (HBO Television).

JOSEPH A. McCARTIN

8 Utraque Unum: *Finding My Way as a Catholic and a Historian*

> The understanding of history, of its possibilities for good and evil, of its direction and its meaning, lies in the field of hope and can be acquired only there.
>
> —Jürgen Moltmann, *Theology of Hope: On the Ground and the Implications of a Christian Eschatology*

It was my threatened excommunication that made me think seriously about the relationship between my Catholicism and my work as a historian. In 1999, I faced the prospect of being officially barred from the Church of my birth, severed from a connection that had shaped my life more than any other except perhaps my family—which itself had been permeated with Catholicism's influence. Catholicism had provided the moral, intellectual, and cultural foundation of my upbringing. Though I had long since left the securely Catholic world of my youth and had grown increasingly critical of the institutional Church as an adult, I had never seriously considered leaving the Church. And yet, by 1999, in my fortieth year, threatened with excommunication, I was no longer certain if I could stay in it. Wrestling with that question during a tumultuous year led me to a reappraisal of my faith and to new insights into how deeply my faith and my work informed each other.

In order to explain those insights, I must first outline my Catholic biography. In many respects, it resembles that of many college-educated, middle-class American Catholics of my generation. Born in 1959, I was raised by parents who loved and practiced their faith, and who considered it the most valuable gift they could give their six children. Our family life was structured by Catholicism. During my youth, it knit my family, school, and neighborhood together in what appeared to me to be seamless, self-contained world. I had absorbed Catholicism's richness through all my senses: guitar masses and murmured prayers; the scent of burnt incense; the taste of communal wine; the flickering light of candles and brilliant stained glass; the starchy feel of the black cassock and white surplice I had worn as an altar boy. My intellectual sensibilities too had been shaped by its influence, communicated through biblical tales, enacted in the rituals of the liturgical cycle, reviewed in the religion classes of my grade school teachers, the Sisters of St. Joseph of Carondelet, and repeated in weekly homilies. Catholicism had helped me locate myself in history and find meaning in the world through its sacraments and symbols, metaphors and mysteries. Prayer, novenas, holy oil, and conversation about faith were integral to the everyday life that I and my five siblings shared.

Both my parents and my time affected how I understood and experienced Catholicism. My parents were deeply faithful people. But, while devout, they were not overly pious. They disapproved of those who put their faith on ostentatious display as if to show that they were "more Catholic than the pope." They also had a healthy appreciation for the human frailties writ large in their Church and did not discourage their children from criticizing the institution. Their love for their Church never morphed into Catholic chauvinism. Perhaps it is because of this that each of their six children are still practicing Catholics. Their spiritual style certainly shaped my encounter with the faith.

So did my relation to Vatican II. I straddled the era of the Church's great changes. I was born prior to the Vatican Council, in the first full year of the papacy of John XXIII. Thus I have some vivid memories of the older rituals and the Latin Mass. My parents were steeped in pre–Vatican II Catholicism and they passed that on to me. My mother was devoted to Sts. Anne and Anthony and took her children on pilgrimages to the shrine of Sainte-Anne-de-Beaupré in Quebec. Her mother, in turn, was a strong believer in the healing powers of St. Anne's holy oil, and liberally administered it to her grandchildren as a cure for everything from earaches to rashes. We attended annual novenas to St. Anne at my grandmother's childhood parish, St. Mary's in working-class South Troy. After I moved away from home, my mother gave me a miniature loaf of St. Anthony's bread, meant to ward off penury. I still keep it in my dresser drawer. Pre–Vatican II Catholic culture permeated the world of my youth and I reveled in its intimate warmth and the sense of connectedness that it imparted.

I experienced the reforms of Vatican II as an enhancement of Catholic spirituality and culture. This in large part was due to my mother's influence. I remember her exhilaration when the altar at my parish was turned around so that the priest would face the people during the consecration. I recall the giddy vitality of the guitar folk Mass at my parish, Sacred Heart, and the symbolic power of attending a Mass in my neighbor's backyard. I believed that all of these signs showed the Holy Spirit at work all around me. I was awed by it. The profound excitement generated by those changes, the belief that the Holy Spirit was actively renewing the Church, provided an important backdrop for my youthful education in the faith.

The influence of my parents and Vatican II was in turn reinforced by a rich, enveloping Catholic culture. I grew up in the small industrial city of Troy, New York, on the banks of the Hudson River. During my youth, it seemed that the city was overwhelmingly Catholic. My world, at any rate, was entirely Catholic: my schools, basketball and football teams, friends, and of course, relatives. The main religious division in our consciousness was not between Catholics and Protestants or Christians and Jews—we rarely encountered such exotics—but rather between Irish and Italian Catholics. Even when I first ventured beyond Troy, I remained firmly rooted in my Catholic milieu. Among the learned Jesuits at the College of the Holy Cross in Worcester, Massachusetts, I discovered how expansive Catholic culture could be, through the poetry of Gerard Manley Hopkins, the peace witness of the Berrigan brothers, and liberation theology.

I never experienced Catholic culture as insular or defensive. The Catholics I grew up with did not see their faith as a counterculture at odds with modern America. We sensed no great tension between the values of liberal democracy and Catholic values. I was raised to be a thinking Catholic, one who did not equate a critique of the Church's failures with disloyalty, nor criticism of its leaders with apostasy. By the time I had finished my seventeen years of Catholic education, I had embraced ecumenism, the notion of a historical Church that was growing to reflect the fullness of Christ's love over time, and a belief that the laity were not subordinate to the clergy but were themselves integral to the mission of the Church.

But both the Church and I changed between my youth and the mid-1980s. As I entered adulthood, I developed a critique of some of the institutional Church's practices and teachings. Church leaders, meanwhile, began a long and largely successful effort under Pope John Paul II to restrict and suppress precisely those theological influences that had helped me formulate my critique. As I entered adulthood, it seemed to me that the Church began shifting toward a defensive posture, forsaking dialogue among the faithful for the security of an increasingly narrow doctrinal orthodoxy. This seemed especially true around the issues of human sexuality and women's rights, where Church leaders increasingly saw dissent as disobedience. The hierarchy's refusal to consider changes in the celibate male priesthood, its opposition to artificial birth control in all instances, and—later on—its opposition to gay or lesbian marriage were not open to discussion. The Church also grew intolerant of Catholic politicians who opposed its call for the blanket criminalization of abortion.[1]

Like many American Catholics, I found myself at odds with Church authorities on these issues. And, like many, my differences with the Church authorities owed as much to my Catholic upbringing as to secular influences. It was my deeply religious mother who taught me that the clergy are not above the people and immune to criticism. It was the nuns at Troy's Sacred Heart School who taught me that every person can be an equal bearer of God's grace and their example made it impossible for me to believe that a priest must be a man. Though my parents followed the Church's teaching on contraception, they did not teach their children that all Catholics were called to do so. What I learned about the sacramental nature of the marital union in theology classes at Troy's Catholic Central High School or in college at Holy Cross, and what I observed about my parents' own example of family-centered fidelity, made it hard for me to understand why a faithful homosexual relationship would be intrinsically sinful and why gay and lesbian couples ought to be barred from formalizing their own family relations through marriage. My conscience, formed by my Catholic faith, cannot justify using the state's power to coerce a woman into carrying a pregnancy to term, regardless of her circumstances or her views of her situation. As inspired as I am by what Joseph Cardinal Bernardin called the Church's "consistent ethic of life" teaching, I cannot translate it into a viable theory of the state that allows me to justify in my own mind the subordination of the wishes of a vulnerable woman to the will of legislators. The crux of the matter for me concerns the proper and practical limits of government power. I agree with the Church's teaching on the sacredness of life, but not with Church leaders' views concerning the authority of the state over a pregnant woman or with their insistence that criminalization would be a just and effective means of ending abortions.

Expressing ideas like these grew more difficult within the Church during the 1980s and 1990s. People who shared my views were routinely dismissed as "cafeteria Catholics" by many of our conservative coreligionists. I heard such critiques so often that I myself came to wonder whether the critics were right. How could I remain Catholic and dissent from official Church teachings in these areas? There was no shortage of voices who urged people like me to admit that we had gradually become "non-Catholics who happen to go to Mass," as Denver's Archbishop Charles Chaput put it.[2] According to the Reverend Richard John Neuhaus, the editor of the conservative Catholic journal *First Things,* people who share my views are part of the "tattered band" of liberal Catholicism that must be isolated and contained. To Neuhaus, we are part of "a past that must be kept safely past"—the liberal residue of mistaken 1960s enthusiasms.[3]

The abundance of such views had shaken my own confidence in my Catholicism before I had reached my thirties. I had become less sure that I belonged in the Church. Still, I wanted to hold on to my Catholicism. I had no plans to leave the Church. And then, suddenly, I faced the prospect of excommunication. It was that encounter that forced me to think hard about my connection to my Church. And it was through that process that I also discovered new connections between my Catholicism and my work as a historian.

My personal crisis came to head on Holy Thursday, April 1, 1999. At that time, I lived in Rochester, New York, and taught at the nearby campus of the State University of New York at Geneseo. That night I attended a Mass celebrated by a priest for whom I had great respect. Among his strengths was his profound sense of the beauty of the Holy Thursday liturgy, long my favorite in the Church. The ritual washing of the feet in imitation of Christ's humble act of service, the consecration of bread and wine as if for the first time, the foreshadowing of both death and resurrection: all of these made this the most beautiful ritual in the Church calendar to me. This particular priest unlocked the power of that liturgy better than any I had known. In fact, his parish celebrated a special Mass every Thursday evening all year long at which the Holy Thursday service was specifically invoked by the placing of a washing bowl and ewer on the altar to remind us all that the washing of feet inaugurated the Church's work on earth.

Ordinarily, Holy Thursday masses had been a source of spiritual comfort for me. But that was not the case on this night. This Mass was held in a Rochester auditorium rather than the parish Church that I normally attended. The reason was that the celebrant that evening, Father James Callan, had recently been excommunicated. This was to be his first Mass since having been defrocked for having defied orders from Rome and his own bishop. Contrary to explicit rules, he had made a woman a deacon in his church, distributed Holy Communion to non-Catholics at Mass, and blessed several gay couples who had been longtime parishioners. It was in fact his prophetic stance on such issues—mixed with an old-fashioned reverence for the Eucharist—that had drawn me to his church, a spiritually vibrant interracial inner-city parish aptly named Corpus Christi.

When I met Father Callan in 1996, I had not been in a parish where I felt truly welcome in many years. The lack of such a place was an increasing concern to me, especially because I had recently become engaged to be married. As my future wife and I talked about how we would raise our children, I felt a desire to settle in a parish where I would feel at home. One evening I saw a photograph of Father Callan on the front page of the local newspaper accompanying a story about his conflicts with a local branch of Catholics United for the Faith (CUF), a lay organization that has taken it upon itself to police doctrinal orthodoxy in the American Church. I learned that CUF members were spying on Callan's outreach sessions to Rochester's gay and lesbian community and sending reports to Rome. "They're absolutely non-Catholic as far as I'm concerned," a CUF activist was quoted as saying after observing the practices at Corpus Christi.

These words touched me even more than the story of Callan's ministry to Rochester's gay and lesbian community. In retrospect, I can see that the CUF activist's denunciation led me to Callan's church. I had heard such painful words directed at me before, and knew their sting. During a marriage preparation session with my future wife in the Archdiocese of Washington, DC, I was denounced by one of my fellow bridegrooms-to-be when I questioned the binding power of the papal encyclical *Humanae vitae* on artificial birth control. Both the Church and I would be better off if I would leave, he advised. "Why don't you just become a Protestant?" he snapped. Sometimes even my friends could be equally blunt. After a wide-ranging conversation we had about our faith, one friend who had converted to Catholicism concluded: "It is people like you who are ruining the Church." Nor were my orthodox friends the only ones who wondered why I remained a Catholic. Over lunch, a former priest who left the Church because he felt ostracized as a gay man told me that by staying in the institution, people like me were helping to perpetuate its sexism and homophobia. Such views made me feel increasingly embattled in my Catholicism. Finding others who were similarly embattled appealed to me. So I looked up Corpus Christi.

What I found there renewed my faith. Under Callan's leadership,

Corpus Christi had been revived from near extinction in the 1970s to become a pulsing and pluralistic inner-city parish with a remarkable congregation, roughly one-quarter of which was African American and Latino. City dwellers and suburbanites, homeless people, a large number of the physically and mentally disabled, and many non-Catholics rubbed shoulders in the pews there. And shoulders did rub, for as many as 4,000 communicants attended masses on some weekends. It was a spiritually rollicking place, especially when the ecstatic gospel choir let loose. Six community outreach missions to the poor, homeless, and imprisoned thrived there. Weekly lunch-hour masses were held downtown for working people. Traditional sacramental devotions were intertwined with the church's social activism, making the place difficult to categorize along traditional liberal/conservative lines. "The thing that holds us together is the love for the Eucharist," Father Callan often said. Over a span of weeks, one might hear homilies critical of military spending, abortion, and the death penalty, the maltreatment of women and homosexuals by both the society and the Church, and the indifference with which the rich treated the poor. It was an exciting place.[4]

Yet while it was deeply infused with Catholic spirituality, the Corpus Christi parish operated at the edge of Catholic doctrine. On the masthead of the church bulletin, Father Callan listed Jesus Christ as pastor and himself as administrator. Moreover, with the encouragement of the congregation, Callan gave a prominent role to "coadministrator" Mary Ramerman, a wife and mother with a graduate divinity degree. Donning an alb and stole given to her by the congregation, Mary stood next to the celebrant and raised the chalice after the consecration to symbolize the day when we would come to finally live out the words from Paul, that in Christ there is "neither male nor female."[5] Such practices outraged conservative Catholics.

Therefore, it should not have surprised me when the CUF's long campaign against Callan and Corpus Christi succeeded. In August 1999, under pressure from the Vatican, Bishop Matthew Clark of the Diocese of Rochester finally removed Callan from his post at Corpus Christi. Bishop Clark was a humane leader who had long sheltered Corpus Christi's unique ministries from their critics while also urging Callan not to transgress Church rules. Reports suggested that Clark was ordered to act against Corpus Christi by none other than Joseph Cardinal Ratzinger, then prefect of the Congregation of the Doctrine of the Faith, now Pope Benedict XVI.[6] Cardinal Ratzinger's intervention through Bishop Clark hit me in a very personal way. Bishop Clark was a childhood friend of my parents; he had hitchhiked back and forth between home and college with my father. I had respect and admiration for him. But in the months after Callan's removal, relations between Callan and Clark grew more strained. After serving a brief reassignment in Elmira, New York, Callan returned to Rochester to await a new assignment from Bishop Clark. Upon his return, members of the Corpus Christi community beseeched Callan to lead a weeknight prayer service they had begun after his removal. Though he was ordered not to do so, Callan began attending and leading those prayer services, which were held in a Protestant church. Callan was subsequently suspended from the priesthood and later excommunicated. The bulk of Corpus Christi's parishioners, meanwhile, began laying plans to continue their parish. The parishioners ultimately named their new faith community Spiritus Christi. It was with the founding of this new parish in mind that Father Callan decided to celebrate his first Mass after his excommunication on Holy Thursday. The Rochester diocese warned that any Catholics who joined the renegade parish were ipso facto excommunicated.

Should I join Spiritus Christi and be excommunicated myself? I did not know what I would do that spring of 1999. But both my own spiritual history and my study of history impelled me to attend the banned Holy Thursday Mass as I wrestled with this question.

From the beginning, I had seen the Corpus Christi controversy as an important historical event unfolding in front of me. Nor was it an unprecedented event. In my mind, it recalled the struggle of Father Edward McGlynn, an American Church reformer whose excommunication had rocked American Catholicism in the 1880s. McGlynn was a popular New York City priest, Irish Land League activist, and founder of the New York–based Anti-Poverty Society. He had been excommunicated in 1887 for his political activism on behalf of labor reformer Henry George, whose ideas were then seen by Church authorities as communistic. When McGlynn was informed of his excommunication, he refused to retract his stances. "No power on earth can excommunicate a child of God from God unless with the consent of that child himself," he told his followers. More than a century later, Callan echoed McGlynn. "I am a Roman Catholic and I have not excommunicated myself," he told one interviewer. "Nobody can change what I am."[7]

McGlynn's story had a happy ending, I reminded myself. Working-class Catholics along the eastern seaboard expressed outrage over the excommunication of the nation's best-known labor priest. In response, the Church came down hard on McGlynn's followers, just as it was doing with Callan's congregation. The New York Archdiocese went so far as to refuse to bury members of McGlynn's Anti-Poverty Society in

Catholic cemeteries. But a spontaneous movement arose in McGlynn's defense that cut Church contributions to Rome and led Church leaders to fret that working-class American Catholics might go the way of so many of their European coreligionists and abandon the Church in favor of working-class anticlericalism. "Dr. McGlynn lost a parish and gained a continent," observed the sympathetic *Catholic Herald*. "He will regain the parish and retain the continent," the paper predicted.[8]

Remarkably, the prediction came to pass. Five years after his excommunication, the Church reinstated McGlynn without his having to retract his previously expressed ideas. In the end, the McGlynn case had helped galvanize the Church's commitment to the cause of labor reform. Nearly simultaneous with McGlynn's restoration to full communion with the Church, Pope Leo XIII released *Rerum Novarum,* the first great Catholic encyclical on the labor question. In so doing, the Church had begun to align itself with the cause that McGlynn had suffered so much to advance.

Could Callan's case have a similar effect on the Church of the late twentieth century? Despite many indications that the Church of my era was not on the verge of a reorientation like the one triggered by *Rerum Novarum,* I still hoped. The Holy Spirit might be at work in this moment, I believed. But what transpired in Rochester in the 1990s diverged from what had occurred in New York City more than a century earlier. McGlynn had not tried to found a new parish while under the Church's ban. Instead, he spoke around the country while his followers organized. With the urging of his parish congregation, Callan had made a different decision. His decision in turn seemed destined to force a decision on me: a choice between loyalty to a parish that had renewed and deepened my faith and loyalty to the Church that had first instilled that faith in me.

Facing that choice, I was forced to think hard about what had led me to Corpus Christi in the first place, to evaluate my dilemma in light of my own history. The more I did so, the more apparent it became to me that Corpus Christi had unified the various strands of my spiritual biography.

At Corpus Christi I had found a parish that could satisfy both my love for Catholic spirituality and my yearning for the sort of open engagement with the world that I had experienced as the spirit of Vatican II. Attending Corpus Christi had also allowed me to reestablish a connection to other aspects of my Catholicism, both intellectual and ethical. In seventeen years of Catholic education, I had been fortunate to find many teachers—Sisters of St. Joseph, diocesan priests, lay Catholics, and Jesuits—who had broken open the Gospels for me, introduced me to the excitement of Catholic theology, and encouraged me to trust my own ability to reason in light of Catholic traditions. At Corpus Christi I had found my intellect challenged in a way that it had not been since I had listened to Jesuit homilies during my college years. In prioritizing solidarity with the poor, Corpus Christi also reconnected me to an aspect of my faith that I had lost touch with as an adult. I had joined the Jesuit Volunteer Corps (JVC) in 1981 after graduating from college, having been inspired by the liberation theology of Gustavo Gutierrez and Leonardo Boff. But after my stint in the JVC, I had not found a parish that kept alive the activist spirit that had attracted me to volunteer work. At Corpus Christi I found a parish that took social justice seriously and made bearing witness against injustice a central part of the community's mission. I was glad to be challenged by that witness.

Corpus Christi parish also appealed to the sort of spiritual pilgrim I had become in adulthood. After leaving college, while in the JVC, I had grown uncertain about my Catholicism. I never lost my faith in Jesus or my love for the Eucharist during these years, but I did acquire growing doubts about the Church and my relation to it. New relationships deepened these doubts. A Quaker woman I met while doing community organizing, and with whom I had a long relationship, opened my eyes to issues of gender inequality. Viewing my Church through the lens of feminism gave me a discerning eye for its hierarchical models of authority. Later, my relationship with a Jewish woman led me to think about whether I could ever leave the Catholic Church. As I wrestled with these questions, I went through a period when my religious practice became irregular. But before I had reached my mid-thirties and fallen in love with my wife, Diane, who is Jewish, I had already concluded that I could not give up my Catholicism. Indeed, by then I had reestablished the regular practice of my religion. Diane understood how important that was to me. Still, I longed to find a spiritual home where she and I could both feel acknowledged and nourished. At Corpus Christi, I found that place. Diane took an immediate liking to Jim Callan, and Callan went out of his way to make her and other non-Catholics feel welcome in his church. Corpus Christi seemed to be the destination I had long been seeking.

Finally, what also made Corpus Christi parish so appealing to me was the way in which it so beautifully lived up to its name. When I was young, nothing stirred my spiritual imagination more than to hear my mother—who was a great devotee of this notion—talk about the mystery of the Mystical Body of Christ. Jesus's body had been broken on the cross, she explained, but the resurrection of that body was ongoing and was incorporating all humanity into a mystical body that transcended time. This body bridged the divide between the living and the dead, and even drew together Christian and non-Christian. Listening to my mother ruminate on the beauty of the Mystical Body during late-night talks in my adolescent years, I felt in my heart a truth that I could not see or understand, yet one that gave a purpose to history. My mother's spirituality prepared me well to understand the Jesuit scientist and theologian Pierre Teilhard de Chardin, who wrote movingly of an evolving universe in which all creation moved toward unity with the Christ.[9]

Because Corpus Christi had connected so well to my own history and spirituality, I could not resist attending the banned Holy Thursday Mass. I decided to go, accompanied by my wife and young daughter, hoping for the return of Edward McGlynn, reluctant to part with the intimation of the Mystical Body I had experienced at Corpus Christi. I did not plan to leave my Church. My struggle over the years of my adulthood had confirmed my desire to stay in it. Yet I did not want to leave my parish either. Perhaps the Mass itself would clarify things, I thought.

As that Holy Thursday night drew near, I grew increasingly conscious of how both my reading of history and my personal history had drawn me into the Corpus Christi controversy. I became more aware than ever of the ways in which my Catholicism and my work as a historian had always been intertwined. At stake for me that Holy Week, it seemed, was not only my relationship to my Church, but my understanding of history and what it taught me.

My decision to pursue a career in history grew naturally from the Catholic milieu within which I was raised. The Catholicism I encountered growing up was fundamentally about imparting meaning to the trajectory of history and the unfolding of each individual life. Father Andrew M. Greeley once argued that Catholics stay in their Church primarily because of the stories they hear there. Over most of the Church's history, most Catholics learned their tradition "almost entirely by story, ritual, ceremony, and eventually art." The images created by these narrative forms are absorbed early in life and prove tenacious for many Catholics. Even those who break with the institution, Greeley observes, "cannot escape the images" conveyed in the stories of our faith.[10]

Stories exerted that sort of powerful influence on me. Indeed, it was the power of stories that led me to my vocation. Although I entered college determined to become a doctor and then revised that plan and decided on law school, I was drawn away from my these professional dreams by the stories told by two of my undergraduate teachers. One of them, David J. O'Brien, an eminent historian of U.S. Catholicism, became my advisor. The other, Nick Salvatore, who was then writing his sweeping biography of the great American socialist Eugene V. Debs, awakened my interest in labor and working-class history. Through the narratives I absorbed in the courses of O'Brien and Salvatore, I came to better understand who I was and to better grasp where I stood in history. This was personally transforming for me. I was a shy student and did not make friends easily. But in my history courses I found ways of transcending my isolation and experiencing a deeper sense of connectedness to the world around me. Novelist James Carroll once wrote: "To be made in God's image is to do this: arrange memory and transform experience according to the structure of narrative." Ultimately, the "story is what saves us," Carroll argues.[11] This certainly proved true for me. Since I first began constructing historical narratives as an undergraduate, I have found the act of "transforming experience into narrative" to be liberating. Doing this work has connected me to others—colleagues, students, subjects, readers—and in doing so helped me find my own voice. From the beginning, it seemed to me that the historian participates in a special way in the work of the Creator, who "gives life to the dead and calls into existence the things that do not exist" (Romans 4:17).

If my Catholicism helped draw me to my profession, it also helped determine the sort of history I would write. I had been instinctively aware of class divisions as a child. I was a middle-class boy whose father was a civil servant. But each of my parents were the first college graduates in their family. Our middle-class status was newly won, and our family straddled the worlds of working class and middle class. Most of my childhood friends were the sons of fathers who had not attended college, who worked as postmen, plumbers, salesmen, construction workers, or auto workers. I was one of only two people in my circle of close high school friends to go away to a residential college. Salvatore's classes helped me understand why my life had diverged from the lives of my friends. O'Brien's classes in turn exposed me to social Catholicism and its vocabulary for criticizing class injustice. Catholicism thus became a bridge into the world of American working-class history: the Catholic Worker movement, the American socialist (and ex-Catholic) Michael Harrington, and the influence of religion on the 1912 Lawrence textile strikers were the subjects of my longest college research papers.

Yet I was also drawn to working-class history as a vehicle for looking beyond my Catholic world for forms of community and solidarity that transcended religious lines. Catholics may have played a large role in American labor history, but to study American workers meant encountering the staggering diversity of American working-class experience. This attracted me. So did the opportunity that labor history gave me to learn from the secular left, which increasingly fascinated me. Thus, as an undergraduate I became intrigued by the Jewish socialist movement of New York's Lower East Side and, upon graduation, I joined the Democratic Socialists of America. Remaining rooted in Catholicism and yet reaching beyond it to find common ground with others who were committed to social justice in turn seemed in line with the spirit of the Vatican II Church to me. Thus I experienced no great sense of discontinuity when I went from college into the Jesuit Volunteer Corps for placement as a community organizer in African American neighborhoods of Houston, Texas, and from there to graduate school at the State University of New York at Binghamton in 1983 to study under my Jewish mentor, and now friend and collaborator, Melvyn Dubofsky.

In many ways, Catholic influences had helped direct me to graduate school in history. But my attachment to Catholicism weakened during my years as a community organizer and graduate student. I did not begin to seriously revive my spiritual practice until my last years of graduate school, as I completed work on my dissertation and recovered from the painful breakup of a long romantic relationship.

In retrospect, it seems clear that the revival of my spirituality and my dissertation work were related in ways that I did not fully understand at the time. The two processes certainly ran parallel courses. Through my dissertation and subsequent book, I attempted to reconcile aspects of the "new labor history" of the 1960s and 1970s with the institutional labor history that had preceded it. Institutionalists like John R. Commons and Selig Perlman had studied working-class history through the institution of the trade union. But new labor historians, such as Herbert G. Gutman and David Montgomery, looked at labor history "from below," tracing workers' histories through the dynamics of the shop-floor conflict, community building, and cultural reproduction. Whereas Commons and his colleagues had devoted attention to the structure of labor markets, unions, and labor relations practices, the new labor historians attempted to get at the lived experience of workers. Although the new labor history was ascendant during my graduate school years, I felt dissatisfied with its approach. "History from below" seemed incomplete to me. My wise mentor, Mel Dubofsky, had his own reservations about the new labor history and he encouraged me to elaborate my views. With his support, I sought to reconcile the new labor historians' focus on workers' experience on the shop floor with the institutionalists' appreciation for the structural frameworks created by the trade union, labor markets, laws, and the state.[12] I wanted to write narratives that connected "bottom-up" history to "top-down" history in order to produce a greater sense of the whole. My goal was to write narratives that not only illuminated human agency, but also showed how institutional structures can constitute or constrain that agency. In many ways, my scholarly vision was an intellectual analogue to my spiritual effort to reconcile my experience of faith with the institutional Church.

The book that resulted from this effort, *Labor's Great War: The Struggle for Industrial Democracy and the Origins of Modern American Labor Relations, 1912–21*, reflects aspects of both my Catholicism and my struggle as a Catholic at odds with Church authorities. It argued that national political developments and struggles in the workplace shaped and informed each other during the tumultuous years surrounding the First World War, when enduring patterns of U.S. labor relations took shape. Teasing out this dialectic led me to connect the disparate worlds of Alabama steel mills, New York electrical plants, Connecticut munitions factories, Woodrow Wilson's Democratic party, the internally divided American Federation of Labor (AFL), and a fractious group of corporations and their managers. The integrative impulse of the book owes a good deal to my Catholic imagination.[13]

But the book also focused on the politics of loyal dissent, and in this it may have been influenced by my conflicts with institutional Catholicism. *Labor's Great War* described workers' response when President Woodrow Wilson led his nation to war in 1917, promising to make the world safe for democracy. In return for their support of that war, many workers demanded that democracy be extended to their workplaces in the United States where they were subjected to the arbitrary rule of their employers, what they took to calling "industrial Kaiserism." To secure union recognition and thus accomplish the "de-Kaisering of industry," workers staged an unprecedented wave of wartime strikes. Employers called them traitors. "They positively have not patriotic feeling," claimed one coal operator (in words that reminded me of those who condemned Corpus Christi's parishioners as "absolutely non-Catholic"). But workers laid claim to a higher sense of patriotism. "We are doing all that we are able to do so that Democracy in the true sense of the word will be a reality and that Monarchy, Aristocracy, and Autocracy shall be forever banished from the Earth," argued one group of strikers. So deeply did many wartime strikers view their struggle for union recognition as consonant with their loyal defense of American democracy that the two merged in their minds. When asked by a government investigator about the nature of his union sympathies, one wartime striker surprised his questioner with this answer: "In a way, I didn't have any [union sympathies]," he explained. "I might say I had an American feeling, that is all. . . . I didn't have much thought in the matter . . . of union stuff."[14] As both a progressive American and a Catholic sometimes at odds with his Church's leaders, I found workers' defense of their wartime activism instructive for its refusal to accept the terms of their critics and its loyalty to what they saw as their nation's highest values.

My desire to further explore issues of loyalty and dissent in turn led me to the book project I had begun to research at the time the Corpus Christi controversy erupted in Rochester. The subject was the 1981 strike by members of the Professional Air Traffic Controllers Organization (PATCO), the union of federal workers who guided aircraft in and out of the nation's airports. PATCO strikers tended to be military veterans with middle-class aspirations. Many had loyally served in Vietnam. They believed their 1981 strike demands were just. Yet their walkout violated a law that prohibits federal workers from striking. When they did not return to work within forty-eight hours, President Ronald Reagan fired and permanently replaced them. I was interested in the PATCO strike because it proved so influential in setting the tone for U.S. labor relations at the end of the twentieth century. But I was also fascinated by the strikers. What had led seemingly conservative workers to such a militant act? How did strikers wrestle with their loyalty to their coworkers and the union on the one hand, and their government on the other? How did they respond to their own version of excommunication, being permanently barred from working the air traffic control jobs that they passionately loved? Only months after interviewing some of PATCO's leaders, I found myself thinking of the parallels between their situation in 1981 and my own: How would I deal with being barred from a church that I loved, one whose spiritual treasures I had only recently begun to rediscover and reappropriate?

As I took my seat for Mass that night in April 1999, the auditorium was packed and a sense of joyful anticipation filled its ample space. As I looked around the room at faces I had come to know well during the difficult months leading up to this night, all of the influences that had brought me to that place swirled through my head: Catholicism's stories, my own story, the stories I had told through my work. And yet I was uncertain of what this night meant for me. Did attending this banned Mass mean I was leaving the Church? Was I still Catholic? These troubling questions were quieted only somewhat by the familiar liturgy, which was celebrated with great joy and emotion. Yet as the liturgy unfolded, I focused increasingly on one question: Should I receive Communion from an excommunicated priest? Would doing so mean that I too was excommunicated?

As the moment to decide drew near, I remained uncertain as to what to do. Thomas Merton once composed a prayer that would have been helpful to me had I the presence of mind to recall it at that moment. "I do not see the road ahead of me," Merton prayed. "I cannot know for certain where it will end. Nor do I really know myself. The fact that I think I am following your will does not mean that I am actually doing so. But I believe that the desire to please you does in fact please you."[15] I did not recall the prayer, but at that moment I felt its emotion nonetheless. As Father Callan held aloft the bread and pronounced, "This is my body," those words seemed as real and powerful to me as they had ever been before. Nor had they ever seemed truer. So I received Holy Communion from the excommunicated priest.

Afterward, I wondered about what this night had meant to me. Did it mean I was leaving the Church? As with all historical events, the significance of that night became apparent only in retrospect, in the light that subsequent developments shed on that moment. Some months later, I found an entry in a journal that I had written eighteen years before, while undertaking a retreat based on the Spiritual Exercises of St. Ignatius, the founder of the Jesuits. To "grow in my understanding, appreciation, reverence of the Eucharist," I had written in 1981, "I must make it the center of my efforts at self-transformation." Of course, when I wrote those words, I could not foresee the unusual Holy Thursday Mass I attended in 1999. But rereading those words in light of that night helped me see that Mass as an affirmation of my faith. Facing the possibility of excommunication made that affirmation all the more real to me.

In the end, I did not leave the Church. History helped determine this for me—quite literally. Just as the Corpus Christi crisis came to a head in the spring of 1999, I was offered a teaching position at Georgetown University, the nation's oldest Catholic and Jesuit university. This was a welcome opportunity in many ways. It brought me to one of the nation's finest universities and renewed my contact with the Jesuit spirituality that had inspired me in college. It introduced me to brilliant colleagues and highly motivated students. But, more immediately, the Georgetown job allowed me to avoid deciding whether to join the former parishioners of Corpus Christi in their new faith community, Spiritus Christi, a decision I would have had to make had I remained in Rochester. Although

I missed the inspiring spiritual vision that I had witnessed at Corpus Christi, I was happy to avoid choosing between the parish that renewed my faith and the Church that first instilled that faith in me.

Having avoided one choice, I made another. I decided to deepen my connection to Catholicism. Only by sinking deeper roots could I survive in a Church that seemed determined to marginalize or drive out people like me. And only through prayer could I find a way to sink those roots. As I live out this decision, I feel less troubled by my differences with Church leaders and more willing to raise my voice in loyal dissent when my conscience demands it. I still wrestle with feelings of anger and alienation, as I did in the wake of the recent pedophilia scandal. But to an increasing extent, those feelings have been counterbalanced by the realization that my marginality within the Catholic Church may be both a spiritual and a vocational blessing. Assuming the posture of a dissident can be difficult, I have found. It can tempt one toward either cynicism and despair on the one hand or defensiveness and self-righteousness on the other. And I have indulged in both excesses. But, if one manages to find momentary equipoise between the extremes, experiencing the marginality of the dissident offers one the chance to receive the gift of humility. This can be good for the soul. As Simone Weil observed, "humility . . . is a far more precious treasure than all academic progress." But humility is not merely medicine for the soul. It is also necessary for the intellect. It is what allows the mind to enter what Weil liked to call a state of "attention," open to new discoveries.[16] Thus it is humility that makes all learning possible. And to the extent that my spiritual struggles have humbled me, they have no doubt made me a better historian.

My Catholic experience continues to shape my approach to history. In the aftermath of my experience in Rochester, my interest in questions of loyalty and dissent has deepened. As I have continued to work on my PATCO book, I have also looked for other ways to explore the nature of loyal dissidence. This led me to the story of Leamon Hood, an African American public-sector union organizer who struggled to balance his loyalties to his union on the one hand and the cause of racial justice on the other. It also led me to edit a book with my friend and colleague, Michael Kazin. In *Americanism: New Perspectives on the History of an Ideal,* we gathered essays that illustrated how Americans, dissenters and orthodox patriots alike, have fought over the meaning of their national ideals since the country's founding.[17] Those essays explore versions of the same problem I have faced as a Catholic: how to remain loyal to a community within which one can often feel marginalized.

But my Catholic experience has left its mark on my work in a more subtle way as well. This is evident not so much in the subjects I have chosen to write about as in the way I look for meaning in history. As a student of labor history, it is difficult to be an optimist. The struggles of poor and working people rarely end in unambiguous victories. In part for this reason, historians are tempted to write stories that rescue optimism from despair, searching for the what-ifs and the turning points where, if the characters had made different choices, victory could have been snatched from the jaws of defeat and justice could have prevailed. Unfortunately, such stories too often exaggerate workers' agency, and thus do them a disservice. The plight of American workers cannot be explained primarily by the perfidy of conservative union leaders, as some in my field would suggest. The causes of class injustice extend too far into history and reach too deep into the human heart to be explained by facile theories. To accurately tell the story of workers' struggles, we must move beyond easy answers and confront harsh, seemingly intractable realities. In that sort of work, optimism is a far less reliable guide than hope. Indeed, I believe that any durable effort to build a more just world must be founded on hope rather than optimism.

Reinhold Niebuhr once wrote that because "nothing worth doing is completed in our lifetime," we must be "saved by hope."[18] The hope of which Niebuhr wrote avoids the twin pitfalls of acquiescence and optimism. Whereas optimism can be shattered by defeats or undermined by unintended consequences, unforeseen events, or the capacity of humans to do evil, hope exists in light of these realities, and in light of the knowledge that defeat is often not only probable but—like the defeat of death—unavoidable. Catholicism has helped me rely on hope, and this has affected how I pursue my craft. Rejecting mere optimism in favor of hope has allowed me to ponder the mystery of how, as William Morris once put it, "men fight and lose the battle, and the thing that they fought for comes about in spite of their defeat, and when it comes turns out not to be what they meant, and other men have to fight for what they meant under another name."[19] To the extent that I have been able to contemplate tragedies, without either acquiescing to the injustices that produced them or trying to redeem them through my feeble words, I think I am a more effective practitioner of the historian's craft. Hope thus gives meaning and direction to history as I understand it. And it was my Catholicism that taught me, in the words of poet Seamus Heaney, how to make "hope and history rhyme."[20]

Just as my faith has helped me clarify my historical vision, my work has helped me along my spiritual journey. It led me to Father McGlynn's courageous witness, the story that encouraged me through the dark days of the conflict in Rochester. It taught me that the tradition of my Church is replete with dissent, dialogue, and change over time, and allowed me to see with historian Eamon Duffy that "the richness of the Church's past is a liberation, not a straightjacket."[21] Indeed, if I have learned anything from my work, it has taught me that nothing God has made is unchanging. Nothing lacks a narrative of change over time. Legend has it that after recanting his findings that the earth orbited the sun under pressure from the Inquisition, Galileo muttered under his breath: "Eppur se mouve" ("And yet it moves"). In saying this, Galileo could have been talking about history itself. For as my work continually reminds me, not only the planets move and change: all things do. In their unfolding across time, they thus reflect the infinite dynamism of the Creator who says, "Behold, I make all things new" (Revelations 21:5). By reminding me daily of the restless movement of creation, my work nourishes my faith. In so doing, it also helps me maintain hope for my troubled Church. It is unlikely that I will live to see a Catholic Church that reflects the Mystical Body of Christ as vividly as the Corpus Christi parish or as generously as my mother's spirituality did. But I believe that the Church, like all things God has made, will change. The arc of history sustains my hope.

When I arrived at Georgetown University in 1999, I was interested to discover the university's Latin motto: "*Utraque Unum.*" It refers to the controversy in the early Church over who was authentically Christian. Some believed that only Jews could become Christians. But St. Paul argued for a broader view of the Church. In his letter to the Ephesians (2:14), Paul reminded his readers that, in Christ, barriers between Jews and gentiles are transcended, divisions resolved: "For he himself is our peace, who has made both one." Both made one: "*Utraque unum.*" After my experience in Rochester, I was pleased to find that my new university took as its motto a statement of unity that emerged from the Church's first great controversy. But the motto held another personal meaning for me. By then, I had begun to see how deeply my struggle to remain a Catholic was connected to my development as a historian. That motto encouraged me—and encourages me still—to believe that this connection will deepen in the years ahead.

Notes

I am indebted to the following people for offering suggestions and criticism: Tom Boland, Tula Connell, Tony Dresden, Philip Gleason, Michael Kazin, Diane Reis, Nick Salvatore, and Tracy Strauss. For their reactions to the conference paper on which this essay was based, I would like to thank Jim McCartin, Mark Noll, and

Robert E. Sullivan. Of course, none of these people bears responsibility for my views. I am especially grateful to Nick Salvatore and my parents, Joe and Marybeth McCartin. Long ago Nick helped me find my voice as a scholar. In recent years he has helped me strengthen that voice. My parents read an early draft of this essay and, as always, encouraged me to follow my heart. They did not live to read this version, but their influence pervades it.

1. A point of clarification: Catholic teaching does not condemn indirect abortion; that is, abortion that occurs indirectly in the process of an act undertaken to save a mother's life. But all instances of direct abortion, including abortion in cases that result from rape or incest, are defined by the Church as "always gravely immoral." Church leaders have called for criminalizing abortion even in such cases. The Church's teaching on abortion is outlined in John Paul II's encyclical *Evangelium Vitae.* See *Evangelium Vitae: Encyclical Letter Addressed by the Supreme Pontiff Pope John Paul II to All the Bishops, Priests and Deacons, Men and Women Religious, Lay Faithful and All People of Good Will on the Value and Inviolability of Human Life* (London: Catholic Truth Society, 1995).

2. Chaput's full quote was: "We're at a time for the Church in our country when some Catholics—too many—are discovering that they've gradually become non-Catholics who happen to go to Mass." Quoted in Peter J. Boyer, "A Hard Faith," *New Yorker,* May 16, 2005, 65.

3. See Richard John Neuhaus, "The Catholic Reform," *First Things* 143 (May 2004): 59–76.

4. Joan Collins Lambert, "Resurrection: The Rebirth of an Urban Church," *City: Rochester's Alternative Newsweekly,* February 29, 1996, 7–11; James Brady Callan, *Can't Hold Back the Spring: The Blossoming of Corpus Christi Parish* (Rochester, N.Y.: Corpus Christi Publications, 1997). Callan is quoted in Lambert, "Resurrection," 11.

5. In May 1998, the *Rochester Democrat and Chronicle* carried a picture of Mary Ramerman raising the consecrated bread and wine aloft at a Communion service. Ramerman later speculated that this picture was the immediate trigger for Rome's intervention. See "Pastor of Liberal Parish Blames Transfer on Rome," *National Catholic Reporter,* August 28, 1998, 3.

6. *Rochester Democrat and Chronicle,* October 7, 1998, 1A; "Pastor of Liberal Parish Blames Transfer on Rome," 3.

7. McGlynn is quoted in Stephen Bell, *Rebel, Priest, and Prophet: A Biography of Dr. Edward McGlynn* (New York: Devin-Adair, 1937), 134. Callan is quoted *Rochester Democrat and Chronicle,* February 25, 1999, 10A.

8. Quoted in Bell, *Rebel, Priest, and Prophet,* 98.

9. Pierre Teilhard de Chardin, *The Phenomenon of Man* (New York: Harper & Row, 1965); Pierre Teilhard de Chardin, *The Divine Milieu* (New York: Harper & Row, 1968).

10. Andrew M. Greeley, "Why Do Catholics Stay in the Church? Because of the Stories," *New York Times Magazine,* July 10, 1994, 40.

11. James Carroll, *An American Requiem: God, My Father, and the War That Came between Us* (Boston: Houghton Mifflin, 1996), 15.

12. I touched on some of my criticisms of "history from below" in "Industrial Unionism as Liberator or Leash? The Limits of 'Rank-and-Filism' in American Labor Historiography" *Journal of Social History* (Spring 1998): 153–63.

13. The underlying view of this book has led me more recently to critique contemporary labor's rights–oriented political language. My critique bears the influence of Catholic social thinker Mary Ann Glendon's *Rights Talk: The Impoverishment of Political Discourse* (New York: Free Press, 1991) in which she writes of the "exceptional solitariness of the American rights-bearer" and criticizes the "hyperindividualism that pervades our American rights dialect" (75). Sharing some of Glendon's views, I argue that the inescapably individualistic character of contemporary labor's rights talk provides a poor basis on which to build workers' solidarity. See Joseph A. McCartin, "Democratizing the Workers' Rights Dialogue: Toward a Re-Framing of Labor's Argument," and "Reply to Lance Compa and Sheldon Friedman," *Dissent* (Winter 2005): 61–66, 70–71.

14. Joseph A. McCartin, *Labor's Great War: The Struggle for Industrial Democracy and the Origins of Modern American Labor Relations, 1912–21* (Chapel Hill: University of North Carolina Press, 1997), 104.

15. Thomas Merton, *Thoughts in Solitude* (New York: Farrar, Straus & Cudahy, 1958), 83.

16. Simone Weil, "Reflections on the Right Use of School Studies with a View to the Love of God," in *Waiting for God* (New York: G. P. Putnam's Sons, 1951), 109. "Attention is an effort, the greatest of all efforts, perhaps," Weil argued. "Attention consists of suspending our thought, leaving it detached, empty, and ready to be penetrated by the object. . . . Above all our thought should be empty, waiting, not seeking anything, but ready to receive in its naked truth the object that is to penetrate it" (111–12).

17. Joseph A. McCartin, "Managing Discontent: The Life and Career of Leamon Hood, Black Public Employee Union Activist," in *The Black Worker: Race and Labor Activism since Emancipation,* ed. Eric Arnesen (Urbana: University of Illinois Press, forthcoming); Michael Kazin and Joseph A. McCartin, eds., *Americanism: New Perspectives on the History of an Ideal* (Chapel Hill: University of North Carolina Press, 2006).

18. The full text of Niebuhr's quotation reads: "Nothing worth doing is completed in our lifetime; therefore, we are saved by hope. Nothing which is true or beautiful or good makes complete sense in any immediate context of history; therefore we are saved by faith. Nothing we do, however virtuous, can be accomplished alone; therefore we are saved by love. No virtuous act is quite as virtuous from the standpoint of our friend or foe as from our own. Therefore we must be saved by the final form of love which is forgiveness." Reinhold Niebuhr, *The Irony of American History* (New York: Charles Scribner's Sons, 1952), 63.

19. William Morris, *A Dream of John Ball and a King's Lesson* (London: Longman's Green, 1903), 39–40.

20. Seamus Heaney, *The Cure at Troy: A Version of Sophocles's Piloctetes* (London: Faber and Faber, 1990), 77. One need not be a Catholic or a Christian, of course, to rely on hope. It seems to me that Italian Marxist Antonio Gramsci was speaking about hope when he urged his followers to embrace "pessimism of the intelligence, optimism of the will." On that idea, see Joseph A. McCartin, "Power, Politics, and 'Pessimism of the Intelligence,'" *Labor History* 40 (1999): 345–49. In this piece I addressed Gramsci's formulation in the context of Melvyn Dubofsky's work on the Industrial Workers of the World.

21. Eamon Duffy, *Faith of Our Fathers: Reflections on the Catholic Tradition* (New York: Continuum, 2004), x.

CONTRIBUTORS

JAMES R. BARRETT, professor of history at the University of Illinois at Urbana-Champaign, graduated from the University of Illinois at Chicago and studied comparative working-class history at Warwick University and the University of Pittsburgh, where he received his Ph.D. in 1981. His books include *Steve Nelson, American Radical* (1981), *Work and Community in the Jungle: Chicago's Packinghouse Workers, 1894–1922* (1987), and *William Z. Foster and the Tragedy of American Radicalism* (2000) as well as critical editions of Upton Sinclair's *The Jungle* (1988) and Hutchins Hapgood's *The Spirit of Labor* (2004). He is coeditor of the University of Illinois Press series The Working Class in American History. Barrett is currently working on two books—*Americanization from the Bottom Up,* a study of the role of the Irish in the multiethnic cultures of American cities, and *In the Neighborhoods,* which combines autobiography and social history to convey a sense of life in Chicago's ethnic working-class neighborhoods in the 1950s and 1960s.

ANNE M. BUTLER, Trustee Professor, Emerita, from Utah State University, and a scholar of the American West, taught U. S. history for thirty years and for fourteen served as associate editor, coeditor, or senior editor of the *Western Historical Quarterly.* She is known for her work concerning criminal women and is the author of *Daughters of Joy, Sisters of Misery: Prostitutes in the American West* and *Gendered Justice in the American West: Women Prisoners in Men's Penitentiaries,* both published by the University of Illinois Press. Her current research focuses on Roman Catholic Sisters in the late-nineteenth-century West, and she is coeditor, with Michael E. Engh, S.J., and Thomas W. Spalding, C.F.X., of *The Frontiers and Catholic Identities.* Butler has written about Mother Katharine Drexel, SBS; Mother Caroline, SSND; and Mother Amadeus, OSU. Other published articles deal with the Sisters of Charity of Providence and the Sisters of the Holy Names in the Pacific Northwest, the Daughters of Charity in Nevada, and the Sisters of the Holy Spirit in Texas. An earlier version of this article, "Western Spaces,

Catholic Places," won the 2001 Arrington-Prucha Prize of the Western History Association.

DAVID EMMONS is professor emeritus of history at the University of Montana. In addition to *The Butte Irish,* Emmons is the author of *Garden in the Grasslands: Boomer Literature of the Central Plains* as well as a number of articles on Irish American and Western history. He is currently completing the last chapters of "Beyond the American Pale: Irish Outlanders and the American West, 1840–1930," which he hopes to publish in the University of Wisconsin Press series on the history of Ireland and the Irish Diaspora.

MAUREEN FITZGERALD is an associate professor of religious studies and American studies at the College of William and Mary. Her book, *Habits of Compassion: Irish Catholic Nuns and the Origins of New York's Welfare System, 1830–1920,* was published by the University of Illinois Press in 2005.

MARIO T. GARCÍA is a professor of history and Chicano studies at the University of California, Santa Barbara. A Guggenheim Fellow, he is the author of numerous books on Chicano history, including *Desert Immigrants: The Mexicans of El Paso, 1880–1920; Mexican Americans: Leadership, Ideology and Identity, 1930–1960;* and *Memories of Chicano History: The Life and Narrative of Bert Corona.* He has received a UCSB Faculty Teacher of the Year award.

PHILIP GLEASON, professor emeritus of history at the University of Notre Dame, is the author of *Conservative Reformers: German-American Catholics and the Social Order* (1968); *Keeping the Faith: American Catholicism Past and Present* (1987); *Speaking of Diversity: Language and Ethnicity in Twentieth-Century America* (1992); and *Contending with Modernity: Catholic Higher Education in the Twentieth Century* (1995). He now lives in Evanston, Illinois.

JOSEPH A. McCARTIN is an associate professor of history at Georgetown University. He is the author of *Labor's Great War: The Struggle for Industrial Democracy and the Origins of Modern American Labor Relations* (University of North Carolina Press, 1997), coeditor with Melvyn Dubofsky of *American Labor: A Documentary Collection* (Palgrave Macmillan, 2004), and coeditor with Michael Kazin of *Americanism: Essays on the History of an Ideal* (University of North Carolina Press, 2006). He is now working on a book about the 1981 air traffic controllers' strike and the decline of the U.S. labor movement. He lives in Bethesda, Maryland, with his wife Diane Reis and daughters Mara and Elisa.

NICK SALVATORE is the Maurice and Hinda Neufeld Founders Professor of Industrial and Labor Relations and professor of American studies at Cornell University. He is the author of *Eugene V. Debs: Citizen and Socialist* (1982), which received the Bancroft Prize in History and the John H. Dunning Prize, and *We All Got History: The Memory Books of Amos Webber* (1996), which received the New England History Association's Outstanding Book Prize. His third biography, *Singing in a Strange Land: C. L. Franklin, the Black Church, and the Transformation of America* (2005) examines the life of one of the most influential preachers of his generation in the black Baptist tradition. See www.nicksalvatore.com.

INDEX

The University of Illinois Press
is a founding member of the
Association of American University Presses.

Composed in 9.5/12.5 Trump Mediaeval
by Jim Proefrock
at the University of Illinois Press
Manufactured by Thomson-Shore, Inc.

University of Illinois Press
1325 South Oak Street
Champaign, IL 61820-6903
www.press.uillinois.edu